Julian Curry

Julian Curry has extensive stage credits, including leading roles with the Royal Shakespeare Company, the National Theatre, and in the West End. He has acted in twenty-one of Shakespeare's plays. Other highlights include Webster's *The Duchess of Malfi*, Shaw's *Back to Methuselah*, Osborne's *The Entertainer*, Miller's *The Crucible*, Beckett's *Company* and *Krapp's Last Tape*, Bernhard's *Elizabeth II* and *Eve of Retirement*, and the two musicals *Lust* and *Love*.

Julian is well known as Claude Erskine-Brown in the popular television series *Rumpole of the Bailey*. Numerous other TV credits include *Inspector Morse, Sherlock Holmes, The Misanthrope, King Lear, Kavanagh QC, The Wyvern Mystery, A Fine Romance* and *Midsomer Murders*. Among many movies are *The Missionary, Fall from Grace, Rasputin, Sky Captain and the World of Tomorrow* and *Escape to Victory* (starring Pelé).

Julian holds a Diploma from the Wine and Spirit Education Trust, and was for some years a member of the Circle of Wine Writers. His one-man entertainment *Hic! or The Entire History of Wine* (*abridged*) has been performed over a hundred and fifty times, from Hong Kong to Bermuda to San Francisco, and sold out as a cartoon-illustrated book. He has also written and recorded *A Guide to Wine* for Naxos Audiobooks.

Other Related Titles from Nick Hern Books

Talking Theatre
Interviews with Theatre People
Richard Eyre

Performing Shakespeare
Preparation, Rehearsal, Performance
Oliver Ford Davies

Freeing Shakespeare's Voice
Kristin Linklater

Hamlet: A User's Guide
A Midsummer Night's Dream: A User's Guide
Twelfth Night: A User's Guide
Michael Pennington

Year of the King
Antony Sher

Julian Curry

SHAKESPEARE ON STAGE

*Thirteen Leading Actors
on Thirteen Key Roles*

Foreword by Trevor Nunn

NICK HERN BOOKS
London
www.nickhernbooks.co.uk

A Nick Hern Book

Shakespeare On Stage
first published in Great Britain in 2010
by Nick Hern Books Limited, 14 Larden Road, London W3 7ST

Cover design by Peter Bennett
Author photograph by Finn Curry
Front cover photograph of Jude Law in *Hamlet*
(Donmar at Wyndham's Theatre, 2009) © Johan Persson

Photographs accompanying each interview are by
Donald Cooper/Photostage, except those of Judi Dench (V&A Images,
Victoria and Albert Museum), Rebecca Hall (Tristram Kenton/Lebrecht
Music & Arts), and Penelope Wilton (The Stephen Moreton Prichard
Collection/Mander and Mitchenson/ArenaPAL).

Typeset by Nick Hern Books, London
Printed and bound in Great Britain by
CPI Antony Rowe, Chippenham, Wiltshire

A CIP catalogue record for this book
is available from the British Library

ISBN 978 1 84842 077 9

FSC
www.fsc.org

MIX
Paper from
responsible sources
FSC® C013604

For Mary

Contents

Foreword

Trevor Nunn

Sir John Falstaff tells the enthralling story of how he was ambushed by a gang of thieves, and fought with 'fifty of them'. In detail he recounts how he took on two, who as his tale progresses become four, who a moment later become nine and then eleven men, all intent on killing him. But we know that the truth of the matter is quite different. We have seen Falstaff approached by Prince Hal and Poins only, causing the fat knight to run away in terror, offering no resistance. It is a seminal comic scene, because we all of us have heard tall stories, and probably have *told* tall stories, and we all recognise how stories can be improved with the telling, and the retelling. Anglers vouch that the fish they nearly caught was 'this big' and by the end of the evening in the pub, that fish has grown from a foot long to the size of a shark.

Theatre anecdotes are notoriously and usually hilariously apocryphal. Shakespeare was an actor, so he must have witnessed any number of small mishaps onstage expanding in the telling, or in the tavern, to full-blown disasters of epic proportions. If not, his theatre company was very different from every group I have ever belonged to. Falstaff would seem to prove the point. But if actors are frequently embellishers of the yarn and the anecdote, are they to be believed when they are remembering the influences and the train of events contributing to their performances, particularly their great performances?

I would say the answer is emphatically yes. Hindsight may colour things, sometimes in a rosy hue, but the reminiscences in this book are very much to be believed. Over and over, what the actor is remembering is the *feeling* of a situation, of a rehearsal, of a role – the feeling of creating something; and this record of feeling is more valuable than all of Mr Gradgrind's facts put together.

The actors doing the remembering in this book were all working through a period of enormous and exciting change in approaches to Shakespeare in this country. The age of rhetorical delivery gave way to the discovery, particularly aided by the influence of small-theatre intimate productions, that Shakespeare was at times an astonishingly naturalistic dramatist. In consequence, the 'voice beautiful' and what became disparagingly known as 'mouth music' gave way to the search for and presentation of meaning above all, and in consequence to the ceaseless search for the underlying thought.

It would have been fascinating had a precursor of Julian Curry interviewed a list of successful actors from the early and middle years of the last century, so that we could compare just how differently actors now speak about approaching Shakespeare to how they did back then. The fashion continually changes, and we in the twenty-first century should continue to have a sense of history. In the future, a time will come when the refreshingly personal approaches to playing Shakespeare remembered in this book will seem to be antiquated and, heaven forfend, comic. But at present, these passages of times remembered contribute vividly to the sense of a teemingly creative period when Shakespeare seemed to have been rediscovered.

Introduction

Julian Curry

It tends to be a mug's game, getting actors to talk seriously about their craft. Ralph Richardson used to maintain that acting was 'the art of stopping people coughing'. Michael Gambon describes his work as 'shouting at night'. Anthony Hopkins says all he does is 'learn the lines and show up'. And so on. The more experienced they are, the more reluctant to define and analyse what they do. Marlon Brando said he'd rather do anything than discuss acting. And when actors talk about what they do for a living, they all too easily disparage it, reducing it to putting on funny clothes and pretending to be someone else. 'One day when I grow up,' goes the refrain, 'I'll get a proper job.'

This leaves a void which begs to be filled. Paintings are housed in art galleries, books line the shelves of libraries, and music is superbly recorded. But theatre is written on the wind. Even the most brilliant performances exist only in the moment, and will endure nowhere but in the memories of those present. Sure enough a film is sometimes made, in an attempt to preserve a record of a great performance. But it rarely matches the original. A camera can't capture the special aura of a live show. The actor/audience relationship that produces the unique chemistry of theatre will be lacking. Critics write reviews, but as often as not they contradict each other, with diametrically opposed views of the same piece of work. Who is to be believed?

What better, it seemed to me, than that the actors themselves should describe the event? What would I not give for Edmund Kean's own account of his King Lear! We have at least this vivid description from his contemporary, Coleridge: 'To see him act, is like reading Shakespeare by flashes of lightning' – which simply makes one long to know more, in particular what the man himself might have had to say.

Shakespeare's major roles are amongst the most challenging and potentially rewarding for any actor. I decided to see if I could persuade some of those who had played them recently to recollect and describe their performances. I hoped they'd be willing to reveal if not *how they acted*, at least *what they did*. I also wanted to know how the show was set, what they wore, and what went on around them. This in itself seemed to have the potential to be a fascinating document.

Who would I approach? The point of departure was a wish list with one very basic criterion: excellent actors who had played leading roles in memorable Shakespearean productions. Having been lifelong in the business, I'd worked with many of my intended targets. Some are friends who were easily accessible, and turned out to be most generous with their time. But not everyone was so cooperative. Certain doors remained firmly shut. My attempts to interview Al Pacino about Richard III were thwarted by his agent, a lady so fiercely protective of her clients that she is known in Hollywood as 'Dr No' or 'The Suppress Agent'. Paul Scofield, on the other hand, sent a charmingly self-deprecatory postcard asking to be excused, claiming not to be much good at interviews.

Preparing for the encounters was a labour of love. Of necessity it involved a thorough refresher course, going back to the plays and spending long hours with nose in text. I also read critical studies and pestered archivists for back copies of reviews. I was determined to approach the interviews as well briefed as possible, in order to frame productive questions. And indeed at times it felt like the work of a barrister. The difference is that whereas a barrister's questions are designed to steer the witness towards a desired answer, mine were simply intended to get juices flowing and tongues wagging. I concentrated on mechanics rather than theory. As far possible I made the question 'What did you do?' rather than 'How did you do it?'

The conversations were tape-recorded, usually at the actor's home or in their current dressing room. I followed, as closely as possible, the following sequence: (1) Put the performance in the context of its time and place, director and designer. (2) General questions about the production and the character. (3) Specific questions about the performance, working through the play from start to finish. (4) Summing up.

Interviews are listed alphabetically by actor's name. To try to impose any other arrangement didn't seem helpful. The order does not follow a pattern, and chapters can be read at random.

This book is an account of thirteen performances, by the actors who gave them. They span almost fifty years, from Judi Dench in 1960 to Jude Law in 2009. It is not intended as a study of any particular aspect of the works of Shakespeare, still less as a series of thespian pen-portraits or an acting manual. Each chapter focuses on a single performance, and the production in which it featured. What they have in common is a uniquely personal account of a creative process. But there the similarities end. I'm not aware of any particular continuities or recurring themes. On the contrary, each one quite naturally occupies its own territory, and I'm very happy with that. It also seems that, as an inevitable by-product, the actors have in fact revealed a great deal about themselves and their own work methods. As such, I hope the reader will enjoy the range and diversity of responses, and that it will be of interest to other actors, students and theatregoers alike.

Acknowledgements

Fervent thanks to Sue Webb, Matt Wolf, Jonathan Dudley and Patrick Curry for their invaluable help and support with this book. And, most especially, to the actors who kindly gave their time to be interviewed.

Brian Cox
on
Titus Andronicus

Titus Andronicus (1591–2)
Royal Shakespeare Company
Opened at the Swan Theatre, Stratford-upon-Avon
on 12 May 1987

Directed by Deborah Warner
Designed by Isabella Bywater
With Jim Hooper as Saturninus, Estelle Kohler as Tamora,
Peter Polycarpou as Aaron, and Sonia Ritter as Lavinia (also pictured above)

The whirligig of time has brought about vivid changes in attitudes to *Titus Andronicus*. Shakespeare's earliest tragedy, first performed in 1594, is by far his most bloodthirsty work. It's a heady brew – a story of revenge and political turmoil, full of appalling brutality, featuring multiple murders, rape, mutilation and human sacrifice. The horrors are leavened by a vein of black comedy, as for instance when two characters meet their end by being baked in a pie. The play was hugely successful in Shakespeare's time, but for centuries *Titus* was written off as a sensationalist example of the blood-spattered drama that was popular in the 1590s. The critic John Dover Wilson likened it to 'some broken-down cart, laden with bleeding corpses from the Elizabethan scaffold', while T.S. Eliot went one better, describing *Titus* as 'one of the stupidest and most uninspired plays ever written'. However, critics have recently taken *Titus Andronicus* more seriously, largely on account of its various themes which presage Shakespeare's greater plays. Like Coriolanus, Titus turns against his native Rome. Like Macbeth, he becomes dehumanised. Like Lear, he divests himself of power in the first scene. And foreshadowing Hamlet, Titus appears to go mad with grief, but leaves us unsure of the extent to which his madness is genuine.

Robert Atkins' 1923 staging at the Old Vic was the first revival of a fully unexpurgated text for two hundred and fifty years. It caused audience members to faint. Peter Brook's famous production in 1955 starring Laurence Olivier was a major turning point in the play's popularity. *Titus Andronicus* was again a tremendous success with Brian Cox's performance in Deborah Warner's 1987 RSC staging in the Swan Theatre, Stratford-upon-Avon. It was hailed as one of the greatest Shakespeare revivals of the 1980s. When working out a wish list of performances I hoped to include in this book, Cox's Titus was a leading contender. I was stunned by it. A play which is most certainly not normally considered one of Shakespeare's best was made plausible, contemporary and extremely hot. I talked to Brian on a pleasant morning in 2006, sitting outside a pub in Camden Town, with only occasional interference from a passing helicopter.

Julian Curry: Titus Andronicus *is a play full of harshness and horror. It confronts bloody revenge, dismemberment, rape, cannibalism and murder.* Titus *opens the action by killing one of his sons and closes it by slaughtering his already maimed daughter. In the intervening acts, hands and tongues are cut off almost at random before doting parents eat their own offspring served up in pies. How can we take this seriously?*

Brian Cox: Well, I don't think, especially nowadays, we have to look too far for the horror. But you've got to remember that *Titus* is written by a young Shakespeare. It's written by a Shakespeare who around the same time wrote *Richard III*. It's all about authority and those who become disconnected from reality, so it has a young man's rebellious nature. Titus is an old fart who forgets what he's there for in the first place. He had twenty-five sons, twenty-one have been killed in battle, and it's only when he's down to four that he realises that he's lost most of his children, in horrific circumstances. And he has suffered accordingly. He's become brutalised, he's maimed. He has served his idol, Rome, for so long, unquestioningly, and has been away for so long fighting the wars, that he's forgotten the corruption at home. And it's only when he finally comes home that the corruption brings all things closer.

The Emperor Saturninus immediately takes his prize, Tamora the Goth, and does the unthinkable by marrying her. So suddenly her boys are elevated, and his one-time captives are now princes of the realm. There are so many modern versions of that, political plays where groups of people take over from other groups of people, and they combine to get into bed together. And these are the last people to get into bed with, to shore up a state which is already crumbling, as Rome is. But Titus is old-fashioned – you know, 'No questions asked. Do your duty. Serve.' Rome is his great master.

Shakespeare tries out a lot of ideas in *Titus Andronicus* that he later develops in other plays, like *Othello*, like *Lear*, like *Coriolanus*. There are lots of themes in those plays which are reiterated. I think it's a truly great play, and not very well understood, because he does it under the guise of extremely black humour. Now most productions in the past – even Peter Brook's production – cut a lot of the laughs because they thought they were detrimental to the play. But I think the laughter in that play is absolutely vital. If you take the masks of comedy and tragedy, and put them together, you create another mask which is ludicrousness. The state of ludicrousness. And life as we look at it now… we look at Iraq, and we look at what's happening since Saddam Hussein has gone. The insurgency outstrips the IRA by a mile. It's a brutalised situation. But it's ludicrous, it's hysterical, it's ridiculous. And I think that's what Shakespeare's touching on. Those are the themes he touches on very carefully in the play. He deals with them so that, point/counterpoint, one ludicrous act follows another ludicrous act, so it's all about shocking, shocking, shocking. And it's very twentieth-century, it's very Artaud, it's very Theatre of Cruelty. You look at Brook, you look at Brook's development. You can see how a play like *Titus* would start him thinking about emotional Theatre of Cruelty which then, seven years later, he does at the LAMDA Theatre. And he starts his French-based theatre company. I think that's very much based on what comes out of *Titus Andronicus*. In a way he couldn't really do justice to *Titus*, because the main stage wouldn't allow it at the time. So it was very stylised. And although Olivier, I think, managed to sneak in a few of the jokes, most of them were excised.

You've written about the image of Archie Rice [in John Osborne's The Entertainer] *being much more vivid than the image of Hamlet. What did you mean by that?*

I think there's the performing element with Titus.

You think he's an actor?

Yeah. Because he has to pretend, which again anticipates Hamlet in feigning madness. How much does he feign madness, and how mad is he? I think he's so far gone that he's mad, nor'-nor'-west. He *does* know a hawk from a hand-saw, but he is kind of motoring, he uses his madness. First of all he uses it to seduce Tamora, and also to seduce the boys and win the boys' confidence, and then finally to murder them and bake them in the pies, and set them up for the mother. Now that's a mad, brutal act.

You're talking about the end of the play. Do you think he was mad earlier on?

Oh yeah. I think he realises his own insanity after the rape. The most incredible poetic piece is 'I am the sea', after his daughter has come out ravished, with her hands cut off and her tongue cut out. She's the only female in that world, they're all sons except for this one girl who is brutalised. Then of course at the end of that scene they bring on the heads of his sons. And suddenly his connection for family, which he's not made before, all comes at once. So there's a shock value like in a great Ibsen tragedy, that promotes something extraordinary. It's like Titus crying, and his tears melt the snow that brings down the ice that creates the avalanche. When finally he cries, it kills him. So the final part of his destiny is set in progress. And that's what's so extraordinary about the play, that he motors towards this diabolic end, but taking everything down with him, taking all the fabric of what is a corrupt society with him. It's a fascinating play, because I think that Shakespeare, as a young writer, is dealing with things in a way that is offbeat. The reason why the play seems to lack cohesion is that people can't accept the humour. They have difficulty with the humour. And that makes them go 'Oh, it's not really a very good play,' because it's a farce. But actually it's the humour, it's the black humour that is cohesive, it's the glue of the play.

It's in the text.

It's in the text. It really is.

'Bear thou my hand, sweet wench, between thy teeth!' [3.1]

Exactly. It's all there. And the whole thing with the fly, the murdering of the fly. The debate about whether you should kill a fly. First he's shocked and says 'Marcus, what did you do?' and then he goes nuts and starts beating the fly up. It's the sheer shock value. So you see Shakespeare experimenting, as he does in *Richard III*. He experiments with something slightly different in *Richard*. I remember going on to direct *Richard* because I was in a production which I found totally unsatisfying. I wanted to rediscover the play, and what this young man was intending and why is it a tragedy. It's called *The Tragedy of Richard III*. It doesn't seem a tragedy, but then if you dig close, here is a guy who was ostracised by his mother and by his sister, and he's been treated in such an offhand fashion that he's become this wicked, wicked boy. And of course it's different again with *King Lear*. Shakespeare in his forties starts to write this play, which is about his own rejection. Lear is a much more circumspect man who's looking back on his life, and seeing his children's rejection of him. And having played Lear later on, I can tell you it's a very depressing play to do. Whereas the great thing about *Titus* is that it's a blood and guts play. It's very energising, you have to be up there because of the humour. The whole thing has a kind of Burt Lancastrian dynamic to it.

I read that 'Cox took the audience into his confidence with nudges and winks'. You brought 'a spirit of dangerous jocularity' onstage with you.

Exactly, and I think that's in the text. I was at a stage in my career as an actor… over the years I'd often felt a bit of a fish out of water with stuff that I did in the theatre, and I never could find my way in. Because I wasn't conventional. I looked quite good as a young man but I wasn't conventional in terms of my playing. I wasn't your kind of effete young Englishman, or your poetic Welshman, you know, I didn't have that. I was a sort of rough-hewn Scot. Titus represented for me a kind of release. As a younger actor I was always asked to be tasteful – there was a decorous element about what one did, for fear of going across into bad taste. And what Deborah encouraged in me was the opposite. She encouraged my clowning, she encouraged my roots which lie in Jerry Lewis as opposed to Laurence Olivier. She encouraged that element which actually is where I come from, those wonderful comedic Scottish actors like Duncan Macrae and Fulton Mackay. Alastair Sim. There's an extraordinary element to them. And also John Laurie, who was a great, classic Scots actor. He was one of the leading men of the immediate post-First World War Shakespeare revival at the Vic. He played all those Hamlets. I remember John Laurie telling me this wonderful story. He said 'D'ye know I had this idea, son. When Hamlet... ye know... I thought... ye know... when Hamlet's finally stabbed in the fight and he turns to Horatio, I thought... ye know... it's a great idea just to say, "I'm dead, Horatio." And I thought it should get a laugh! But of course the powers... Lilian Baylis didn't like that at all. She said "Oh, ye cannee do that, John," But they'd laugh!' If you think about it there is a black humour in the play. And the setting of *Titus* was really very fortunate.

Can you describe the setting?

We did a thing they'd never done at Stratford. We started without any designer or any set, and we designed it as we went. Basically we had the idea of this big sandpit, like an extended children's sandbox. And we had images of clay, that came up through rehearsal. Then we had a wonderful designer called Isabella Bywater. Originally there was a leaning towards a Mafia kind of thing, but then we felt that located it too much in a specific environment, which always becomes limiting. So we decided against that – it wasn't going to work, so we threw it out. And then we came up with what we felt served our production, which was much more classical, much more Brechtian, using Roman artefacts and leather, swords and all that. But very, very simple.

But not set in the Roman period?

Well, we didn't exaggerate the Roman period. At one point we used a light bulb. But we were dressed sort of pseudo-Roman. If you look at Elizabethan Roman plays, they were often set in Elizabethan dress with elements of Ancient Rome. We did a similar thing with the twentieth century. We had a flavour of guerrilla soldiers, say Cuban rebels, Che Guevara, with armour and rough khaki and rough hessian. And off-greeny-grey linen clothes. We did a twentieth-century version of a Roman idea.

Lets the play breathe more.

That's right. And keeps the play much more plastic, which is what it requires.

Most directors come with a strong idea of a production from day one. You're describing a totally different process, aren't you?

Deborah doesn't do that. Deborah has a very strong aesthetic, but she always keeps her aesthetic up her sleeve. I think subsequently as a director, she's allowed the aesthetic to come much more to the fore. But in those days that wasn't the case. In those days she played better poker with it. She didn't allow the aesthetic to rear its head too early. You'll see it more in Deborah's later productions like *Richard II* and *The Good Person of Szechuan*. And then she moved on to work with Hildegard Bechtler, and it became omnipresent. But with Isabella, who she only worked with the once, it was a developing thing. It was much more organic. We took what was in the rehearsal room, and converted it. She would take implements, like these ladders that we used during rehearsal. We hit upon this brilliant idea of the boys – Titus' captives on their first entrance – being locked into the ladders, chained to the ladders. We used the ladders horizontally as yokes. And then we thought 'Well, sitting on the ladder, could be Titus.' So we devised this most extraordinary entrance for Titus, that he was carried in on the ladder held by these boys in a yoke. They're all supposed to be chained up anyway, like slaves. So the image was Titus coming on and being greeted, followed by his sons, with Tamora and her two boys and Aaron the Moor in their yokes. It was a brilliant image. But it came within the rehearsal process, it came one day when somebody grabbed a ladder and put his head through it. It's got the Brook influence on it, and it worked, it worked incredibly well. Deborah had that trust all the way through. I remember Estelle Kohler found it really difficult because she'd worked in such a traditional Royal Shakespeare way. When the sons were given to illustrating the stories, it was kind of fantastical, which Estelle found very throwing and she had to rethink.

What do you mean? I haven't got that. What were the sons doing?

Well, during their scenes the sons would do these pantomimic acts. They'd do all kinds of jokey things. Estelle found that tricky because she's used to classical Shakespearean enunciation, and 'This is *my* moment, this is Tamora's moment.' But Deborah wouldn't cut that business, she allowed it. She wanted much more of a sense of immediacy, rather than something that was beautifully rehearsed and beautifully presented. But in fairness to Estelle, she really took it on. She had worked in Stratford with a particular style, and suddenly she had to start again. She developed a much better sense of improvisation. And it worked. It wasn't improvised in the end – what we did was very clearly set down, it was like learning dance steps. Same thing in the scene towards the end where I was mad and started serving imaginary tea, I was miming teapots and counting the cups. It was a preamble to my dressing up in the chef's outfit. And we did the 'Heigh-ho'!

That took a lot of stick from the critics.

That took a lot of stick from the critics but it…

Were they right or wrong?

We only used a phrase of it. We wanted to do 'Off to work we go'. We wanted to constantly knock the audience off-balance, so they weren't getting what was expected, they were having to rethink very quickly. And it worked. Of course the purists get on their high horses. I've done it before. I did it in a production where John Peter damned me for using saxophones instead of trumpets. I used saxophones in *Richard III*, because I prefer the sound, I just like that sound.

One review said 'Every line of text seems to have been worked over with scrupulously colourless intelligence.' Which I thought was an odd sort of backhanded compliment. What do you make of that?

I don't understand that. 'Scrupulously colourless.' It was certainly scrupulous, but I don't think colourless. We worked over every line in terms of the meaning, or in terms of what the trajectory of the play was. You have to get the trajectory very clear in terms of where the textual intention of the play is going. You have to be absolutely clear on that front. Especially when you're doing a lot of very physical things as well. You can't just make it a purely physical production. I remember warning Deborah about this. I said 'There was a famous *Midsummer Night's Dream* that Brook did, which was a very liberating production, but parts of the text went out the window. And sometimes you didn't quite get the rhymes, or why they moved from verse into rhyming couplets.' I felt we had to be very careful, we couldn't just make it a bunch of young people's rants, we had to be meticulous. Maybe it's a subeditor's misprint – maybe he meant colour*ful* rather than colourless!

The play's full of violence and horror. Could you describe how some of the violence was staged?

Something implied is always much more scary than what is actually visible. So when my sons' heads were cut I off I said 'Don't let's have phoney imitation heads, let's have heads that are covered in muslin, blood-soaked, so you imagine that the contents are really pretty horrific.' When they were brought on, I'm with Marcus and I literally chuck one at Donald Sumpter, so he has to catch it like a goalkeeper. And of course with the head flying across the stage in a muslin bag, and Donald having to catch it... you'd hear a gasp from the audience because it just happened so quickly. And for cutting off my hand, we put a bag over it and used a wire cheese-cutter. Once the bag was over my hand I curled it up like this (I had a big enough sleeve) and Aaron put the cheese wire round and pulled it through. It appeared that my hand was in the bag, which then filled with blood. Everybody gasped, people fainted. We had people literally being carried out, especially when Lavinia came on. Her stumps were all wrapped, bloody, but again there was no bare flesh. It was always what seemed to be underneath – that was pretty horrific. That element of the production was very powerful.

I've got a recollection of people being stabbed, not in the corny old way under the armpit or in the ribs, but straight up between their legs in the groin.

Yeah, yeah. And the other thing was when I killed Lavinia [5.3]. Instead of stabbing her I used her like a ventriloquist's dummy. She sat on my knee, my child sitting on my knee, and then I broke her neck.

With one hand?

Using the stump, holding her neck against the stump, I turned her head away like this and broke her neck with the other hand. It was a very quick action. Donald was sitting behind me and he had a stick which he broke, so you heard this snap. Again it was so quick.

Tasty stuff.

It was all part and parcel of what the play is about. The play is about violent acts, sudden violent actions. But it was never pantomimic, because the grief element of the play is so powerful. David Bradley came to see it about five times, and I remember him saying it was the best play about grief he'd ever seen. The mourning element, the mourning of the daughter. And 'I am the sea' [3.1]. That scene, which is all about grief, about the realisation of losing his sons, it's just fantastic stuff. Here's this writer experimenting with ideas, and you see so many that have not left us, that's what's so fabulous about the play. People went 'Ah well, you know, Titus is just a grumpy old beast, it's not as great as the other plays.' But I quarrel with that.

He's got more cause to go mad than King Lear.

Oh yes, much more cause to go mad than King Lear. Lear has really just got his ungrateful daughters…

It's a picnic by comparison.

Exactly. *Lear* is a picnic! It's a deeper thing in *Lear*, though, but again the themes are there. I didn't enjoy *Lear* as much as *Titus*. It's just an enjoyable play. You came offstage and you felt that you'd had a workout by the end of it. And it did mark the card a little bit on the play, because people saw it and went 'Wow.' And then, you know, there have been productions since which have tried to go down that route, but haven't quite come at it from where we came at it. Because I think, historically, we hit a very interesting time. We liberated the play from its Victorian mythology. Brook was a great fan of it. He came to see it and said 'I couldn't have done that in 1955. I couldn't have done what you did. We didn't have the actors, in terms of an ensemble, who were prepared to do that kind of stuff.'

Most of the characters seem fairly straightforward, apart from Titus. But he's wonderfully complex. Going back to the beginning of the play, why did you turn down the candidacy to be Emperor? And why did you support Saturninus?

I think it's the fact that he's a soldier, he's not a politician. And he's not of royal blood. There are feudal elements to the play, and he sees very clearly where he is on the feudal ladder. He makes the wrong choice in supporting Saturninus, but he does it in order to safeguard something which... he believes that things are going to be better served by Saturninus. And he makes a massive error of judgement. Actually the reason he doesn't take on the candidacy of Rome is because he doesn't want it. He doesn't want to be Emperor, that's not who he is.

He says 'I'm too old, too tired, you'll have to elect somebody else tomorrow...' But do you think he really means it? Does he want to be asked three times?

No, I don't think he does, I think that's his honesty. He's an honest, bluff old soldier. That's what makes him an attractive character. Alright, he becomes wiry and wily, and he does all these tricks later on, but basically he's served Rome, and he's served Rome pretty well. His relationship to Rome is a very good one, because he's not done anything for himself. He's never feathered his own nest. He's given, given, given. And this is why the act of betrayal is so great. It suddenly dawns on him, 'I've given my whole life to the idea of Rome. I've given to the Royal Family, I've given to what I believed was right, I've followed traditional values.' He's very much a traditionalist. It's like Mountbatten or somebody, who's gone on doing certain things in a certain kind of way for truth, and finally he gets treated so badly that he flips. He suddenly says 'Well, hang on a second, I don't think this is right. I think this is wrong, and I've got to do something about it.' It's a bit late in the day, but I think he is a servant to Rome, and that's what he sees in himself.

Would you say Titus has a tragic flaw?

Yes, his tragic flaw is that he doesn't ask questions. He's unquestioning, he's a killing machine, and as a result he becomes brutalised. He sees the death of his sons as being rather noble. But then it impinges on him. When you've got thirty sons you don't notice it, but when it's down to four you begin to think 'Hang on, they've all gone!'

So what's his journey through the play? What does he learn?

The journey is to realise that he's lost his humanity, and to try to reclaim it. Which is what he does, in a sense, even by the dastardly killing of his daughter. And his line is guaranteed because at the end of the play his son takes over. It's really interesting that at the beginning of the play he was obviously a bit of a hero. He was a very popular figure. But if you are in the face of such action for so long, and you're used to serving, serving, serving, you begin not to be able to see further than the end of your nose. It happens to a lot of old soldiers, you know. Soldiers on the whole tend to live long lives, and they go through changes. They can emerge quite wise, but sometimes they behave brutally.

Looking at the play, you'd be tempted to think Titus pays a price that's way in excess of what he deserves for his faults.

Yes, I think to a certain extent that is true. But Shakespeare's a young man who's rubbing authority's face in the dirt. He's always playing with that, Shakespeare. His whole attitude to authority is questioning. 'Thou ladder which overreaches itself,' or words to that effect, Richard II says to Northumberland. He talks about the ladder, in the sense of people going beyond what they're supposed to. And neglect. Lear: 'I have taken / Too little care of this' [3.4]. He talks about neglect constantly, about these great figures who neglect their responsibility. There's a very powerful moral imperative throughout his plays. He talks about it in *Richard II* and in *Henry VI*, with the King wandering around saying 'Oh, I haven't really done what I should have done.' The Lancastrian wars, all of that. He's seen people who have neglected something very vital, a human responsibility or one of state. We think that the time we live in has become debased, but so many things go way back. They had Walsingham, they had the Cecils, and all the internecine struggles of these people who were running the country on Elizabeth's behalf. And I think Shakespeare thought 'These guys are a bunch of wankers. They're bastards, and they've let us down very badly.' His plays are full of references to 'We've allowed things to slip, we've allowed things to go', and *Titus* is about that. *Titus* is about this man who finally realises he's been fighting for the state so long, he hasn't noticed how decadent it has become until too late, and he has to pay the price. And Shakespeare says 'In order for you to redeem yourself you're going to have to walk barefoot on coals,' and that's what he puts Titus through. So there is a sense of redemption. It is heroic, ultimately. But it's quite interesting, where that kind of heroism comes from. Because we don't think of it as a heroic play. We think of other plays being much more heroic than *Titus Andronicus*.

Can you describe your appearance?

In the first scene I came on caked in mud, and later as I got madder the mud increased. My image was all to do with a corroded statue. It was to do with the statue of a once young, healthy soldier that over the years had been corroded, and then bits had broken away, and the nose had gone. I wanted this sense that the brutalising nature of his life had corroded him physically, and this was the last bestial act of corrosion. There was also a self-amelioration, in the sense that as he gets crazier and crazier, he comes to recognise his corrosion.

What about the chef's outfit at the end?

Well, it's a sudden… it's way off… it's outfield. But it's also to do with waking the audience up, and saying 'Now we're in this Walt Disney world.' Suddenly there's this guy coming on like one of those French chefs with a moustache, and doing that 'Heigh-ho! Heigh-ho!' And they think 'My God, this is weird!' It's also distressing, because the audience don't quite know what to do. They go 'What is this?' And then that's taken to its extreme with the baking of Tamora's sons in a pie, and getting her to eat it. He's gone, because he's played madness to a point where the line has been crossed. And then of course he comes back out of it again. It's an astonishing play, a truly astonishing play.

In the final scene there are three murders in three lines. Deaths purge, up to a point, and scores are settled. Your son Lucius becomes Emperor. Is there anything more positive, more upbeat that you recall?

I think, just relief. Relief it's all over.

For?

For everybody! The evening. The war is over. It's like the Iraq conflict. What a relief it'll be when we get out of there, if we sort it out. It's not sorted out. Looks as if it's not going to be sorted out… But a sense that after the events of the night, you don't need to comment on them by going into a big celebration. You just have to say 'Alright, he's King now. We've stopped. Enough. Now we're moving on.' Which is life.

Can you sum up?

He wrote a crowd piece, but he wrote it under the guise of all these ideas. He thought 'How can I do what I want to do, and at the same time make the money, make it successful?' And as you said, *Titus* was one of the most successful plays of the period. But he just threw everything at it. He threw the whole kitchen sink at it, and said 'I'm going to have a riot, I'm going to go nuts, I'm going to put in every idea.' And I reiterate: *King Lear, Coriolanus, Othello, Macbeth*, every single play is in that play.

A returning warrior, who doesn't know how to cope with life back home…

Exactly. It's fascinating, it's absolutely fascinating.

How was doing it in a small theatre? That must have been helpful?

It was, especially when people kept fainting! And in The Pit they used to wander onto the stage. One time I was mid-performance and I heard this woman go 'Help me, help me!' She was sitting in one of the side seats. I had to take her, still acting at the same time, and walk her off the stage into the vomitorium. I said to the ushers, 'Get her out of here!' As soon as she got past, she was on the floor, out for the count! That happened twice.

I'm not surprised.

They were so overcome. We had a man die in Paris.

Really?

Oh yeah. It's nothing to be proud of, but somebody actually died, at the end of the first act.

Of a heart attack?

Yeah. At the Bouffes du Nord. He sat in his seat and he didn't get up at the interval. It's a thing to go out on. Good God!

Judi Dench
on
Juliet

Romeo and Juliet (1595–6)
Opened at the Old Vic Theatre, London
on 4 October 1960

Directed and Designed by Franco Zeffirelli
With Thomas Kempinski as Tybalt, Alec McCowen as Mercutio,
Peggy Mount as the Nurse, and John Stride as Romeo

Romeo and Juliet is Shakespeare's early tragedy of 'star-cross'd lovers', whose youthful deaths ultimately reconcile their feuding families. Since its first performance in the mid-1590s it has remained one of his most popular plays. The lovers are united by their passion yet doomed to separation, and the fact that they have so little time together lends intensity to their relationship. They fall instantly in love, are married almost immediately, and enjoy just one single night together before their enforced separation. *Romeo and Juliet* brilliantly evokes the ardour of youth. A testament to the immortal power of what is frequently billed as 'The Greatest Love Story Ever Told', is the fact that each year thousands of letters are sent to 'Juliet in Verona' from young lovers, seeking her blessing or advice. The volume of mail is such that a local organisation, Il Club di Giulietta, devotes itself to replying on her behalf.

Romeo and Juliet has been revived, revised and adapted countless times on stage and film, and in musical, opera and ballet. The play draws much of its power from discord, and powerful versions have been made in areas of genuine conflict. It was famously transposed to 1950s New York for the musical *West Side Story*, depicting the rivalry between teenage street gangs, the Puerto Rican immigrant Sharks, and the 'True American' Jets. In 1994 it was set in Bosnia with a Christian Romeo and a Muslim Juliet. *Romeo and Juliet* has been filmed some sixty times, starting in 1900. Franco Zeffirelli's 1968 movie recreated much of the atmosphere of his stage production.

I was delighted when Judi Dench agreed to talk about playing Juliet, not least because my first job was as a limping, hunchbacked citizen of Verona in the same production, when it was recast for a long tour. By then the newspapers with their mixed notices were turning yellow, Judi was quite sensational, the show was eight months into its run and well on the way to becoming legendary. It was thrilling to be involved. I was a walk-on without a word to say but felt part of a rich onstage community. I knew what my character's job was, who I was married to, where we lived. I can still remember the fabric of noises, the whistling and shouting, grunting and groaning, dogs barking, birdsong, the tolling of bells and general din, street cries, distant offstage snatches of song and vendors bawling their wares.

I went to meet Judi for this interview in 2006 at her beautiful Elizabethan home in Surrey. Having played Juliet forty-six years earlier, some details had necessarily become hazy. But others were still razor-sharp, and the longer we talked, the more memories came flooding back. It made perfect sense that, for all her later triumphs in Shakespeare, this was the part she chose to discuss.

Julian Curry: You've played most of the great parts for actresses in Shakespeare. But Juliet holds extra-special memories for you. Why's that?

Judi Dench: Well, it was at the end of my second year at the Old Vic, I think. I'd been there since '57. And I'd played lovely things – Maria in *Twelfth Night*, the First Fairy in the *Dream* and Ophelia. But it came very much from left field when Michael Benthall [the Artistic Director] said he wanted me to do this. He was casting for Franco Zeffirelli, who'd never directed a Shakespeare play before, and so he was casting in the dark. I remember being absolutely thrilled – John Stride as Romeo and Alec McCowen as Mercutio. And then worrying that Zeffirelli would arrive and I might not be what he would want.

So you didn't audition for Zeffirelli?

No. Michael cast us, and I've never known whether Franco had been over and seen us all in something else beforehand.

Sent a spy, maybe. So it wasn't quite your first Shakespeare, but it was very early days.

We were in everything at that time, we weren't out of a play. *Merry Wives*, *Twelfth Night* and *Hamlet, Lear*. If you weren't actually in them, you were walking on and understudying.

Or playing a soldier.

Or playing a soldier. We played a lot of soldiers in the *Henry VIs*. I remember when we got Asian flu, all of us, they said 'Go, one of you, and pull down The Savoy.' And I ran off carrying a ninety-foot pole with a toffee apple on top of it, to tumultuous applause. And then they said: 'Let four captains / Bear Hamlet like a soldier to the stage' – and during the Asian flu, there were only four girls! So we'd been through quite a lot, yes. Learnt a lot.

Did you know the play well, did you have preconceptions?

What I knew is the Prokofiev music very, very well, and the Tchaikovsky music very well. I knew the play, but I had no preconceptions. The way Franco worked was very much on instinct, tremendously on instinct. You would be rehearsing and, out of the corner of your eye, you'd see him doing it beside you… much, much better than you were doing it!

So he was a demonstrator-director?

Well, he didn't want you to actually watch him, but he kind of wanted to share the emotion with you. And of course, it did make you share the emotion. I remember him saying 'I don't want anything stately about these two. They're children, they're little, young children, and they're entirely imbued with the passion of Italy and the passion of the feud between their families, and the passion between the two of them. There's nothing bridled about them. They're fast and impulsive. They're not contained in any way. They're completely free emotional spirits, passionate spirits.'

What do you remember about the production in general?

I remember there was a gasp on the first night. Because the Vic, I don't think, had ever seen anything quite like it.

Zeffirelli not only directed, but also designed the sets himself, isn't that so?

He did. He designed the sets. It opened with people putting their bedding over verandahs, and a marvellous sense of heat, and a fountain in the middle. It was spectacular to look at. And there was an incredible gasp when the lights went up. He taught us all. Franco didn't really have a regard for the verse, which is a great pity because we didn't know enough, and we were much criticised for that. But instead of the verse, he got the youth, because everybody looked and was very, very young.

The costume designer was called Peter Hall, wasn't he.

Yes. Not Peter Hall the director, another Peter Hall was the costume designer.

I read that 'he brought from Verona a collection of coloured pebbles picked up from the tessellated squares of that city, to act as a guide to the tones of the costumes'.

Absolutely. I'm sure that's exactly right. I had a wonderful old dresser who couldn't carry one of my dresses upstairs because of the weight. It was all soft browns and ochres and gold and cream. It looked like a painting.

A Renaissance fresco?

Yes. Exactly like that. Everybody dressed exactly like that.

The lighting was very warm and Mediterranean, wasn't it.

Yes, fantastic. Sometimes there were streaks of sunshine coming through a window or lattice. But when it was dark, it was really dark.

There was a beautiful lullaby during the blackout at the beginning. Tell me about the music.

It was Nino Rota who wrote the music. And his melody that he wrote for us, I think was later used for that radio programme on a Sunday, where people would write in and say 'my boyfriend's left me' and 'my father's died', and all that. I kept hearing that music, thinking 'That's vaguely familiar!'

I believe you were short of music just before the first night. So they locked Nino Rota away in a room and said 'Compose some more music!' When they came back two hours later he hadn't written a note. And they said 'What have you been doing?' He said 'Massimo [the assistant director] came, and we were talking about love.'

And I remember also, after a day's work, John Stride and Franco and I used to go to dinner in Soho. We were very relaxed about it, weren't we! I supposed that helped.

That was his first Shakespeare, but had he worked in England before?

An opera... had he done an opera before? I think he had, at Covent Garden. While we were doing *Romeo* we were asked to the first night of *Tosca*. The very first night with Callas and Tito Gobbi. I'll never forget it. Wonderful to think that we were there.

The fights were sensational.

Who did the fights?

Bill Hobbs.

Yes, he did. They looked really as if people were having a proper fight. I mean really, really. They were really animated and up and over everything, and up and down stairs. I can't imagine how long they must have rehearsed.

On the death of Mercutio [3.1], he and Tybalt were half playing at it until Romeo intervenes, and there's an accident.

Don't you remember how Alec used to be so surprised?

These days there are frightful street brawls with gang warfare and stabbings, every day you read about them, don't you. Do you think the guys in Romeo *are similar? Or are they more just showing off, being very cocky?*

Well, I don't know, I would have thought a bit of both. They were rival gangs. The beginning of *Romeo* is just two gangs challenging each other to see how far they can possibly go, saying rude things to each other. Then it gets serious. I mean, how very similar.

You were talking about the emphasis on youth, and saying how he seemed to improvise the production. But how much do you think was pre-planned, and how much made up as he went along? Could you tell that?

Well, of course, he has a strong idea about what he wants before he starts, but I always get the feeling with Franco that he kind of senses it as he goes along. I remember filming *Tea With Mussolini*, suddenly he said to me 'Oh, I know, we should have you with the vet with the dog.' I said 'The vet with the dog?' He said 'Yes, we will make this scene.' And I said okay. So we went on working, and about quarter-past five that afternoon he said 'Here is the scene with the vet with the dog.' He had cleared out the whole of his office, it was full of animals, and there I was sitting with my dog. I think that's why Franco was so wonderful with the play because he is a creature of instinct, very much, and passion. And although he would know the play, he would know the surroundings of the play, he would know intimately the detail, he would know what he wanted it to look like, and then he would throw himself in. That's what you got from him, that's what I remember. I loved it, that total instinctive thing.

Was he patient, or was he dictatorial? Particularly in those days, directors could be very dictatorial, couldn't they.

Yes. But I don't think he was, in the slightest.

The whole cast was rather in love with him, I think.

Oh, we were absolutely passionate about him. I have a photograph somewhere of him with my face looking sideways. I'm blurred in the foreground, he's looking with a cigarette in his mouth, at the way the plaits went, curled up like this at the back. It just summed up the care he took. We were absolutely mad about him.

The production rather divided the critics.

Oh, it didn't divide them about me. They all thought I was frightful, except Kenneth Tynan and Milton Shulman. Those two. Oh yes, I remember it clearly.

You weren't exactly showered with praise, it's true.

What was wonderful was when we went... were you with us in Venice?

Yes, I was.

It went up an hour and a half late because of a gondola crash, do you remember? And then all Franco's relations came round in the interval and took the champagne from our rooms. I'll never forget it. I didn't have one single bottle left. I was given champagne and they took it all and drank it in the interval. I didn't have a single bottle left.

The devils! I remember the technical rehearsal in Venice being interrupted at two o'clock in the morning because Anna Magnani – or Sophia Loren maybe – had come in to greet Franco, and the whole tech would have to stop and wait until they'd finished partying at the back of the stalls.

And the rake. I'll never forget in 'Gallop apace' [3.2], lying back on that bed and seeing two stagehands standing at the back of the bed like this, going *'Ohh-ohh, amore!'* Holding the bed. And also holding the wall. They were all braced by real people... I left it in Venice. That was my last performance. That was an emotional night. Crikey. I left it to go to the RSC.

To do what?

Anya in *The Cherry Orchard*. Franco never spoke to me for a long time.

Kenneth Tynan, as you said, loved it. He called the production a miracle and wrote 'Nobody on stage seems to be aware that he is appearing in an immortal tragedy.'

Yes. That's just as it should be. Franco was very anti that thing of being two statuesque lovers standing and saying the lines. And of course we swung, perhaps, too far the other way. But nevertheless I wouldn't have foregone any of it for anything.

Milton Shulman wrote 'It looks and feels like Verona. The citizens might be Veronese. Everything about this production pulsates with radiant light, and the picturesque seediness of Italy.'

That's right! Everything was really broken down. Do you remember? The bottoms of walls and things like that, he spattered the base of walls with dirty water to look like dog pee. Edith Evans said 'The costumes are disgusting. You all look so dirty!' It did exactly look like a painting.

On the other hand, critics wrote 'The poetry is lacking... The lyric poetry is underplayed... The beauty of the poetry was lost.' Why do you think that was?

Well, I think it's because we were very young. We were twenty-three or something.

Did you have any kind of dialogue coach?

No. Franco, as I said, was dead against any statuesque delivering of poetry. He said that you must imbue it with all the passion. With what I know now it would be different, but we didn't know then about the verse. Because we didn't have dialogue coaches at the Vic, or people like Peter Hall or Trevor Nunn or

John Barton, we didn't have that. Therefore there wasn't the attention paid to speaking Shakespeare, as I now believe there always must be. It would have been an asset had we had that knowledge. Michael Benthall taught me all I knew about speaking Shakespeare from 1957. But it obviously wasn't enough to hold me in good stead through all the things that Franco wanted us to do.

There was another even earlier famous Romeo and Juliet *when Gielgud and Olivier alternated playing Mercutio and Romeo. Olivier was also criticised for mangling the verse when he played Romeo.*

Isn't it interesting.

About the lovers – this will make you laugh – R.B. Marriott said 'The lovers are the best I've seen in many years.' But Harold Hobson wrote 'What has happened to youth? Where is its spring, its élan? Are there no high spirits in the world except for Mr Khrushchev's?'

'Except Mr Khrushchev's'? Was he a madman? He was already losing it, wasn't he!

So in general they loved the settings, the fights, the crowd scenes, the vivid evocation of Verona, the youth, vitality, ardour, the urgency. But they harrumphed about the neglect of poetry. And fussy bits of business. They didn't like you fiddling with Romeo's collar while you talked about nightingales and larks, at the end of the dawn scene [3.5] when you've just been to bed together for the first time, and he has to go. They were very old-fashioned and picky in their attitudes.

That's why you must learn never to read them. It was very soon after that that I refused to read another notice.

They're summed up in the London Theatre Magazine*: 'It's hard to remember a production that's won such flatly contradicting opinions, from "appalling" and "worst ever" to "the best London Shakespearean production since the war... If Mr Zeffirelli has ignored our time-honoured traditions, then it's only time someone did, for the English theatre is becoming petrified in its own conventions".' What do you make of that?*

Well, I suppose they welcomed a kind of other glance at it, and somebody not being so reverential, do you think? Was Shakespeare petrified? I remember seeing some wonderful productions at the Vic before that.

There was a temptation for actors to look for steps, and stand with one foot up and one foot down.

Absolutely. Oh, that, certainly. And all the make-up. Everyone putting a mark here. Everyone had cleft chins. Don't you remember, it got a notice once that everybody at the Vic had cleft chins!

It was a completely groundbreaking production. But in rehearsal, were you all aware of that? Were you thrilled by it in rehearsal?

Franco was very different, because of his passion and his glamour. He was very glamorous. And because he would be very witty and camp, and that was wonderful. So of course we were, as you said, absolutely charmed. And it was thrilling working with him. Thrilling. So fuck them.

But during rehearsals, I'm curious to know if you realised then that you were on to a winner. With Brook's Midsummer Night's Dream, *before it opened some of the cast thought it was going to be terrible, a mess. They really didn't know it would work, because it was so different.*

I don't know. I just remember having a lot on my plate, thinking this is a lot to do.

So, talking about the characters. Do you remember a difference between the two families, the Montagues and the Capulets?

No, I don't think there was any difference at all.

Romeo is described at the beginning of the play in courtly lover terms, isn't he. 'With tears augmenting the fresh morning's dew' [1.1]. Daniel Day-Lewis, after having played Romeo at Stratford, described him as 'a wanker'. But Stride wasn't very much like that, was he.

Not remotely. I suspect he was probably one of the best Romeos that's ever been. He had those rounded features, very, very boyish-looking. I thought he was just spectacular.

He was very energetic. No kind of a drip at all.

Not at all.

What about the balance between the two of you? Was one more mature than the other?

I don't think so. Well, not the way that we approached it. I remember watching the ballet and seeing Juliet come in with the doll when she's called to her mother about Paris at the beginning, and I thought 'Oh yes, that's just wonderful.' Because, although they were expected to marry very young, nevertheless what's so important is the immaturity, and that fantastic innocence of both of them. When he talks about Rosaline, I think Romeo is in love with an *idea* of a person. But this is like nothing either of them has ever experienced. So in their passion and in their practice, they're as unpractised as each other.

Alec McCowen was described as a 'beatnik Mercutio'. Can you make sense of that?

No. No, that's rubbish. A beatnik? Why? Just because he was rather anarchic and waspish? Well, I suppose in that sense every Mercutio should be a beatnik. But it's a curious expression to use.

I remember you talking about Juliet as a 'running, laughing and falling down performance'.

George Baker said to me 'That's the swiftest Juliet I've ever seen.' Well, I don't want to be a sitting target!

You gave an interview to the Evening Standard *when you said 'Looking back to my own fourteen-year-old experiences, I would never have taken love as seriously as that. I was thinking more about hockey and that sort of thing.'*

Was I? Did I say that? Well, I don't think that's Juliet. But I do think that the wonderful thing is that she grows up during it, and has to come face-to-face with her own youth and the consequence of what she's done. But at the beginning I don't think she should have that awareness at all, she's a child. Otherwise, if she's knowing... it's like Lady Macbeth coming on and if you think 'My God, she looks rough, she's a bit sinister...' there's nowhere for the character to go. You cannot believe at the beginning of *Macbeth* that that woman is going to do what she does. Otherwise, why does she invoke the spirits? And Juliet, as a child at the beginning, suddenly runs into something which is completely overwhelming. Impulsively it all builds, builds, builds, and she has to take stock and grow up, as it were, during the play. Become wiser and calmer.

All sorts of other things were written about you. 'A vigorous, mischievous teenager, instead of the usual highly lovesick heroine.'

Yes, I don't think she gets lovesick, she doesn't know what lovesick is about.

'She's too much given to paraphrasing the lines.'

Oh my God, I hope Peter Hall, Trevor Nunn or John Barton don't hear that!

'We see Judi Dench change from eager girlhood to womanhood onstage.'

Good. Who wrote that? What a discerning person. Fuck the rest!

'She flits about the stage like a brown butterfly.'

'A brown butterfly', that's nice. Yes, it was a brown dress.

'Miss Dench sheds her kittenishness when she lolls on the bed aching for love, and even more effectively when she stands wide-eyed and soul-stabbed at the threat of her husband's exile.'

Good. They all saw different performances!

'Exciting and moving. Gets stronger as the play progresses, instead of weaker as usually happens.'

Well, so it should be. It has to be that way, doesn't it. She goes to take the potion, you know. Of course she gets stronger as the play goes on. You stupid man! Or woman… it's bound to be Caryl Brahms, she loathed me.

I'm coming to Caryl Brahms…

Oh God, don't! Is it 'She looks something like an apple in a Warwickshire orchard'?

No, it's quite nice, actually.

Oh, I can't believe it. She never said a nice thing about me.

She said you were 'The merriest tragedian of them all'.

I reckon she'd say that. She used to call me 'Dench, J.' She never called me Judi Dench. So she can fuck herself.

Don't you like being called 'The merriest tragedian of them all'?

No. Because I know the way she says it.

Juliet's an only child, isn't she? There's no sign that she's got friends or siblings.

No. I don't think she needed any. I don't think she sees her father and mother that much. The Nurse looks after her.

I remember someone in the cast saying 'Judi doesn't hang about, she doesn't linger in the wings before a scene.' They said you would time going from your dressing room, so you went straight onstage.

It must be the only time I've ever done that in fifty years.

I was wondering if you were a bit of a Method actress in those days.

No, I've never been a Method actress. I was probably doing something, drawing on somebody's door. There wasn't much time, actually, to linger. I was always going and changing. Hugely quick changes. It was just off and straight back on again.

So it was nothing to do with not wanting your concentration to be broken?

No, no, nothing like that.

The word 'beatnik' cropped up again, connected with you: 'An Italian gives Juliet a beatnik heart.'

I don't know what that means. Does it mean that we don't stand about?

I wonder whether it means that you were a rebellious modern spirit.

Maybe.

Some parts in Shakespeare – even some leading characters – are quite passive, aren't they. But Juliet rather motors the play, she takes important decisions.

She ultimately takes important decisions. She doesn't at the beginning.

She proposes to Romeo in the balcony scene, doesn't she? She says 'If you're serious about this…'

Well, he first declares his love to her, and then she to him. In those days you didn't mess about. You didn't say 'Are you ready for a quick one round the back?' If somebody declared love to you, however soon it was after you met, and you declared love back to them, it would be marriage. It wouldn't be a quick snog anywhere, would it!

I suppose not. But the fact that this innocent fourteen-year-old virgin says 'If you're serious, marry me, and I'll see you round the Friar's tomorrow morning…'

Yes, quite. But you know, she was going to have to go round the Friar's anyway, to meet Paris. Her relationship with Paris comes I think as a great surprise to her. When her mother says at the beginning, 'I want you to look on him, he's a very good catch,' that's quite a surprise. All she can say is 'I'll look to like, if looking liking move' [1.3]. It comes from left field! She thinks 'Good grief, it can't be that already, can it?' The odds must have suddenly stepped up quite a bit for that child.

The parents are quite gentle with her over the marriage, at the beginning.

Yes, at the beginning they just suggest it. Even so, it's quite a surprise to her.

In the first scene, how did you feel about the Nurse, with her endless stories and ramblings?

I remember the opportunity to set up that whole relationship with the Nurse. She is Juliet's confidante, the person she sees much more than her mother. She's the person who makes her laugh, and the person who'd be there if she fell down and cried. And then also a feeling of impatience with her, to say 'Just pack it up for a minute!' That's the real opportunity to set up her life before the play, her childhood.

She could laugh at her and be warm towards her, but also be impatient.

Absolutely. Be angry with her, yes. Much more at ease than with her mother.

You've said it was one of the fastest Juliets, running, laughing and falling down. Is that in danger of undermining the tragedy?

Well, it would depend when you did it. I don't think the person who is a tragedian necessarily doesn't run. Or fall down, or laugh. I think that if you can learn to turn on a sixpence then you can encompass all those things, like a real person. Who doesn't! King Lear gets pretty silly from time to time, but that doesn't diminish what happens to him. It's what circumstance does to you, and then how it affects you, that changes your character. But if it enabled me to show them somebody very young, and then you saw her grow up in front of your eyes, it seems to me that I achieved something for the play.

In the ballroom scene [1.4], can you describe your first meeting with Romeo over the sonnet?

All I remember is that Natalia Makarova came, with Masoud Khan, and we were all going out to dinner afterwards. And as I stood there ready to dance with Brian Spink as Paris, I thought 'Not only am I going to show her that I can act, but I'm going to show her I can dance as well!' I took one step forward, trod on the inside of my dress, and fell up it! The dancing was very formal and extremely beautiful, with all those wonderful colours... red, orange, gold, everything. I can just remember going round and seeing Romeo out of the corner of my eye.

It's described here: 'Juliet slips step by casual step round the periphery of the crowd to find herself with ingenuous surprise, near enough to Romeo...'

To get his hand... did he catch my hand?

'...for him to take her willing hand.' And then it says 'They're at once in a world of their own, quiet and private among the milling guests.'

That must have been what it was. I do remember seeing him first... and then somebody singing...

Elric Hooper.

Elric! Elric singing. And then moving round the outside, yes.

He was upstage-centre with a horseshoe of people round him.

That's right. We moved round the outside, and met downstage, the two of us. That's right, I'd forgotten.

And he pulled you out away from the crowd, towards the audience. It was a fabulous stage picture.

There were always things happening in the background. Because Franco staged it all in such a way there was a proper life going on. It's like at the beginning, with people putting their stuff out over the balcony. It doesn't say that in the text; it doesn't say that there's somebody singing. That was Franco's invention.

At the end of the scene you say 'If he be married, / My grave is like to be my wedding bed' [1.4]. Were you aware of being a star-crossed lover?

I think it's for the audience to understand the dual meaning of those lines. Not her at all. She's somebody who's suddenly so struck with love that she's saying 'That's the person above all that I want to be with, want to be married to. And if he's married, then there's nothing left for me.' But I think that you mustn't ever act with foreknowledge. But you shouldn't pre-empt what actually happens to her. I remember when we did *Macbeth* [at the RSC, 1976; see pp. 143–69], I used to say to Trevor Nunn and Ian McKellen that we ought to approach this thinking that some schoolchildren will come and maybe not know that we kill Duncan. And it was a wonderful thing to keep in mind. Because they shouldn't know until they see that scene of the play. So it may be that *Romeo and Juliet* will end happily, for some people who come to it for the first time. When they went to see the play when it was first put on, they didn't know at all. They went and watched this thing unfold.

Getting onto the balcony scene [2.1], again more diverse opinions. Kenneth Tynan said 'The balcony scene is heart-rendingly good. Their encounter is grave, awkward and extremely beautiful.' Harold Hobson said…

He wasn't having a good evening.

No, he wasn't! He wrote 'In the balcony scene Miss Dench flaps her arms about like a demented marionette.' 'Awkward' is a word that crops up again. Alan Brien said 'The balcony scene was clumsy and awkward.'

Yes, I think that's what Franco wanted.

Why?

Franco wanted it not to be easy, not easy. The balcony too high, and not easily reachable. Sometimes when you see it, he could just leap up there. But it should be awkward, and it should be unprecedented in their lives. Certainly unprecedented in Juliet's. And she's got somebody inside calling her all the time.

How close to each other did you get? You touched hands…

Just touched hands.

Did you kiss?

I don't think so.

Quoting again: 'Juliet runs up and down the balcony, whirling herself about with pleasure at her lover's appearance. Or, she lolls over the side…'

I remember all that.

'She is not a tragic heroine at the outset of a tragedy…'

Good!

'…she's the girl from next door, amused by her boyfriend.'

Not quite.

'He clambers awkwardly up the tree and is always in imminent danger of falling off the balcony edge.' Did you get laughs in the balcony scene?

Well, some – and rightly. There are some wonderfully funny lines. 'I have forgot why I did call thee back' used to get a good laugh. And why shouldn't it. It's not practised, it's two children there.

We were talking about the differences, the balance between them. It seems that Romeo is the wildly poetical and ardent one, and Juliet's a little bit more practical in this scene, isn't she? She's rather more 'How did you get here? It's a high wall.' And he says 'With love's wings…'

He suddenly finds a language for them. But then she says:

> My bounty is as boundless as the sea,
> My love as deep: the more I give to thee,
> The more I have, for both are infinite.

Crikey! They both come out with some pretty sensational things.

'The clock struck nine…' She's not as euphoric and relaxed in her next scene [2.4].

She's not relaxed at all. And she's rather irritated with the Nurse.

You got quite ratty with her.

She imagines everything that's happened. She suddenly thinks 'Is the Nurse reliable in a matter of this kind?'

Is she also worried that Romeo was only fooling around last night?

I think everything. Because her world's completely changed from one day to the next. Totally changed.

But it works out fine and you go to Friar Lawrence's cell to meet Romeo [2.5]. The Friar says 'You shall not stay alone / Till Holy Church incorporate two in one.'

Because just before that, Romeo went to kiss me. And the Friar used to say, 'I'm sorry, but THIS HAS GOT TO STOP!' We were absolutely… we couldn't wait to get into each other's arms, and he actually used to hold us apart.

You were extremely hot.

Mmm. Overexcited.

So he had to hold you apart physically?

Yes.

'Gallop apace…' Another fantastic scene for Juliet [3.2]. 'She's flinging herself about in paroxysms on a great bed.' This was another of the things that upset some of the more staid critics.

Yes, they had a fit, because it usually was said standing and staring straight out.

They didn't like the fact that you were writhing in erotic expectation.

Well, too bad! I remember at one moment falling backwards. Later on a dancer did it in a ballet – Lynn Seymour, I think it was. Somebody remarked, and she said 'Oh, I picked that up from Judi Dench.' I used to lean backwards over the side.

Big shift from the ballroom and the balcony scene. This was raunchy…

Because everything is within reach suddenly. He's going to arrive. That's never happened to her before, it's all new.

What's the Nurse doing when she comes in and says 'Oh, he's dead, he's dead. Oh, woe is me!' Surely she must know that she's misleading?

I think the Nurse is in such a state, having been complicit in the whole plot. She doesn't know what she's saying, does she. And obviously Tybalt is a great favourite of hers. Crikey!

But the way she goes on and on and on…

Well, she's not bright. But she's not wilfully unkind. I think she's completely bemused and wrapped up in her own feelings.

It's very different from the earlier scene with the Nurse [2.4], when you're asking 'What's the news? What's the news?' and she says 'Ah, my back, my back!…'

Yes, that's wonderful, because it's the Nurse sending Juliet up. Ros Atkinson, when she took over from Peggy Mount, instead of 'Have you got leave to go to shrift today?', she said 'Have you got leave to go to Shrifton?' I'll never forget it. It's a wonderful place, obviously in Wiltshire. But no, I just think in the later scene the Nurse is beside herself, because of the enormity of what is happening. I don't think it's wilful, thinking 'I'll give her a terrible fright.'

Then you've got this extraordinary oxymoronic speech [3.2] – 'A damned saint, an honourable villain!', etc. And she moves from saying 'O serpent heart, hid with a flow'ring face!' to 'Shall I speak ill of him that is my husband?' in the space of a few lines…

'Where is my father and my mother, Nurse?' – 'Here we are, darling, in row H!' You know, that was my father.

What?

That's an absolutely gospel true story. Franco had me on the ground, in a nightie – he had copied a child's nightie, a most marvellous shape – and instead of being all poetic, he had me crouching on the ground. I said 'Where is my father and my mother, Nurse?' My parents had come down from York to see it, and Daddy said, loud enough for them to hear around him, 'Here we are, darling, in row H!' He was completely carried away.

How did you react?

I didn't hear it.

It would have been difficult if you had.

Desperate.

There's a huge journey during that one scene, isn't there?

To maturity.

Then you have the dawn bedroom scene [3.5].

Of course. 'It was the nightingale, and not the lark…'

You have to cry a lot in that scene.

I don't remember crying a lot. I can remember Johnny Stride sweating a huge amount.

This is a lovely thing said by Penelope Gilliatt: 'I've never seen the dawn love scene played with greater documentary truth of euphoric tiredness and clandestine departure.' And then there's another of those premonition lines: 'Methinks I see thee, now thou art so low, / As one dead in the bottom of a tomb.'

Well, it's a premonition again, a signpost perhaps, for the audience.

So it's not in her mind?

Well, if it is, I think it's only momentarily. Otherwise it erodes from his death when it actually happens. It's not in the play that she has a premonition of any ghastliness happening, or that their plan shouldn't work...

Unless you play that as a premonition.

Unless you play it, yes. Some nights you might, I suppose; some nights not.

You might change it from night to night?

I might. You know how when you get a chance to play something over a run, you change it ever so slightly all the time. I would never make a hard and fast rule, I don't think, except about some key pointers. I remember in *Antony and Cleopatra* [with Anthony Hopkins, 1987–8], I was absolutely certain there was a laugh on one line. We did a hundred performances at the National Theatre, and on the last performance I got the laugh. And I knew it was there, I just knew. It's funny, isn't it!

Carrying on with the same scene [3.5], the father turns into a brute.

It's just simply terrible. And after the emotion of that night too, the first night she's spent with Romeo, and then quite suddenly that happens – banging doors and saying 'Come on, you're going to be dragged to church...'

To marry somebody else. She turns to the Nurse and says 'Comfort me, counsel me.' Very vulnerable. And the Nurse says...

'Get on!'

'Get on, marry the other fella. Romeo's a dishclout...'

She's isolated. Left to her own device.

So you go to the Friar's cell and you meet Paris, who flirts with you in a rather tacky way [4.1]. And then you go back to your parents, and find that you can lie to them about marrying Paris [4.2]. Is that easy?

Once she's made her decision. Her resolve is much bigger than her lying. Her mind is on what she's got to do. She's just going to say yes, and agree to anything on the way. She knows at a certain time matters will be out of her hands, and out of theirs.

And then you've got the potion speech [4.3]. Juliet's got a lot of soliloquies. It's a wonderful thing to have soliloquies, isn't it.

It certainly is. Well, if they step the play on, yes. It's like a song in a musical. If the song doesn't step the story further, cut the song. You've got to find a way with those soliloquies that moves the story on. And of course they do. 'Gallop apace...' [3.2], there can't be anything greater than that to describe the state she's in. They're thoughts spoken out loud in the midst of some great emotion. And the fear – that's when I cracked my ribs – the fear of deciding to take the phial, and thinking 'Christ Almighty, I'm going to be put into the family tombs. What if the ghost of Tybalt... what if all that... what if...' You know...

You cracked your ribs in the potion scene?

Mmm. So that wasn't for the audience. It was real, real fear. I remember Franco saying maybe she hasn't got the courage to do it, and starting very quietly, with 'I'm going to do it...' Then I got myself into a really terrible, terrible state. Because he said, when she says 'Methinks I see my cousin's ghost', she should actually do so, the fact should be that she's seen him. And then the extreme fear was what made her go 'For Christ's sake, don't think about it any more, just do it!' A very different person from the girl you see at the beginning. I think she drives herself with her imagination, and fear of what she's got to do, to a point where she suddenly takes the potion.

Then the final scene [5.3].

It was very dark, really dark, I'll never forget it. There was that huge long catafalque...

Big and gaunt.

It was really grey and cold, icy cold and no light.

Were you ever tempted for a moment by the Friar's suggestion of going off into a nunnery instead of killing yourself?

I don't think for a single minute. That's not an option for Juliet. No, I don't think so. Not for a second. I remember being given a note saying it's very, very hard to kill oneself – she stabs herself, doesn't she. I remember not really realising how difficult it is to push the blade of a knife. I got that note quite late on. I saw an exquisite thing when Ian McKellen and Francesca Annis did it. As he kissed her, when he was dying, her hand just moved behind him. It was heartbreaking. Because it's, you know, life and death, just balanced like that. Her hand just flickered. Too late for him to see it. Wonderful.

It wasn't easy to kill yourself, but you had really no option.

Oh, there was absolutely no option. No option at all. I think she just thought that once he is dead, there is no… what life is about. And then they played that melody at the very end, the same as at the beginning, with all the families.

Can you summarise Juliet's journey through the play – what she's learnt, what's she's lost, what she's gained?

Well, I think it has to be the journey of a young girl to an incredibly mature woman. And she of course learns courage, and she learns passion, she learns what love really is. I think there should be a marked difference from the person you see in the first scene to the person you see at the end. It's a great, huge, life-changing experience, that happens in a very short time.

Do you think Juliet's got a tragic flaw?

I don't know. I've never thought in those terms about it.

I thought that production of Romeo and Juliet *was so wonderful, I've never particularly wanted to see it since.*

I've never seen it since, apart from Ian and Francesca. Not because I think ours was so wonderful, but because I just haven't seen it since.

You take a little shareholding in a part, don't you, especially when a production's that special…

Yes. You feel proprietorial about it, because you've worked on it and you've done it night after night, and therefore you kind of think that you discovered it… or sometimes that you *didn't* discover the play! I see wonderful productions of *The Merchant of Venice* – I thought ours was lousy. But I don't like the play. We had the luxury at the Vic, as you do at Stratford and the National, of playing for months in repertory. Therefore being able to think 'No, that bit's not right, that bit's not right, but I'll get it right tomorrow.' Like the laugh in *Antony*. I remember some performances of *Romeo* when people were absolutely… the wonderful excitement of that feeling catching in the audience and catching in the cast. I think it happens less and less as you get older. But there were times when, somehow, it fell into place for that night. And when that happens, it's wonderful. It happened on the first night of *Antony*. Our first night of *Antony* was the performance that we did the best up to that moment. Afterwards, I think we got it much, much better. But that night, that wonderful gratifying thing of thinking 'Well, that's it. That's what we've done so far.' Whereas you can get to a very good stage in rehearsal, and suddenly the first night comes and it falls short of where you've reached. With *Macbeth*, I feel that we really cracked something, we really cracked it with that production at The Other Place. Because the journey of it all was so clear to me, so clear. I used to wonder, why did Edith Evans think there was something missing of Lady Macbeth? There cannot be, because it's as clear as bright daylight.

Ralph Fiennes
on
Coriolanus

Coriolanus (1608)
Almeida Theatre Company
Opened at Gainsborough Studios, Shoreditch, London
on 14 June 2000

Directed by Jonathan Kent
Designed by Paul Brown
With Oliver Ford Davies as Menenius, Emilia Fox as Virgilia,
Barbara Jefford as Volumnia, and Linus Roache as Tullus Aufidius

Coriolanus is a Roman history play and Shakespeare's last tragedy. It is a natural choice in times of political turbulence. The play focuses on the political divide between democracy, as favoured by the tribunes, and the autocracy represented by Coriolanus. He can be seen either as a hero deserted by a fickle populace, or as a villain whose arrogance threatens dictatorship. In 1930s Paris it was suppressed as the cause of pro- and anti-Fascist street demonstrations. The Nazis identified Coriolanus with Hitler as a model of leadership. Conversely, Brecht's adaptation of the play presented it as a tragedy for the proletariat. And a production in Communist Moscow stressed Coriolanus's treachery and aristocratic pride. It was hailed as a lesson in the betrayal of the people by an individualistic leader in the Western mode.

Shakespeare introduced a human dimension, in Coriolanus's dependence upon his mother Volumnia. She prides herself on having moulded her son, and his identity relies to a pathological degree on her esteem. The tone of the play is serious throughout, without any of the comic characters, low-life scenes, or other devices that Shakespeare often used to leaven his tragedies. What little comedy there is resides in Coriolanus's unbending attitude, the tribunes' wily manipulations, and the cowardice, hypocrisy and fickleness of the plebeians.

When I asked Ralph Fiennes if he was willing to be interviewed for this book, he was adamant that this was the role he wanted to talk about. Despite his brilliance on the battlefield, Coriolanus is amongst the least sympathetic of Shakespeare's tragic figures. He is haughty and anti-democratic, sneers at hungry plebeians and is completely devoid of political tact. This is part of the character's fascination. I'd worked with Ralph years earlier when he was playing the saintly, unworldly Henry VI at the RSC. But he is not an actor who needs to be taken to the audience's heart. He put down a strong marker to that effect as the sadistically amoral Amon Goeth in *Schindler's List*, and has since notched up several other very nasty pieces of work. When I went to meet him, one morning in July 2007, I thought there must have been a mistake about the address. The East London street was narrow and dingy, a knock at the door produced no response. Not a predictable film star's residence. However, I phoned up and Ralph answered, having just got out of the bath. He let me into a pleasant, relaxed dwelling – open plan with bare brick walls – and made tea and toast. He proceeded to speak about the character with tremendous enthusiasm and urgency. I had to suggest a break in recording or I thought he would never get round to eating the toast.

Julian Curry: You've played plenty of the great Shakespearean parts. What's special about Coriolanus?

Ralph Fiennes: It's an odd role for me. I did it paired with *Richard II,* always a part I'd had my eye on. Jonathan Kent suggested a double bill with *Coriolanus.* There's no particular connection between the plays, except they're both about people who aspire to power and abuse it. They can't handle it, and fuck it up. And I just became obsessed with this man. He's one of the hardest characters to like, I think. The play is like a horrendous, uncompromising cliff face. It doesn't have any of the warm, human, lyrical moments that you associate with Shakespeare. It seems to be a relentlessly uncompromising, jagged piece. Likewise, he is this peculiar, twisted, repressed machine. He's pulped and conditioned, malformed by his mother. But I love the anger in it. And he has this aspiration to unbending purity. It can be repellent and fascist, but it's also… he's trying to be something distilled. I think it is a real tragedy. And interestingly, most people I spoke to seemed to dislike him initially, and then feel he is the victim of political manipulation and Machiavellian intrigue. Which he is – he's manipulated by the tribunes, by the people.

And by Aufidius later on.

Yes. Well, he's betrayed by Aufidius.

You've worked with Jonathan Kent a lot, so presumably that gives you a useful kind of shorthand. Can you describe his processes?

He comes with a strong design concept, look – whatever you want to call it – that's well thought out. But I don't think the cast ever felt pushed into anything. Maybe with *Richard II* (which Jonathan had been in before, as an actor) there was more sense of that. I remember thinking sometimes, 'Why should I do that?' But with Coriolanus I felt free. It evolved between us. He's very open to see what happens. The best thing for me, the way I love, is when you both have ideas. The director and the actor each has an idea, a sketch in their heads.

Two-way traffic.

Yeah. You can put things on the table. You're not sure about this, but that was good, and what happens if you do such-and-such. The setting was very strong, because the two plays were designed to be in the Gainsborough Studios, the old Hitchcock film studios in Shoreditch which have since then, tragically, been turned into modern-style apartments. But because the developer was about to knock them down, we could mess with the structure relatively cheaply. We had in essence what was originally built, a Victorian or Edwardian power station. There had been a thick, heavy, concrete floor across the middle that I think had been put in later, which we took out. So we created this big, big, high space. Acoustically it was very difficult, especially for *Coriolanus*.

It had a giant gash down the back wall.

Yes, we smashed through the wall to get this jagged effect. It was like a split in the wall, and it went from being wide at the top to quite narrow at the bottom, just enough so you could walk through, and that was your upstage entrance. There was reasonably good wing space on stage-right. Left, there was not enough. Where there would normally have been wing space, there was none. The stage went right up to the exterior wall, so the only entrance on that side was the upstage-left doorway onto a sort of platform. There was a permanent little gangway or catwalk, which was visible. But it worked.

You had a glass panel in the middle of the floor, I think.

Yes. It was toughened perspex or something, with lights in it. It was there that the senators sat on little stools or chairs, as a way of spatially defining the senate area when you wanted it to. It was not great to be on because it was very slippery. I think probably it looked quite good, like an installation piece. But I don't know that it quite did what we were told it was meant to do.

What about the costumes? They were described as 'A mixture of modern chic with trappings of ancient Rome.' Is that what you remember?

Yes, they were loosely modern. No one was conventional except Oliver Ford Davies, who played Menenius, he had a suit. The other senators had sort of Nehru-collared-style suits. I had an extremely military tunic, reduced as it were. There were no decorations, just a simple tunic, very dark green, and dark trousers.

So it wasn't rooted in any particular period?

No, it wasn't. It was a loosely modern, minimalist style, and then for the senate scenes we had these toga-like robes. Actually I've seen a number of productions do that, Roman productions. They stick people in suits, and they've also got all these sort of toga-y things. They did that in Deborah Warner's *Julius Caesar.*

The play is abnormally rich in stage directions. Shakespeare also actually specifies the clothes at certain moments, very humble clothes.

The 'garment of humility' [2.3].

Yes, and the disguise 'in mean apparel', when you go to Antium to join Aufidius [4.4].
Something else about the play that struck me is the language. A lot of it is very diffi-
cult.

We cut a fair amount. I think Jonathan would like to have cut more. It is very, very difficult. It seems deliberately obtuse sometimes, and you feel as if Shakespeare's really trying something odd. But interestingly, despite the language being nubbly and difficult, the energy of the play is very clean. It doesn't go off into little subplots or anything, it's like a streamlined missile.

There's no subplot at all.

No, there's not. It's just like this hard metal chomp.

It's one of Shakespeare's most political plays, and it's had very diverse interpretations.

Well, I can see all those things. We were more interested in the psychology of what happened between him and his mother Volumnia, which Barbara Jefford played, to make him what he was. Jonathan and I agreed that although he's full of pride, and there is a kind of vanity, I suppose, in the end he's got a set of rules he's determined to live by. They're rules that she has created, and she has brought him up by them. We were interested in why he was like he was. So the emphasis was on that relationship, and it was not political at all. I think you say 'Here is the man and you judge, you decide what you think.'

Did you have any particular influences, any particular way of preparing for it, any
modern resonances that came to your mind? War heroes are not very fashionable these
days. Suicide bombers are more topical, aren't they?

I remember feeling that the physicality of soldiers is very important. They're very held, they don't like giving anything away. I tried to show the repression, and that military thing of being conditioned. It's in lots of modern films, American films about soldiers going to Westpoint. You see that sort of mask that comes into play. I don't necessarily think it's sexy, it's a male way of being, a particular code. It's Samurai-like: 'There is only one way and this is the way, and I will never deviate from this path and I'm prepared to go to my death to defend the way of the code, the code of honour, this is the way.' And I looked at a lot of paintings – Victorian paintings of soldiers in uniform, holding themselves very taut – with the designer Paul Brown. I remember a discussion about the tunic. Actually it felt a bit too heavy in the end. If you look at those paintings of warriors, they're very interesting. That was my thing. I've got a whole load of postcards of paintings from those incredibly proud Renaissance princes to the era of Velazquez's Philip II, and onwards. The way men have wanted themselves portrayed with their virility and pride.

There are all these lines about how difficult Coriolanus is, that he's spoilt and vain, and brave to the point of madness, a caricature of disdain and superciliousness. Why should we care about such a prig? Is there a temptation for a star actor to compensate by making him a bit too sexy and charismatic? A lot of leading actors need to be loved onstage.

Oh, I didn't give a fuck about that. I wanted to say 'You can fucking hate me, you fuckers, I don't care! Yeah, this is who I am.' No, no, I loved it. I think it's quite a challenge for the audience.

So, no glamorising of violence. Coriolanus dies a bloodied thug, not a hero. But he has an unusual political purity and emotional honesty. And that's where the part does become attractive, isn't it – that he doesn't compromise, he doesn't court anybody. However, it's also part of his problem, isn't it, that he refuses to court anybody.

It's what I love about the part, that he doesn't ingratiate himself. I love that he doesn't do so, either, with the audience. It's a piece of theatre that says 'You take this. Can you handle this? Because it's where this play is going. These are sentiments that I really mean, and I'm standing here. Can you handle it?' I love it that the play does that.

There are areas of the part that look quite comic. At times his vacillation is almost risible. Did you find comedy in the part?

Little bits. I found comedy in the opening of the scene asking for the people's voices. Also in the scene with his mother, like the stamping of the feet. And some other things on the text – they liked 'mildly' for instance: 'I'll speak to them mildly', seemed to get a laugh [3.2].

Also I imagine when Menenius and the women are talking about your twenty-seven wounds [2.1].

Yeah, that was funny. And then there was a thing I used to think was amusing – it got a titter more than a laugh. It was where he goes back to the market-place again, after his mother has persuaded him, and says:

> Th'honour'd gods
> Keep Rome in safety and the chairs of justice
> Supplied with worthy men; plant love among's,
> Throng our large temples with the shows of peace,
> And not our streets with war.

In a priestly tone.

Yes. Or like an official statement. 'Yay, "plant love among us"!' In the context it was quite funny.

Let's go back to the beginning of the play. Before you come on you're described [1.1] as 'chief enemy to the people', and 'a very dog to the commonalty', etc. You then arrive and immediately start haranguing these poor hungry citizens. It's as if the mere sight of a plebeian is enough to set you off. Why this high-octane abuse as soon as you walk onstage?

Well, first of all, they are rioting, and he doesn't know them. This is his weakness: his ignorance, there's no question. But as the actor you have to find his vision of the world, which is that these people are wanting to be fed, yet when the chips are down they won't go to war. And that's how Shakespeare writes them, buckling and running.

But they're not soldiers – not everyone's a soldier.

Yes. But I suppose in Shakespeare's time very few people were. Now we have professional soldiers, which then was probably less the case.

So in those days they would all have been expected to turn out, would they?

Well, I'm guessing this, but I think probably at that time you were mustered for armies. The concept of the professional soldier hardly existed. There were trained mercenaries, famously, in the Thirty Years War. But really a nation's army was its people. Anyway, I think that no one in the audience would know that, it's a programme note. The point is, I suppose, he's decided that they are fickle. His haranguing of them is because they just don't stand up. They're not what the Americans call 'stand-up men'. When the going's good, fine. But when they have to confront, they won't do it. Coriolanus's attitude of course is not a good one, because they are hungry people. But he's prepared to die. He's absolutely prepared to die. The way he lays into them probably makes him unattractive, but it's what he feels. 'I am prepared to go into battle. I am prepared to die, and I don't think any of you are.'

That's why I asked if you thought there was anything of a suicide bomber in his outlook.

Yes, I'm sure there is.

It's all for the cause?

I also think he's unhappy. He's longing for the release. There's a release, there's an ecstasy in battle. I don't think his mother showed him any affection. It's all to do with that. I think he's a deeply disturbed man. If you create someone like that, of course he can go the distance, but he's emotionally dried up. He's not emotionally intelligent, because of how he's been made. I think the audience understand him more as the play goes on. Initially they think 'What?!' Dramatically, it's a piece of strong writing to have a man come in and go 'You fucking scum, you should do it like this. Hang 'em, hang 'em, hang 'em. Fuck off, hang 'em!' But later I think there's a chance that you can understand, when you see the way his mother manipulates him in Act 3. She says 'Go back to the people' and he goes. I think he's like... you know when horses are trained very specifically to be ridden a certain way, if you give them a wrong instruction they hate it. I always thought he was like a horse. His mother said go back, and he went.

What, tossing his head, as you did just now?

Well, inwardly. It's 'You've always trained me. How can you, of all people, tell me to do this?' I think we can understand those earlier scenes retrospectively.

It's interesting that at the end of the first scene, when you smell military action, you're transformed. You're a different person. You're energised and positive in a way that you haven't been before. There's a line about venting 'our musty superfluity'. I wonder whether that is a collective thing about the plebs or whether it's personal – the reason for your spleen on your first entrance...

Inaction. I hadn't thought of that, that's very good.

... kicking your heels and becoming splenetic.

Well, even if he says it about the other people, a psychiatrist might say that it's really about himself.

If you're not onstage, you're being talked about. Which is nice, isn't it, because it does part of your job for you, I suppose.

It's quite an exhausting part. When you read it, you think you have free time. At first I thought 'Oh fine, there'll be little rests, it's not like a Richard or a Hamlet.' But actually when you're off, you're changing or you're preparing. You come on and have quite a big scene sneering at the people, saying 'Hang 'em!' and giving a litany of reasons why they are repulsive. Then you go off and there's a gap in which you are changing or getting ready for the battle scene. After that it's relentless. I felt I had to bring that adrenalin of a man going to war. There's the siege of Corioli [1.4], there's the cursing of his own soldiers, the going in, the coming back out. You feel as an actor that you must be pumped up for this to be convincing.

The fights got wonderfully reviewed: 'Lethally choreographed... thrillingly dramatic off-stage battle... war simply yet terrifyingly evoked.' How was it terrifyingly evoked if it was an offstage battle?

What happened was when Coriolanus takes the city, there was a vast abattoir-like door that slid vertically upwards. As it opened there was just a huge light coming at us, a massively bright light and smoke. There were no people visible, just a sense of something horrific. It was all done sort of elementally, if you like. There were sound effects and a lot of dry ice. A searing light, screams, and a noise like scraping metal or something horrendous.

An abstract evocation.

Yeah, an abstract evocation of war. I go in through the gates saying 'Follow me!' And immediately the doors come down – ZZZZZZZHHHHH!!! And the soldiers say 'See, they have shut him in.' 'To th'pot, I warrant him.' And they start to speak little eulogies about him, because they assume he's definitely dead. Then the door goes up – ZZZZZZZHHHHH!!! The lights blaze again, and out comes this figure covered in blood, going 'COME ON!!!'

'Fiennes displays a ferocious ecstasy as he runs into the very jaws of death.'

So Coriolanus takes the city and then he goes to help Cominius, the other Roman general, his superior. He arrives covered in blood, saying 'Come I too late?… Come I too late?' [1.6]. Cominius says 'You must rest.' He says 'No, we mustn't rest, we must go on.' And he has this wonderful speech like a mini Henry V moment, where he says to the soldiers: 'If any such be here… that love this painting / Wherein you see me smear'd…' He gets them all shouting and waving their swords, and then he goes off again into battle. And we're still in Act 1! So that in terms of theatre energy, you've done more fighting in the first act than in other plays happens at the end. You have expended massive amounts of adrenalin. He gathers the soldiers to him in that one moment.

'O, me alone! Make you a sword of me!' he says [1.6].

I adore that line.

You lingered lovingly on the phrase. Why was it so special to you?

I felt it was a moment of self-definition, of self-realisation. 'Yes, I'll do it on my own, on my own.' It was like 'This is what I am. I'll be the perfect sword.'

A real 'raison d'être'.

Yes. Cominius says 'Take your choice of those / That best can aid your action.' He replies:

> Those are they
> That most are willing. If any such be here –
> As it were sin to doubt – that love this painting
> Wherein you see me smear'd, if any fear
> Lesser his person than an ill report,
> If any think brave death outweighs bad life

> And that his country's dearer than himself,
> Let him alone, or so many so minded,
> Wave thus to express his disposition,
> And follow Martius.

Then they all shout and wave their swords and take him up in their arms and cast up their caps. He says 'O, me alone! Make you a sword of me!' It was an ecstatic moment of a man doing all he does best, and being acknowledged for it by his soldiers. We cut the rest of the speech, because he then goes into this funny qualification which is difficult to follow. And it sort of dwindles away.

After the victory, you request freedom for 'a poor man' [1.9]...

A great moment.

...then you forget his name.

Yeah, that's fantastic.

It's quite out of character, isn't it.

Well, that's what I love about it. There are these little moments where you glimpse this other person that he could have been. He's gone into the city, and at one moment in this horrendous act of violence – he was probably killing people and being wounded – and out of the blue a figure came up and shielded him, or he ran into some Volscian shopkeeper's store and this little man gave him a glass of water. This is what I imagined for myself. He suddenly had this bit of simple humanity. Afterwards he just remembered. And I think that's the genius. You say it's out of character, but then, well, what *are* our characters? People think we're one thing, and then we say or do something, and they go 'Oh, I didn't think that's like you!' But it is me.

There aren't many moments in the part that surprise you like that.

No, there aren't. As an actor you leap on that moment.

He's terribly bad at receiving praise. 'No more of this, it does offend my heart,' he says [2.1]. He won't receive praise and he won't show his wounds to the people. Why not? You know it's the custom. Why won't he let them see his wounds?

I've done the work, why should I? I feel like that with journalists. I've done the work, why should I talk about it? 'Well, you know I fought in the battle, why should I prostitute myself?' It's like a prostitution for him. Flaunting. 'Why should I flaunt these things to you? I've actually put myself on the line.'

It's a matter of pride.

Yeah, pride.

It involves having an intimate relationship with people you think are beneath you, isn't that it.

I suppose so. For me it was more like 'Why should I be a commodity, why should I display my wounds in order to get your votes?' I guess that's pride, but in his head it's 'I've done it. I have taken Corioli. I have the name.' It's true, he is proud, he doesn't want to talk to them about it. He makes little noises. 'I have wounds to show you, which shall be yours in private,' he says [2.3]. Whatever that means. It means 'I won't ever do it.'

He's supposed to share his wounds with the people at large. And there's this whole episode about the gown of humility, whether he's going to put it on or not. It's kind of comic in a way. But it makes you wonder how much he actually wants to be consul, because the gown is also part of the deal.

I think he really wants it.

He really does want it?

Yes.

Why?

Power. Prestige. But much as they're manipulating him, I think they're right when they say that he shouldn't be consul. He's totally unpolitical, he's contemptuous of the whole body of the state, the people. He's like an ambitious little child wanting the top prize. It's power and prestige, it's position and it's the highest honour.

Professor Anthony Clare wrote a note in your programme saying 'From a psychiatrist's point of view, pride is often a mask to cover up a deep-seated insecurity.'

Yes, I think that's right. It goes back to the whole mother thing I was trying to explain. That the pride was a layer, a carapace to protect him. I saw something I wish I'd done. I was watching Alan Howard in the BBC TV production (which you feel is made on a shoestring, to its detriment really). But he does this wonderful thing when he's talking to the people. He simply doesn't know how to talk to them, when he asks for their voices. I think I played it a bit too much on the note of a sneer, a sort of 'You reptiles' tone. But when I saw Alan, after I'd played the part, I thought it was really interesting, because he actually didn't know how to form a sentence to these people. It seems like contempt, and it partially is contempt, because that's the only thing he's been trained to feel for them. But a man comes up to him and says 'Why are you standing here?' Alan did it brilliantly. He said 'Well... you *know* the reason why I'm standing here.' There was something slightly hesitant and held at the same time.

Yet there are times when you can see he's a man with acute political insights, and he's obviously a terrific orator when he's got his steam up.

Yeah, he's a good speaker.

But he has no people skills at all, and that's basically why he couldn't hack it, isn't it. It's so interesting at the beginning of Act 3, Scene 1, everything seems to be fine. He's been given the vote for the consulship and he's got Aufidius in his sights. Then he meets the tribunes and just flies off the handle. He's totally self-destructive, isn't he? He's his own worst enemy.

I know in my rational, balanced, *Guardian*-reading way, that what he says is repulsive. He's not electable. But dramatically I just love his uncompromising attitude, his imagery of 'Bring in / The crows to peck the eagles'. He has these wonderful speeches. He obviously hates the idea of any kind of unrest. He says, about letting the tribunes have any sway:

> ... and my soul aches
> To know, when two authorities are up,
> Neither supreme, how soon confusion
> May enter 'twixt the gap of both, and take
> The one by th'other.

Then he argues at length about giving a voice to the people, what harm it does, and he concludes with:

> Thus we debase
> The nature of our seats and make the rabble
> Call our cares fears, which will in time
> Break ope the locks o'th'senate, and bring in
> The crows to peck the eagles.

Isn't that great stuff?

Terrific.

And you see his vision that the patrician establishment rules the best. They keep the strength, they keep the solidity, they keep the power, and Rome can survive with this hierarchy. But if we allow this little middle road of debate and the people's voice, it's the way to unrest. It's not something I personally feel, but it's great to play. And actually, in this fucking New Labour world of spin, I'm getting more intolerant. I like to hear the voice of 'Get out of the way, let's speak it how it is.' I loved it when a couple of army officers said Tony Blair should be impeached for what he's done. I love it when people speak out. The press go 'Oh, Sir General Downing should never have said the army is in a bad state...' Well, good for him for saying it.

I wonder whether there's a problem for a modern actor in terms of the part being very much to do with heroism, but we don't have superheroes these days. Also because of film and TV, grand-scale acting is not current. Was that a problem?

What's a real problem is that his anger is so often talked about, and the way he flips into white-hot rage so quickly. The challenge of the part is finding the gradations and moments of subtlety, nuance. So much of what he says about the people is quite repetitive. He goes into the marketplace, wearing the gown of humility [2.3]. He starts in a rather obtuse, ironic, contemptuous tone, all in prose. Then he segues into verse, saying 'Why should I stand here begging? I *deserve* this!' But then suddenly he switches and decides to play it right down the line, like 'Right! I am doing it. I've said I would hate to do it, I would despise myself for doing it because I don't see I need to. But fuck it, I'm gonna do it.' And he does it. 'Your voices! For your voices I have fought, / Watch'd for your voices.' Bang bang bang bang. Menenius comes in and says 'Right, you've done it, now it's fine.' So it's done.

But then in the following scene [3.1] he's confronted by the tribunes who say 'You haven't done it correctly. You didn't ask for the people's voices with enough humility, so you have to do it again.' And he goes mad at this, he says 'I have done it!' And he has done it. So he has this extended moment of building rage. It can be quite funny because everyone says to him 'Come, enough.' 'Enough, with over-measure.' He says 'No, take more.' They go 'Has said enough.' But he goes on and on and on. He keeps going on and on, it's relentless. The language is very difficult, and the rhetorical arguments that Shakespeare gives him are tortuous. But I loved playing it, it was a wonderful... [*Ralph makes Wild Western shoot-out sounds and gestures.*] The rage just builds and goes on and goes on. You have to keep topping yourself and topping yourself and topping yourself. And within that, not let it become a shout or a rant, but keep the arguments at high octane, and keep inventing. On a good night, at some kind of speed, it really seemed to work. Jonathan always said to me, if you take time to lay everything out clearly, you can lose it. I remember trying to find the right balance, because you can sometimes over-speed, and then you also feel you've lost it. To keep the argument active and present, and the rage building without it becoming too extreme, that was the hardest thing. So it was quite athletic, vocally and emotionally.

Another review said 'Rarely can a leading actor have strained so little to attract sympathy. No charismatic histrionics, but a portrait of the killing machine as schoolboy cipher, stamping his feet like a spoilt child when he meets resistance from his mother.' Tell me about that moment.

It's in the next scene [3.2], where Volumnia persuades me to go back again to the people. She says 'Go to them, with this bonnet in thy hand...' It became one of those things that was funny when I first did it, and then it got a bit over-heavy. 'Look, mother, I'm going... [*Stamping feet.*] Yaaahhhh!' [*Making a face and putting his thumbs in his ears.*] Well, it wasn't quite that extreme. But he becomes the little boy saying 'I'm going, look! You've told me to go and I'm going. Here, you see, I'm going. Okay? Are you happy now?' I remember that with my own mother, she'd say 'Go and tidy your room. You go and do this.' And I'd say 'I've done my room, look. Look, it's all done. Can you see? Are you happy now? My bed, is it good enough for you?' It was that sort of thing.

So back he goes, and immediately there's the final flare-up.

I think it's all part of the spiral of what's happened. His own emotions and temper have taken him to the first confrontation with the tribunes, then back to the mother. 'Go back to the people,' she says, 'speak softly to them.' So he goes back again to the people, and says 'Plant love among's, / Throng our large temples with the shows of peace...' etc. [3.3] But then they say 'You're a traitor.' A TRAITOR???!!! That's when he goes off like a machine gun – 'Ba-ba-ba-ba-ba-ba-ba'! – 'You common cry of curs...' And he loses it:

> I banish you!
> And here remain with your uncertainty!

And in the heat of the moment he says:

> Despising,
> For you, the city, thus I turn my back.
> There is a world elsewhere.

So you depart to go into exile [4.1]. As you say goodbye to your family, you seem at your most informal and relaxed, almost happy. It's odd, isn't it. Because you've just been banished from Rome, and apparently you don't know where you're going.

I don't think he does. It all happens in the moment. There's no planning. I think there's a release in him, a huge release. There's a huge sense of 'I'm getting out of here.' It's not necessarily a conscious thought. And talking of laugh lines, there's the one about six of Hercules' tasks. He says to his mother as he goes, trying to cheer her up:

> Nay, mother,
> Resume that spirit, when you were wont to say,
> If you had been the wife of Hercules,
> Six of his labours you'd have done, and sav'd
> Your husband so much sweat.

Yes, he's on the move. They would pick him out, he's going to be killed. So it's a hurried farewell on the corner of some street. I remember playing it quite fast. 'Goodbye. Yes yes, come on. Bye. Don't worry, don't worry...'

Arriving in Antium, you say 'My birthplace hate I, and my love's upon / This enemy town' [4.4]. Your defection seems very abrupt. For other parts, in other plays, Shakespeare might have written a soliloquy showing a spiritual crisis, the inner turmoil that leads into that statement. But there's nothing like that. Do you think it's underwritten, or is it appropriate for Coriolanus?

I found a new vocal placement for this scene. Having earlier been 'Ba-ba-ba-ba-ba!', suddenly here he is in Antium, and he's covered up. But I think he's someone who relishes a feeling and then says it. 'My birthplace hate I, and my love's upon / This enemy town.'

He's not a Hamlet, not a cogitator.

No, I don't think he is. But he registers that he might be killed there, doesn't he. And actually he does have a couple of bits of cogitation just before that. He says:

> many an heir
> Of these fair edifices 'fore my wars
> Have I heard groan and drop. Then know me not,
> Lest that thy wives with spits, and boys with stones,
> In puny battle slay me.

And then:

> O world, thy slippery turns! Friends now fast sworn,
> Whose double bosoms seems to wear one heart,
> Whose hours, whose bed, whose meal and exercise
> Are still together, who twin, as 'twere, in love
> Unseparable, shall within this hour,
> On the dissension of a doit, break out
> To bitterest enmity.

That's a reflection on the world. It's not really depicting personal inner turmoil.

He recognises the capriciousness of everything – it's all just turned in a moment.

So you go over to Aufidius, and seem quite calm on the surface.

It's funny, that speech [4.5]. It's incredibly controlled and articulate, telling Aufidius why he's here. 'I'm ready to die.' It has a formal clarity, and it's more accessible than many other speeches with all the raging stuff. His mind is very clear, with the clarity of hatred.

It's a long speech and for nearly forty lines Aufidius doesn't react. Shakespeare doesn't give him anything to say.

Well, Coriolanus is here in front of him, out of the blue. I think he hears him, and he's annoyed. And the speech has a clear line running through it.

Menenius says 'He and Aufidius can no more atone / Than violent'st contrariety' [4.6]. *In spite of that it does seem to be remarkably easy for that alliance to be formed. Does* *he expect it to be so easy?*

He doesn't know what to expect, but he knows exactly what he's going to say. 'I hate Rome, it's betrayed me. I want to destroy my country. If you wish to use my skill against Rome, so be it. If not, kill me.' It's very, very, very simple.

Aufidius says earlier that Coriolanus is 'Bolder, though not so subtle' [1.10], which is *accurate, isn't it.*

It is true, yes. That relationship is very interesting. Aufidius has intense hatred and envy of Coriolanus, but when they meet he uses language almost of infatuation with him.

A homoerotic relationship?

I think that's there. We didn't play it as full-on as we might have done. But it was there. Linus Roache played Aufidius, and he definitely indicated that. He behaves like a betrayed lover. And he's vicious, he is… vicious.

When the play was done at Nottingham in the 1960s, with John Neville as Coriolanus *and Ian McKellen as Aufidius, it was apparently an overtly homosexual relationship.* *But you didn't go that far, I take it.*

It depends what you mean by 'overt'. In our production there was clenching and hugging and touching.

When you fight in Act 1?

That's right, yeah. There was a moment when we held each other and looked [1.8]. But I don't think we ever wanted to sledgehammer home overt homosexuality, it was about intimacy and proximity…

But now after you defect, Aufidius is speculating as to why you couldn't carry on as a *noble servant of Rome [4.7]. He says 'Whether 'twas pride… whether defect of judge-* *ment… or whether [inflexibility in] not moving / From th'casque to th'cushion…'*

'…but commanding peace / Even with the same austerity and garb / As he controll'd the war.'

Do you think it's any one of those things in particular, or all of them?

I think it's a bit of everything.

Going on to Act 5. When your wife and son and mother come in, even before they arrive you say 'Shall I be tempted to infringe my vow / In the same time 'tis made? I will not' [5.3]. It rather sounds as if you will! And then before they speak you say 'I melt, and am not / Of stronger earth than others.' So the vacillation is evident.

I found it very hard to know the pitch of this stuff. He has his asides which are odd, because they describe what the audience is seeing: 'My wife comes foremost, then the honour'd mould... I melt... My mother bows...' I found the formality of it quite difficult. He kneels, he rises, she kneels, he raises her. And this strange character of Valeria. It's an odd formal meeting of the three women coming to Coriolanus, in which Shakespeare gives him these funny little descriptions of his inner state, which are hard to pull off. Then the idea that Volumnia has knelt to him. He says:

> What's this?
> Your knees to me? To your corrected son?
> Then let the pebbles on the hungry beach
> Fillip the stars. Then let the mutinous winds
> Strike the proud cedars 'gainst the fiery sun,
> Murd'ring impossibility, to make
> What cannot be, slight work.

The idea that she would ever kneel to him 'murders impossibility'.

Strong stuff.

But it's hard to play. You can feel the audience going 'What's happening?' The scene sags. It seems to kick in when he says:

> I beseech you, peace!
> Or if you'd ask, remember this before:
> The thing I have forsworn to grant may never
> Be held by you denials. Do not bid me
> Dismiss my soldiers or capitulate
> Again with Rome's mechanics. Tell me not
> Wherein I seem unnatural. Desire not
> T'allay my rages and revenges with
> Your colder reasons.

'Don't do this, don't tell me this!'

Nonetheless, from the moment of their entrance you feel he's going to be won over.

I think the audience genuinely don't know his feelings. The tension is that they shouldn't.

In Harley Granville Barker's Preface to Coriolanus *he says 'Coriolanus is no renegade, his striving to be false to Rome is false to himself.'*

Yeah, he hates it, he knows he's false to himself. I think you can feel the conflict in him. He sees his mother and says:

> But out, affection!
> All bond and privilege of nature break!
> Let it be virtuous to be obstinate.

Then:

> I'll never
> Be such a gosling to obey instinct, but stand
> As if a man were author of himself,
> And knew no other kin.

But that's not the way he carries through the scene, is it.

No, that's what I'm saying. It helps the audience to not know. If they followed those little asides, they really don't know. And when Volumnia starts her long speech, they still don't know where it's going to go. I think not all elements of our production worked, by any means. But you know that great moment when a Shakespeare play cuts to the chase – it cuts to what everything's been building towards – and you feel the audience catch fire? It was like that. She's going on and on, and he's not giving in, and he's not giving in. And then the collapse.

There's a stage direction about silent hand-holding…

'*Holds her by the hand, silent.*' We did that. I love that stage direction. Just as a sentence it's wonderful. The main thing for me in the play was the relationship with the mother. Barbara turned to walk away from me, and as she turned I grabbed her. She stopped and I went to pieces, fell to my knees, so I was looking up at her. There's the line:

> What have you done?…
> But for your son, believe it, O, believe it,
> Most dangerously you have with him prevail'd,
> If not most mortal to him.

Meaning 'You know what you've done? I'm going to die.' And she had this look as if to say – actually it would have been great in close-up – as if to say 'Yeah, I know.'

But she's happy with that, isn't she? She's got no problem with you dying, as long as you die gloriously.

Yes yes, she can live with that. She says earlier on 'Had I a dozen sons… I had rather had eleven die nobly for their country than one voluptuously surfeit out of action' [1.3].

You had a tremendously affecting breakdown.

I saw it as a breakdown. I hope I didn't overextend it as the production went on, but I remember that I ended up on the floor literally trying to pull myself together. And to face Aufidius, who's looking down disdainfully at Coriolanus in tears. I had a great line: 'Would you have heard / A mother less? or granted less, Aufidius?' And he just says, with a sneer, 'I was mov'd withal.'

What is it that makes you so emotional at that moment?

I don't know. It felt like a huge release that I've never really examined. It's like a little boy pleading with his mother in the most open, innocent way. 'Mummy, Mummy, please don't do that, Mummy, please say it's okay…' It's the little boy pleading with his mother on the most basic, most simple, most childish level. I think that's what's moving.

Tell me how you died.

I went back to Tullus Aufidius bearing a formal presentation [5.6]:

> We have made peace
> With no less honour to the Antiates
> Than shame to th'Romans…

'We're all fine.' Then he starts. He calls me 'thou boy of tears'. He insults me to the point where I have the final Coriolanian explosion:

> If you have writ your annals true, 'tis there,
> That like an eagle in a dove-cote, I
> Flutter'd your Volscians in Corioles.
> Alone I did it. 'Boy'!

So he throws the insult back at Aufidius. And then everybody says 'He killed my son!' 'My daughter!' 'He killed my father!' And I was grabbed from behind by Volscian soldiers, in cruciform, and had my throat cut.

By Aufidius?

Yes. He came up to me and did it.

Would you like to play it again?

Yeah.

Would you change it much, do you think, if you played it again?

Yes, I would. But I'm reticent to talk about it, it's too early. [In 2010, Fiennes played Coriolanus again, this time on film, also marking his directorial debut.]

It's quoted as the tragedy of a great man whose moral and psychological failings bring about his downfall. Does that seem accurate?

Yeah, that's right. I see it as a tragedy of some little boy being made into only one thing, with this rigid attitude. Rigidity snaps, whereas if you've got any fluidity, you have more chance of surviving. There's a whole mass of experience he's never been allowed to have. So he becomes this rigid thing, he can only be a sword. 'O me alone! Make you a sword of me!'

Rebecca Hall
on
Rosalind

As You Like It (1599–1600)
The Peter Hall Company
Opened at the Theatre Royal, Bath
on 13 August 2003

Directed by Peter Hall
Designed by John Gunter
With Rebecca Callard as Celia, Joseph Millson as Orlando,
Michael Siberry as Touchstone, Eric Sykes as Adam and Sir Oliver Martext,
and Philip Voss as Jaques

As *You Like It* divides critics. 'A work of great literary value,' say some. 'Lacking artistry, a mere crowd-pleaser,' say others. Nonetheless, it remains very popular. On the surface the play is a simple pastoral romantic comedy with little of the darkness of Shakespeare's other mature comedies, and a happy ending is never in doubt. But at a deeper level it touches on a host of subjects such as love, nature, ageing and death. The comedy's genius lies not in its paper-thin plot but in its characters. Jaques prides himself on his abilty to 'suck melancholy out of a song as a weasel sucks eggs' [2.5]. His sardonic commentary and Touchstone's restless bawdy innuendo are balanced against Rosalind, whose generosity of spirit, complexity of emotion and subtlety of thought make her one of Shakespeare's most fully realised and beguiling characters. Rosalind blends front-foot energy with vulnerability; she dominates all around her, then proceeds to faint at the sight of Orlando's blood.

Gender reversal is central to the play. Rosalind disguises herself as the boy 'Ganymede', whose name, taken from one of Jove's lovers, carries homoerotic overtones. Orlando enjoys acting out his romance with Ganymede, almost as if the beautiful boy who looks strangely like the woman he loves is even more appealing than the woman herself. *As You Like It* lampoons the conventions of courtly love. Characters lament their sufferings in love, but their anguish is skin deep. 'I to live and die her slave,' writes Orlando, but his verses are mocked by Rosalind as a 'tedious homily of love' [3.2]. She asserts that 'men have died from time to time, and worms have eaten them, but not for love'. But whereas Touchstone and Jaques merely focus on romantic folly, Rosalind champions love so long as it is grounded in the real world. She knows that 'Men are April when they woo, December when they wed' [4.1].

My own experience of acting in *As You Like It* is limited to a cough-and-a-spit at Stratford in 1968, when a weird thing happened. (Old Actor's Anecdote coming up...) One midweek matinee I'm one of a bunch of lads making up the numbers onstage, listening to the First Forest Lord describe the death of a stag. It's late in the season and advanced boredom has set in; we've heard this stuff many times before. 'Must be about 2.45,' I think to myself. 'If I was to nip across the road to The Duck I could get in a quick pint before closing time... Hmmm, tempting... Yes, to hell with it, that's what I'll do right now!' I'm about to sneak off the stage and over to the pub, when I realise that I am the actor I'm listening to. I am playing the First Forest Lord. I've become disembodied, and am listening to myself delivering the stag's death speech on autopilot.

Rebecca Hall was twenty-seven when we met, by some years the youngest contributor to this book. She was already well on the way to a highly successful career, having started six years earlier with an award-winning debut in Shaw's *Mrs Warren's Profession*. She had arrived with a bang. Her Rosalind followed immediately afterwards, and created waves on both sides of the Atlantic. It was easy to understand why she had dropped out of Cambridge in mid-degree, from sheer impatience to get cracking as an actress. I interviewed her in the summer of 2009 at the matchbox flat in central London where she was staying, during her run at the Old Vic Theatre playing Hermione in *The Winter's Tale* and Varya in *The Cherry Orchard* for Sam Mendes' Bridge Project.

Julian Curry: You played Rosalind in Bath in 2003. And soon afterwards in New York and California. And you'd have been – what?

Rebecca Hall: Twenty-one, just. I turned twenty-one the day before we started rehearsals.

An excellent age to play Rosalind.

Yeah, it felt like a good age.

It was your professional debut in Shakespeare?

Yes, it was. Before that I'd just done Shaw's *Mrs Warren's Profession* and *The Fight for Barbara*, which is a very rarely performed D.H. Lawrence play. So it was my third professional production.

The director was not a debutant though, was he?

No, not at all. Long-standing.

He was your dad, Sir Peter Hall.

Yeah.

How was it, being directed by him?

Well, we'd figured out how to work together by that point, in *Mrs Warren's Profession*, which he also directed. That was much more about how we'd collaborate, would it be okay, or would it ruin my career chances? By the time we got to *As You Like It* those things had stopped being a concern because we'd already established a strong working relationship, with a sort of ease. He started talking about *As You Like It* towards the end of *Mrs Warren's Profession*, saying I should do it. He was quite passionate about it, because he'd never done the play before. Ever since he knew I wanted to be an actor, and thought I was talented, he was always making noises about it, saying 'You'd be a really good Rosalind, you must do it one day.'

Can you remember why he thought you'd be a good Rosalind?

Probably because I'm 'more than common tall' [1.3]!

There were lots of wonderful things written about your performance, but it doesn't sound like the sunniest Rosalind. 'Downcast' was a word used.

I don't know whether she was downcast...

Somebody else said '... brings out a profound sadness in the character as if her inability to declare her love was a source of spiritual frustration.'

Yes, I think that's probably accurate. It was clear to me from the first reading that this is not someone who is easy with love. I don't think anyone really is, and that's ultimately what Shakespeare's doing. He's writing a play about many different aspects of love. Falling in love is a dangerous business, with all sorts of possibilities of rejection. The backdrop to Rosalind's story is that she's brought up in a horrible court with her evil uncle, her father's been banished, she's alienated, she's got no parental guidance. I think she's very fragile and vulnerable, and desperately wants to love, is open to it. For people with those defence mechanisms and problems, I think when they do fall in love it can be all the more beautiful and joyful because of the hardship that comes with it.

Did you know the play well beforehand?

No. I'd never seen it, and I didn't know it. I didn't study it at Cambridge for some reason, and I didn't study it at school, therefore I was completely fresh to it.

So you had no preconceptions.

No, none at all, and I was happy about that. I deliberately didn't look at any books or hear about other people's opinions, to keep it as fresh as possible.

How did you prepare?

Text, text, text, and then in the rehearsal room. I started with the text, allowed it to resonate with me and worked out what I thought it all meant, unpicked it. All the choices were made from there.

One of the main things about Rosalind is that for much of the play she's disguised as a boy, which is very strong dramatically.

Yes. Especially as she would have been played by a boy in the first place.

The chemistry of it is fascinating. Can you say what the disguise did for you?

Well, it's a mask, isn't it. I found it a liberation. As soon as she starts being a boy she's much more herself. She feels more at ease with herself, and able to say what she's feeling and what she's thinking. But it's less, I think, about performing a boy and more about daring to be yourself to the outside world, with the protective mechanism that you're not really yourself.

It's a paradox, isn't it.

Yeah, it's a total paradox. But for me it was crucial not to do a lot of 'Oh, here I am, I'm a boy, swagger, swagger', slapping my thigh and doing all of that. I just played it straight in boy's clothes. In doing that you embrace a certain amount of ambiguity about her. I think there's something genderless about Rosalind. She has aspects of femininity and she has aspects of masculinity. And I thought the ambiguity would work better if I stopped worrying about playing one or the other and just delivered the truth of the text.

In boy's clothes.

In boy's clothes.

Rosalind really is an actor, isn't she – she flies when she's playing a part. Did you find that fun?

Yes, I did, I did, there's no question about it. The first scene with Orlando in the forest [3.2] where she confronts him and really goes for it, was such a joyous scene to play. She just runs with it, the adrenalin is up in your throat because the stakes are so high, she has so much fun and she gets away with it. And she can hold court, she really can. But I think a lot of it almost comes as a surprise to her. It tumbles out of her mouth before she knows what she's doing. I don't think she's aware that she's a natural born actor. To me there's something almost self-effacing in her nature. And again it's paradoxical. I found the key to this in the epilogue. She just walks down and says 'Okay, I know you don't need to hear this. I won't be much good as an epilogue, and maybe you didn't like this play, or maybe you did…' Apologies, apologies. And I thought actually that runs all the way through: 'I don't know if I'm any good at this. Maybe I am, maybe I'm not. Are you going to accept me?' It's this constant downplaying, a kind of modesty, I suppose.

It's been suggested that the relationship between her and Orlando is often more like master and pupil than a couple of equals. Did it feel like that to you?

No, it didn't. I think she's learning as well, not so much from him as from the whole set-up. You have to bear in mind that when they fall in love it's this crazy, I guess sexual, attraction that just goes bam. They've hardly spoken a word to each other, they don't know each other. So I think it's less 'I'm going to tell you how to love me', and more 'Let's find out if we can love each other, is it possible, and how are we going to do it?' And also 'Will you love me for *me*?' I think that's actually what's going on. Earlier on you read that quote about sadness. Maybe that's how it would come across, as I was playing someone who was vulnerable. But I don't believe she's sad in her relation to love, I think she's just uncannily realistic. She's got an innate wisdom which takes her beyond being a starry-eyed young girl, almost as if she becomes Shakespeare's voice. She's constantly telling people to cut out any trace of hyperbole. She says 'Don't laugh too much', or to Jaques 'Don't be so sad.' And she really tells Orlando off when he makes overblown declarations that don't make any sense to her, because in her mind 'We met, but you don't know me yet. You can't make these grand statements. If you are going to love me, you have to accept me for who I am. I haven't grown up yet, but I could potentially be a complete basket case.' I could be:

> more clamorous than a parrot against rain; more new-fangled than an ape; more giddy in my desires than a monkey. I will weep for nothing, like Diana in the fountain, and I will do that when you are disposed to be merry. I will laugh like a hyena, and that when thou are inclined to sleep. [4.1]

He then says…

'But will my Rosalind do so?'

And you say…

'By my life, she will do as I do.'

Which is a funny line.

Yes. Hilarious.

I don't believe a word of it.

No. I don't think it's true for a moment.

She's making herself out to be perverse and coquettish, which Rosalind isn't, surely?

Oh no, I completely agree with you. But there's a grain of truth, in the sense that she's saying, 'I'm a little frightened about this whole set-up. Would you still love me if I was like this? Would you still love me if I did that?'

I want to ask you some more about the production. Arden seems to be all sorts. It's in Warwickshire, yet it's described as desert and bleak and barren, yet it's got olive trees and palm trees, a lioness and a snake. Was that a concern?

There was a lot of discussion about it, and Peter came to the conclusion that because of the fantastical elements, it should be as hostile a place as it is a magical, warm place. I suppose that informed the whole production, and my thinking about Rosalind. When we first enter and I say 'Well, this is the Forest of Arden' [2.4], I remember it being winter and freezing. The snow's falling, and we're all bundled up in coats and jackets, and it's frightening. And then we move into the next act and spring has sprung and it's beautiful and green and lush.

So it's both.

Yeah, it's both. I suppose we created a place that was non-specific and fantastical, where you can believe it if a snake suddenly appears, without worrying about making it somewhere specific.

A lot of the play seems to veer in and out of fairytale or pantomime. How naturalistic were the performances?

We didn't go for any of the choices that would take it off into fairytale territory. For example, at the end Hymen wasn't a god that suddenly descended, he was the shepherd Corin who got dressed up and wheeled on as for a village fête. Rosalind stage-managed the whole event. It was very realistic, with a sort of folksy, earthy base to it, I suppose.

What about the set and costumes?

Very minimalist. Everything was based around a large square on the floor, inside a box set. In Duke Frederick's court at the beginning there was a large red mat, and that was it. There was no furniture or anything, just the red square with a couple of doors. Everyone was dressed to suggest some sort of fascist, vaguely militaristic society, with lots of black and lapels. I was in a very constricting red dress with a kind of built-in corset. It wasn't set in any specific period. And then in Arden the square initially got covered with a large, white sheet to represent snow, and there were a couple of tree stumps. After that, when spring came, the mat turned to grass, and we had some beautiful trees. It was very, very simple.

What about the text, was it much cut or rearranged?

Not really. There were a few cuts, but it was pretty faithful.

There's a fair amount of Shakespearean 'witty repartee', which doesn't look all that witty on the page.

Well, we got a lot of laughs. I don't know how!

So that was all left in, was it?

Oh yes, I never stopped speaking. That sort of antithetical wit that doesn't really mean much to a modern audience, but somehow we managed to make sense of it. And all of Touchstone's stuff was kept in, which Michael Siberry handled incredibly well, he was a sort of lecherous figure, very funny. His interaction with the countryfolk was really raucous. It was all very sexualised – Audrey was an extremely voluptuous lady that he was desperately trying to get into bed. And there was lots of singing.

I'm going back to the beginning of the play now. The early court scenes, as you said, are grim.

Very grim, very hostile.

There's no mother in sight.

No mother, no father.

Only this oppressive uncle. And with the fascistic uniforms you were talking about, it sounds quite dangerous, not like the conventional opening of a comedy.

No. It was very dangerous. And that was compounded by the wrestling match, which was brutal. It was horrific, very violent. At the end there was the sound of a neck cracking, and we imagined that Charles the wrestler had been killed. We were exploring the similarities between Rosalind and Orlando at the start of the play. They're both alienated and a little unhinged, which she expresses by being slightly melancholy and introverted, and he expresses by being incredibly angry and potentially violent. They recognise each other's angst, as it were.

Were you conscious of seeking freedom before you were banished? You hadn't been allowed to go with your father, therefore I wonder whether part of you might have been hankering to get out. So when you are banished a couple of scenes later, it wouldn't have been entirely bad news?

That's an interesting question. I think I played the banishment as entirely bad news, because the world we'd created was very hostile. You certainly didn't get any sense that it meant she could go off into a more welcoming environ-ment. It meant she was literally going to be cast out with nothing and nowhere to go. And so, essentially, death. How would she survive? Where would she go? How would she make any money? All those sorts of things. It wasn't 'Oh, great, now I can run away from it all.'

But did it rankle at all that you'd been separated from your father in order to keep Celia company? She says 'I see thou lovest me not with the full weight that I love thee' [1.2]. Is there any truth in that?

No.

You perk up when you talk about devising sports, and say 'What think you of falling in love?'

She was very cheeky, Rebecca Callard as Celia. They're such close friends that she doesn't have to handle Rosalind carefully. She can help her to perk up. There's a lot of friendly joshing. And equally a certain amount of light-hearted sarcasm in, for instance, 'Well, I will forget the condition of my estate, to rejoice in yours' [1.2]. There was plenty of back and forth between them.

'Is yonder the man?' you say when you first see Orlando, about to wrestle [1.2]. Was it love at first sight?

Le Beau had come on and been very excited by the extremity of the violence. He talked about the other guy's ribs being broken, and took a lot of relish in describing quite how gruesome it was. Celia and I were pretty queasy about it all. 'Do we really want to see this?' Then everybody suddenly rushes on and we get swept up into it. There's a sense of not really wanting to look, so we did a lot of this...

Half-shielding your eyes with your hand.

Well, *I* was, but Celia was more gutsy, a bit more 'Come on, let's have a look.' We held off the moment where I saw Orlando. The first impact I suppose was that he looked so weak in comparison to Charles. We had a full-on body-builder who was about six foot seven playing Charles, and Orlando looked tiny and weedy in comparison. So the initial emotion and the draw towards him that both Celia and I feel is 'Oh God, this poor man is going to get utterly demolished.' It was less 'Is yonder the man – he's hot stuff!' and more 'You mean *him*? You can't be serious!' Then we go and try to convince him not to fight, because we know he's going to be killed. He was kneeling down and Celia was in front of me; she goes forward to talk to him and tells him 'embrace your own safety and give over this attempt'. I was dawdling behind her, letting her take the lead as she always did in that early part of the play.

Then she clears to let me through, and he looks up for the first time, and we played a moment of not quite having the words, either of us, and being bowled over by the attraction. Eventually I say:

> Do, young sir. Your reputation shall not therefore be misprized. We will make it our suit to the Duke that the wrestling might not go forward.

And then he has this incredible speech:

> I beseech you, punish me not with your hard thoughts... I shall do my friends no wrong, for I have none to lament me; the world no injury, for in it I have nothing. Only in the world I fill up a place which may be better supplied when I have made it empty.

He's saying 'Don't care about me. I am ready to die.' Rosalind then says 'The little strength that I have, I would it were with you.' It is such an emotionally packed statement, which comes so soon. And that, to me, was the moment of falling in love. She sees this man, understands his desolation, feels so much compassion, and recognises the feeling in herself. Then she says 'I wish we could both survive on my little bit of strength.' And he wins the wrestling, having been enlivened by her. Then the comedy moment that we milked every last bit out of was directly after the wrestling, when he does lose all power of speech.

When you put the chain round his neck?

Yeah.

Was that an easy thing for Rosalind to do?

It's an extremely important gift. The moment is erotically charged, he's heavy-breathing, exhausted. She suddenly realises he's going to leave, and she's got to give him something to remember her by. So it's 'Here, take this.' It happens like a lot of things – on the hoof, spontaneously.

When Celia asks Orlando if he's good at keeping his 'promises in love', is she fancying him as well?

No, but she's realised that I do. She gave me a little wink. I'm going 'Stop it, stop it, why are you looking at me like that?' Which is very Rosalind. She's not great at people teasing her, saying 'Ooooh, you're in love!' There's a lot of pride – 'I'm not so silly as that!'

Next scene [1.3], you've just fallen for this gorgeous guy and you're really downbeat again. Why is that?

Oh no, I didn't play that at all.

It's in the text.

'Why, cousin! Why, Rosalind! Cupid have mercy! Not a word?' Okay, it's in the text that she's not speaking. But her answer 'Not one to throw at a dog', struck me as funny. I think she is equal parts irritated to have fallen in love in an instant and then to be separated, and exhilarated that it's happened. Celia is joshing her, she joshes back: 'But is all this for your father?' 'No, some of it is for my child's father.' Now that is very cheeky and very funny. Celia went 'I can't believe what you've just said!' But then Rosalind immediately snaps back from the excitement of 'I want that man to have my kids' to the frustration of realising it might not happen: 'How full of briars is this workaday world!' But I didn't play this scene as melancholy, it was very energetic. We both came in pacing, and I'm going 'Shut up, shut up, don't speak to me, don't speak to me.' It was very excitable:

—   These burs are in my heart.
—   Hem them away.
—   I would try, if I could cry 'hem' and have him.

That makes her laugh.

—   Come, come, wrestle with thy affections.
—   O, they take the part of a better wrestler than myself.

More wordplay – it's hysterical. When Rosalind's excitable or emotional, she tends to filter it with wit. That's how she expresses herself. You know she's functioning on a very high plane right now because the wordplay is so strong. She's taking everything Celia says and twisting it and running with it. It was wonderful, because we got to such a state of energy by the end of the scene that when Duke Frederick comes in and says 'You, you're out', it was a big hit in the face.

You answer him eloquently. But are you defiant or perplexed, how did you play it?

Maybe it's because I'm in *The Winter's Tale* at the moment, but I think these Shakespearean women caught up in male-centric environments are incredibly eloquent and defiant. It's similar to Hermione's trial. I wouldn't say angry, but there's the sense of utter injustice and incredulity. 'What is it with these men? How can they behave like this?' It started off measured:

> I do beseech your grace,
> Let me the knowledge of my fault bear with me.

'Tell me what I've done wrong.'

> If with myself I hold intelligence,
> Or have acquaintance with mine own desires,
> If that I do not dream, or be not frantic –

As I do trust I am not – then, dear uncle,
Never so much as in a thought unborn
Did I offend your highness.

The way you just did that was measured and reasonable.

Yeah – with a lid on it. But then his justification is ludicrous: 'Thou art thy father's daughter; there's enough.' When he doesn't give any reason, I do get angry and say quite rebelliously:

So was I when your highness took his dukedom;
So was I when your highness banished him.
Treason is not inherited, my lord.

She's talking utter sense, but getting worked up about it. She does let rip at him.

It's amusing when the Duke tells Celia 'Her very silence, and her patience' make her untrustworthy. Rosalind's normally a complete motormouth, isn't she?

She is later on, but I think she probably has been silent and patient. If she's out of her element, in an environment where she doesn't feel comfortable, she's more likely to be measured. She's a great observer of people, she's intuitive and understanding and compassionate. I think it shows in this scene, where she says these lucid things about the paranoid nature of tyranny. This is ridiculous behaviour, and she tells him so. I can imagine she has been quiet and measured, and that has probably been an attractive quality to others who were being repressed in this violent environment.

What happens after the Duke's exit [1.3]?

I sank down and pretty much gave up on life at that point. 'What am I going to do? I've got nowhere to go. This is it for me.' Celia's very much the one that gets her back on her feet. She insists:

— I'll go along with thee.
— Why, whither shall we go?
— To seek my uncle in the Forest of Arden.

Rosalind's first reaction comes from her realism: 'Alas, what danger will it be to us, / Maids as we are, to travel forth so far!' I didn't play it scared so much as 'That's a ludicrous idea. We'd be robbed and raped and killed': 'Beauty provoketh thieves sooner than gold.' Then Celia shifted into a different gear and said, half-joking, 'You're right. Okay. I've got a funny idea':

I'll put myself in poor and mean attire,
And with a kind of umber smirch my face…

And we started having this nutty fantasy that was totally unrealistic, but the idea of it became exciting. It made us feel better. 'Ha-ha, wouldn't it be funny if I dressed up like a man?'

> Because that I am more than common tall ...
> We'll have a swashing and a martial outside,
> As many other mannish cowards have
> That do outface it with their semblances...

Thinking about her uncle with that bit of anger hanging over from the last scene, but still not really taking it seriously. And then Celia says 'What shall I call thee when thou art a man?' – dead straight. 'I know we're having a laugh here... but why not?'

What made you choose 'Ganymede'?

The reality of the plan was emerging slowly, but Rosalind's still partly in the game. So she goes 'Well, I want the best possible name there is', so:

> I'll have no worse a name than Jove's own page,
> And therefore look you call me Ganymede.

And it's funny because of the gender, and the mixture of male and female: 'But what will you be call'd?' And they're both scoping each other out. 'Are you serious?' 'Are *you* serious?' That's how we played it. 'Well, I'm serious if you're serious.' 'Well, I'm serious if *you're* serious!' And she says:

> Something that hath a reference to my state,
> No longer Celia but Aliena.

Which isn't funny, there's no element of wit in her chosen name. It says, 'I'm going to *alienate* myself from everything I'm familiar with. I'm deadly serious about this, so are you on board or are you not?' And then we're totally serious for the rest of the scene. And I say:

> But, cousin, what if we assay'd to steal
> The clownish fool out of your father's court?

'We can do this, but we need a man as well.' So we played that scene as a game between two friends that suddenly turned serious out of nowhere.

Into the forest. You arrive in Arden and it's winter [2.4]. What do you think you want? Originally you talked about going to seek your father, but he hardly gets mentioned, does he?

I think a key to the part is that once she finds Orlando in Arden, there's no reason for her to stay in disguise. She could simply stop it all and reveal herself. But I believe that if you can find out why she doesn't do that, then you unlock the character. That's really how we came to the conclusion that it's not just about educating him, it's about her finding out how she's going to be as a woman, and perversely doing it through being a boy for a while. Also she doesn't want to give up the disguise because she really likes it; and she's not yet sure how to be herself without it.

Act 3, Scene 2. It's summer, and you enter without Celia for the first time. You're reading these verses which are romantic tosh, but they're all about you. What do you make of them?

Well, she's not stupid, old Rosalind, she knows they're romantic tosh. But on the other hand I took her to be incredibly excited by them. And gobsmacked, and not quite believing whether it's her or...

Another Rosalind?!

It's 'I can't quite believe that someone would do this for me'. Again it's the adrenalin, and the feeling in your stomach of 'I can't quite believe this', but the big grin on your face. Totally flattering. If she comes on cynical and critical of the poems then there's no pay-off when Touchstone starts mocking her. I think she's incredibly wise and realistic about life, but she's not cynical in any way, shape or form. She's open to things. But of course it's private, so I only allowed myself to show that bewilderment and joy to the audience. As soon as Touchstone comes in and catches her, then the mask goes straight up again. She laughs along with his joshing of the poems, and then tells him to shut up. She shrugs it off – 'I just found them on a tree, I don't know what they're doing...'

Then Celia comes in and reads lots more verses.

I made Touchstone hide behind a tree. I hid behind the other one, and I tried to make Corin go as well. But he was baffled by why I was behaving strangely, cos he was an old country dude, so he just sat there on his tree stump eating his pickled cucumber. Celia's very romantic and excitable about the verses on my behalf; she doesn't realise anyone's there, and she walks straight to the front and gives them out to the audience. Then I come out and surprise her and send her up, doing exactly the same to her as Touchstone has just done to me. A sort of displacement activity, I suppose. 'What tedious homily of love have you wearied your parishioners withal!' Celia says 'How now!' ('What have you been doing?'), then 'Back, friends! Shepherd, go off a little. Go with him, sirrah.' As in 'bugger off' to Touchstone and Corin, so she can have a proper chat with Rosalind.

She teases you at great length about who wrote the poem, and says it's somebody who's got your chain round his neck. But you still apparently don't quite buy it, do you?

I don't know how to phrase this without sounding like some awful self-help manual. But I don't think she is quite comfortable enough with herself to believe that anyone could really be in love with her. I'd say that's the crux of it. And she plays out that very serious thought through wit and deferral and making a mockery of it all.

Orlando then arrives with Jaques, who says to him 'Rosalind is your love's name?' Orlando says 'Yes, just.' And instead of leaping out and dragging him into the nearest shrubbery you embark on this long scene, telling Celia 'I will speak to him like a saucy lackey, and under that habit play the knave with him.' But of course if you didn't do that the play would end a lot sooner, just as if Beckett had written the stage direction 'Enter Godot'.

I think she's still too insecure to go out and say 'Hey, it's me! Are you serious?' It's the paradox of love. Even though he's standing there saying 'I'm in love with Rosalind', and putting his poems on trees, she's still frightened of rejection on some level. And I think that's very true of romance in general. It goes right back to the playground. 'Such-and-such has got a crush on you.' 'Well, go and tell him that I've got a crush on him too, and then you can come back and tell me...' There's the fear of young love, that it can't possibly be easy. She hasn't got the balls to just go out there, so she does it through disguise instead.

The scene is amazing. She's so inventive, it must feel like flying.

It is exactly like flying, it's incredible. When it was on form and everything took off, it would get big laughs. There was the tension of running out there in disguise – will she get found out? There was a very strong audience engagement, with people gasping. It was very powerful, very exciting to play. Like skipping on water.

When Orlando says 'Where dwell you, pretty youth?', it's like saying 'Give me your phone number.' He seems to be coming on to Ganymede, falling in love with this young man who is not you. That's a mixed blessing, isn't it.

No, quite the opposite. I think she wants him to fall in love with her as the boy, oddly, because it *is* her. Yes, she's playing the part, but it's very much her personality. I think what scares her is him falling in love with his image of Rosalind, this fantasy Rosalind that he met for two seconds and has been writing poems about. She wants to be sure that he is falling in love with the real Rosalind.

The real Rosalind who is... the pretend Rosalind.

Well, the real Rosalind who's pretending to be a boy. That's the only relationship they have. Every other relationship he has with Rosalind is in his mind. It's hyperbolised and romanticised, which in her eyes is wrong and terrifying because she might disappoint him.

It's a wonderful mix. She ups the ante all the time, doesn't she? 'There is a man haunts the forest that abuses our young plants with carving "Rosalind" on their barks.' Then she goes on: 'You're not in love, you don't have any of the symptoms of a lover.'

It's very tongue-in-cheek. There are different things going on. Initially she's testing him with 'There is none of my uncle's marks upon you. He taught me how to know a man in love, in which cage of rushes I am sure you are not a prisoner.' ('Come on, show me that you are!') Orlando asks 'What were his marks?' Then – this was very fun, inventive – I started moving round him, and touching his face. It was quite sexy. I went up to him and stroked his face very slowly on 'A lean cheek, which you have not...', and there was a little crackly moment which we let hang. And then I was darting all around him, doing this and doing that... I picked at his shoe, and I tipped his hat, it was very energetic. And yes, initially wanting to know whether he's really in love, but also keeping on talking because of the sexual tension. I'm listing all the symptoms of neglect that show a real lover, and end up 'But you are no such man. You are rather point-device in your accoutrements, as loving yourself than seeming the lover of any other.' He got quite angry with me at this point because I'd gone so over the top, and shouted 'Fair youth, I would I could make thee believe I love.' I pulled it right back, and just went '*Me* believe it? You may as soon make her that you love believe it – ' and suddenly became very serious:

—   ...which, I warrant, she is apter to do than to confess she does... But, in good sooth, are you he that hangs the verses on the trees, wherein Rosalind is so admired?

—   I swear to thee, youth, by the white hand of Rosalind, I am that he, that unfortunate he.

And now here we come to the absolute crux of the scene, that it's all been building to: 'But are you so much in love as your rhymes speak?' She can't quite believe that he is going to say yes, but he answers her better than she can possibly imagine: 'Neither rhyme nor reason can express how much.' And it floors her. It completely floors her. And she realises that she's utterly in love too. The whole thing is terrifying. This next speech is so beautiful and I love it. It's almost my favourite:

Love is merely a madness, and I tell you deserves as well a dark house and a whip as madmen do; and the reason why they are not so punished and cured is that the lunacy is so ordinary that the whippers are in love too.

It was beautifully minor-key and reflective, the way you just said that.

She suddenly has this incredible lucidity about love. It's sort of rueful. I suppose it's that quality of any really great comedian, of having an equal part sadness, because so much of the humour in life comes from the sadness of life. She has that. For every funny thing she says, there's an undercurrent of reality as well, of the slightly frightening nature of it all. And she's not being flippant, she really does think love is completely crazy –'I just stumbled into this man, and he's putting his poems up on trees, he says he loves me and I love him, and here I am in a boy's outfit talking nonsense!' It's all crazy. Love is mad. And yet we run our lives by it.

Celia's been onstage through all of that without saying a word. Did her presence affect the scene?

Oh, it did, massively. We both hid behind a tree when Orlando made his entrance. When I said 'I will speak to him like a saucy lackey, and under that habit play the knave with him,' she was going 'No, no, no!' and trying to hold me back. But I ran out and started the scene, and she sat there looking critical, upstage-centre, so Orlando was never aware of her but the audience was. When he says 'Where dwell you, pretty youth?', I realise I can't quite do this on my own, so I go behind the tree and grab her and pull her down, saying 'With this shepherdess, my sister.' It's totally against her will and she's furious with me. She's very grumpy about it and won't speak, but she's present. But by the end of the scene she visibly softened, because she finds it amusing and enchanting and wants to be supportive of me. Their friendship is very important, and certainly in their next scene [3.4] as well.

Does it change during the course of the play, or remain constant?

I think it changes in the way that the best childhood friends or any good friends feel threatened when one or other of them starts having a romantic relationship that may undermine their friendship. We discussed a lot in rehearsals how Shakespeare deals with every type of love in this play. It's about the love between friends, it's about unrequited love, or the fear of unrequited love, and paternal... the love and separation of parents and children. And then you have the solitary figure of Jaques, who rails against love and walks off at the end of the play, when everyone's getting married, saying 'I hate you all, I'm gonna go and sit in a cave.' So there are people without love, there are people with love, there are people who want to be in love. And there's the lust element with Touchstone and Audrey – there's everything.

Act 3, Scene 4. Orlando's stood you up. And yet again Rosalind seems to start at a low ebb.

That's true. 'Never talk to me, I will weep.' We played this scene very much like two friends not quite hitting it off. Celia's trying to cheer her up, but everything she says only makes Rosalind more irritable. And that, in turn, makes Celia irritable because she can't say the right thing. Rosalind grumpily says 'His very hair is of the dissembling colour.' 'You're right,' says Celia, 'absolutely, he's really ugly.' 'Something browner than Judas's. Marry, his kisses are Judas's own children.' Which makes Rosalind go 'How dare you talk about my man like that? I'm allowed to do that, but you can't': 'I'faith, his hair is of a good colour.' So Celia says 'An excellent colour – your chestnut was ever the only colour,' getting a little bit pissy with her. And then Rosalind says 'And his kissing is as full of sanctity as the touch of holy bread' ('So there, stop it!').

Have you been kissing?

No, no. It's fantasy, prompted by Celia bringing up his kisses. Rosalind says 'If you're going to talk about his kissing, don't you *dare* say they're bad, they're the absolute best!' – 'But why did he swear he would come this morning, and comes not?' [3.4]. Celia's hurt, and she says 'Nay, certainly, there is no truth in him.' But Rosalind, open as always, then looks to her for counselling and says 'Do you think so?' Celia replies 'Yes. I think he is not a pick-purse nor a horse-stealer, but for his verity in love, I do think him as concave as a covered goblet or a worm-eaten nut.'

Does she mean it?

It's complicated. Maybe she doesn't quite know. I think she doesn't want Rosalind to be in love any more.

Because she thinks Rosalind is going to get hurt?

No, it's not that. In this early part of the scene, Rosalind's being a nightmare. She has become very self-involved, all she ever talks about is Orlando, she won't drop the disguise, and Celia can't ever say the right thing any more. So Celia is just annoyed with the situation. She wants things to go back to normal. She was very much a princess, not someone who adapted well to Arden. She missed her comforts and wanted to go back, she was not particularly up with the shepherds and the way of life – whereas Rosalind loved it, which I think is very important in this scene. Celia's motives aren't coming from a genuine place, but Rosalind is taking everything she says absolutely to heart. She says 'Not true in love?… You have heard him swear downright he was.' 'Have I got it all wrong, am I being naive?' She's terrified of being naive and romantic. And Celia's quite cruel. She says '"Was" is not "is"' i.e. he *might* have been in love, but that doesn't mean he still is, which again ties into all of Rosalind's fears. She's aware that love is possible in the moment – being young, in the forest and all the rest of it – but can it last? Her 'Will it last for ever?' preoccupation is quite modern, but I believe it's there in the text.

You mention your father briefly – 'I met the Duke yesterday' – and give him a line and a half. Then 'I'll prove a busy actor in their play', when you hear about Silvius and Phoebe. She seems back in her element, being an actor.

I didn't play that as particularly buoyant, it was more trying to mend her relationship with Celia. Corin comes in and talks about something completely different, nothing to do with Orlando. So I played that as saying to Celia 'Come on, let's go and look at these two, and I promise I won't be a moody cow. I'll be really jolly and be a boy and make you laugh. I promise I won't talk about Orlando.'

You watch the two of them, and you're not at all jolly. You seem to get really angry with her: 'Who might be your mother, / That you insult, exult, and all at once, / Over the wretched?' Is this genuine anger?

Absolutely. She can't bear to see someone so passionate being treated so badly. There it is, right in front of her – unrequited love. She's enraged, it's so unfair. 'Is this what's going to happen to me? Is that why Orlando hasn't turned up? I'm going to take it all out on her.'

You talk about 'Your bugle eyeballs' and 'your cheek of cream'. Are these compliments or terms of abuse?

'Your inky brows, your black silk hair, / Your bugle eyeballs... your cheek of cream...' That's all complimentary, but it's hyperbolic, sarcastic. All those things that will turn people on, they're trash.

So bugle eyeballs are nice eyeballs, they're not nasty eyeballs?

The sound of the word is also a little cruel, so there's ambiguity going on.

'If you will know my house,' she says to Silvius. It's the house that he was going to buy, surely. Why does she say that?

We toiled over this bit for so long. We came to the conclusion that it's pity, and she wants to know what happens to these people.

'Keep in touch.'

Yeah.

Act 4, Scene 1. The most wonderful romantic scene. It's all in prose, as was your previous scene with Orlando, whereas Silvius and Phoebe were all in verse. People say that when the emotional level intensifies Shakespeare tends to write in verse, but this is the opposite. It's an exception to the rule. What did Peter Hall say about that? He's a great man for these distinctions, isn't he?

Oh yes, absolutely. 'Treat the verse like verse and the prose like prose.' But actually most of this play's in prose, which is interesting.

Jaques says 'I prithee, pretty youth, let me be better acquainted with thee.' Is this more sex? What's going on here?

No, it was innocent. I think by this point Ganymede is getting a reputation around the forest for being a little bit interesting. Wiser than one would expect a young boy to be. So Jaques comes along and goes 'Ah, you're that one, I want to know more about you.' And Rosalind is confronted with someone that, similarly, has a reputation in the forest for being a worldly-wise depressive, so she says 'I don't want to talk about *me*, I want to talk about *you*. They say you're a miserable bugger.' And he says 'Erm, I am, yeah.' I think their relationship's interesting and I always enjoyed the scene a lot, because nobody else stands up to Jaques in the way Rosalind does. She flummoxes him in the way she cuts through all the nonsense and says things so directly.

It's quite an odd little scene on the page.

It is. But I enjoyed doing it. There was something wonderful about 'Those that are in extremity of either [melancholy or laughter] are abominable fellows, and betray themselves to every modern censure worse than drunkards' [4.1]. And I loved the way Jaques gets quite defensive: 'Why, 'tis good to be sad and say nothing,' which makes him sound ludicrous. She replies 'Why then, 'tis good to be a post.' 'What's the point in life if you're miserable and don't say anything?' Shakespeare never writes anything arbitrarily, and he puts Rosalind as the protagonist in all these situations that teach her something about herself. Just at the moment when she's feeling low, as if she might end up being miserable, never telling Orlando who she is, never living her life – along comes a person who has spent his life being miserable and alone. And she realises 'I don't want to be a depressive. What's the point of living like that?' So actually it's an important scene.

Orlando then turns up, and she seems to be really angry: 'Where have you been all this while?' No acting required, is there? I imagine that Rosalind and Ganymede become one at that point.

Yes, absolutely. One hundred per cent. There's hardly any acting in this. When Orlando comes in, suddenly this wave of anger comes up towards him. But again she's taking it all out on someone else, she's always deferring. She says to Jaques:

> Farewell, Monsieur Traveller: look you lisp and wear strange suits,
> disable all the benefits of your own country, be out of love with your
> nativity, and almost chide God for making you that countenance you
> are, or I will scarce think you have swam in a gondola. [4.1]

It sounds like one of those bits of nonsensical verbal play you were talking about, but actually it's taking 'I don't want to be like you' and building on it.

She really sends him up and gives him a hard time, and says 'You're an idiot, you haven't done anything, and you spend your life wandering around being gloomy', and it's over the top, totally inappropriate. Jaques leaves, going 'What on earth...?' So when the scene between them starts off, Orlando knows that he's walked in on someone who is angry and tense, and it carries straight on. She doesn't really want to say anything to him. He goes 'My fair Rosalind...' ('Oh, you know, I'm sorry...') And she's absolutely furious. 'Break an hour's promise in love... Nay, an you be so tardy, come no more in my sight. I had as lief be wooed of a snail... for though he comes slowly, he carries his house on his head.' Again, she always gets a little bit of wit in there.

You seem to try to provoke him into a laddish sort of joke about cuckolds and women's promiscuity, which he doesn't pick up on.

Yes, you're right:

— Besides he brings his destiny with him.
— What's that?
— Why, horns.

But then Orlando switches it around: 'Virtue is no horn-maker, and my Rosalind is virtuous', i.e. 'Hang on a minute, what's up with you? You don't even *know* my Rosalind, so don't talk about it. You just calm down and stop behaving like an idiot.' Which is exactly what she needs sometimes. And she also switches round after that. It frightens her, him talking about 'my Rosalind', and being cross with her. That's why she replies 'And I am your Rosalind.'

Then Celia interrupts. Why does she do that?

Because I said it as if I was about to come out and tell. I played 'And I am your Rosalind' full-on. Big silence. He's going 'What?' and then Celia comes in with 'It pleases him to call you so. But he hath a Rosalind of a better leer than you.'

She has to rescue you.

Yeah. I remember feeling quite emotional, wanting to tell him but not wanting to tell him, cross with him but not wanting to be so cross that I'd push him away, as I had done earlier. On top of all that, Celia reminds me that maybe it's not such a good idea to reveal myself. Okay, so I'm going to make it all better: 'Come, woo me, woo me...'

You're bound to think, watching this scene, 'He must *know!' It's fascinating. You can't play that Orlando realises who 'Ganymede' is, and yet it seems crazy that he doesn't. Was there any suggestion that he did?*

No, he didn't have any suspicion. He can't have. I think you just have to accept that it's a convention. In fact he played it quite comfortable with the homo-eroticism. When he said 'I would kiss before I spoke,' he got quite close to me, and was a bit sort of tickly and funny about it all. And then I went 'Nay, you were better speak first,' and again she keeps talking to get over the awkward-ness. The next bit was done lounging around in the sunshine, shoes off, picking at bits of grass and throwing them, and Celia making a little daisy chain. Orlando says he will die if Rosalind will not have him. 'No, faith, die by attorney,' she tells him: 'Men have died from time to time, and worms have eaten them, but not for love' – i.e. 'Let's be realistic about this. Don't ever say anything that's over the top. Only tell me the truth…'

Tell me about the mock-marriage.

It gets absolutely serious. We spoke in rehearsals about the fact that at the time the play was written, just saying the words would have constituted an infor-mal betrothal. So the stakes are really high. I grabbed him and we were on our knees facing each other, and we became very close to the point of nearly kiss-ing. Celia was increasingly furious with me for going so far, and unwilling to say anything. Orlando began by finding it all a big laugh, and then being swept along by how serious I was being, and the romanticism, the electricity between them. So it built from a being joke up to 'I take thee, Rosalind, for wife.' There was a pause. And then he got confused, pulled back and broke away. But he *never* played 'I suspect you of being Rosalind.'

A little later in the scene he suddenly says 'For these two hours, Rosalind, I will leave thee.'

Yeah. 'I've got to go… This is all a bit weird, I've got to go.'

'You have simply misused our sex with your love-prate,' says Celia when he's gone.

And she means it.

Your next scene [4.3] is very odd. Orlando's late yet again, and Silvius brings a love letter to you from Phoebe. First of all you lie to him and say the letter's full of hostility, and then you cruelly read him the real thing. What's your game?

I think she's going a bit mad at this point. She's lost the plot. She's just been through an incredibly emotional scene with Orlando, and now she's got to deal with these people again, who break her heart. It upsets her so much that she's tried to help this poor lovesick man, and only made the situation worse because Phoebe's fallen in love with her. The idea is just ludicrous. We tried so many versions of this. Eventually I started off being protective, going 'You don't want to hear this, it's nothing.' And then 'You want to hear it? Okay. She doesn't love you, she loves me. Listen to this. Are you getting it?' – being deliberately cruel, like a short, sharp shock. She wants Silvius to stop loving Phoebe, so she tries to beat it out of him. It was very cruel, and he ended up baffled, going 'But you said I would like to hear this letter...'

Being cruel to be kind.

Yes. But she's so upset by seeing how love affects people when it's not working. David Birkin played Silvius as a very calm, sensitive, poetic soul. He was in tears by the end of it. And the more I saw him dissolving in front of me, the more it upset me. But I thought it would help him so I kept on going. Eventually we were all in an emotional state, and he just ran off.

Next on comes Oliver, and you're unusually silent while he and Celia have their moment together. Then he describes the lioness and the snake, and produces the bloody napkin which causes you to faint. I love the way Rosalind later says 'Did your brother tell you how I counterfeited to swoon?' [5.2].

She's afraid she's been caught out. She's so mad by this point, so tired and drained, I think she's an emotional wreck. Everything is going wrong and she feels responsible. Phoebe, Silvius, Orlando... And now Celia's fallen in love, and Orlando's been wounded by a lioness – what's going on? So it makes sense to me that she passes out and then comes to and just obsesses about this counterfeit swoon. 'Tell everyone that I pretended to swoon!' She's really lost it.

She describes Celia and Oliver's love at first sight, just like her own. But they get it together immediately, unlike her and Orlando. Then suddenly she seems ready to finish role-playing.

Yes, she wakes up and goes 'Okay, I have to take stock of everything. I have to drop the disguise and take the risk of falling in love, letting it happen, just trusting it. You can't protect and shield yourself for ever, because you'll be unhappy like Jaques. You have to take that risk.'

She seems to turn into a magician-cum-deus ex machina.

At the beginning of the scene [5.2] I haven't quite got there yet, I'm still half in game-playing mode. But Orlando had his arm in a sling and was staring out front, and just says 'Did you hear about Celia and Oliver?' I stayed behind him and played the speech about them to his back. 'They looked, no sooner looked but they loved, no sooner loved but they sighed, no sooner sighed but they asked one another the reason.' And I realised during the course of the speech that it could and maybe should be that easy. 'It's wonderful, why couldn't *we* have been like that?' There was almost a melancholy in this scene, a girding of loins, a letting go. And then he lost patience and was quite snappy with me, and said, still out front, 'I can live no longer by thinking.' I take a deep breath, still looking at his back, and go 'I will weary you then no longer with idle talking…' I'm gonna do it. He sits down and I kneel, so there was again the sense of a proposal. Then the speech 'Know of me, then – for now I speak to some purpose – that I know you are a gentleman of good conceit…' and she waffles a bit, trying to think what to do, and coming up with 'Believe then, if you please, that I can do strange things.' But as always with her, there are the little qualifications. It's all about 'if', this speech – it really got to me how much this speech is about 'if'. There's a lot of irony.

So, jumping on to the last scene [5.4], the 'strange things' had nothing to do with magic, or Hymen descending from the clouds.

No. None of it was magic, it was utter realism.

With you stage-managing.

Yes. There was nothing spooky about 'strange things'. It was matter of fact. 'I can do strange things, just trust me and I'll do it. I can make it all alright…'

Did the production have a happy ending?

Yes, very. Ultimately, extremely happy. It was tentative right up until the last moment, and there were some miserable bits. Phoebe was utterly heartbroken when she finds out that I'm a girl and she's going to have to marry Silvius whom she doesn't love. So their union wasn't exactly ecstatic, but it was comical. She's screaming, and then gets dragged into a big dance. I remember spending the last ten minutes of the play running on and offstage, grabbing people and putting things on them. We deliberately didn't opt for Rosalind suddenly appearing as a woman and everyone going 'Gosh, isn't she glamorous!' I came back still wearing the coat and hat to reveal myself to Orlando, and indicated 'Yes, look, it's been me all along. Sorry. How do you feel about that?' Even then it wasn't 'Oh, great, let's hug, I love you.' He played a moment of 'You mean you've been having me on all this time? I don't know how I feel about that.' And I played a moment of 'Please, please, I'm sorry.' And it was resolved silently, except for those couple of lines at the end. But then everyone gets together. We did a very, very joyful dance all around Corin, and everyone had garlands, and there were flowers… there was a lot of singing and whooping, and it was wonderfully exuberant. Finally they all stayed onstage, and I broke away to do the epilogue.

You played the epilogue as Rosalind?

Yeah, as Rosalind.

Derek Jacobi
on
Malvolio

Twelfth Night (1601)
Donmar Warehouse in the West End
Opened at the Wyndham's Theatre, London
on 10 December 2008

Directed by Michael Grandage
Designed by Christopher Oram
With Mark Bonnar as Orsino, Ron Cook as Sir Toby Belch,
Victoria Hamilton as Viola, Guy Henry as Sir Andrew Aguecheek,
Samantha Spiro as Maria, Zubin Varla as Feste, and Indira Varma as Olivia

Twelfth Night is generally considered to be Shakespeare's most perfect comedy. It was written around 1601 when he was at the height of his powers, and is a brilliant blend of lyricism, boisterous laughter and bittersweet emotion. The threads of an improbable plot involving male and female identical twins are effortlessly interwoven with searching insights into human nature. Romantic love, and the pain it can cause, is a major focus of the play. 'Even so quickly may one catch the plague?' asks Olivia.

Twelfth Night is very attractive to actors, having no out-and-out lead but rather a galaxy of excellent parts. If two roles stand out they are Malvolio and Viola. Shakespeare takes Malvolio on an eventful journey through the play. We first meet him as Olivia's scrupulously correct and humourless servant. He soon reveals himself to be a puritanical party-pooper, thus antagonising Sir Toby, Sir Andrew and Maria. The trick they play on him then exposes his remarkable ambition, which is no less than to marry Olivia and become Count Malvolio. His gullibility and self-delusion turn him into a ludicrous figure, as he dresses absurdly and smiles constantly. Our laughter turns to pity when he is treated as a lunatic and locked in a dark cell. He is released into the midst of a celebration of happy lovers and reunited siblings, and stalks away alone, vowing revenge.

When I first knew Derek Jacobi and acted with him at university, he appeared to have leapt straight from the womb as a fully formed immaculate actor. He'd played Hamlet as a schoolboy at the Edinburgh Festival, and already seemed impossibly accomplished, with enviable physical and vocal ease. Since those days he has been awarded two knighthoods, one British and one Danish. Nonetheless, he has remained reassuringly ungrand. We met and talked one morning, with a boisterous interruption from his dog, at his home in Belsize Park. It was February 2009, during the run of *Twelfth Night*. He had just been nominated for the Olivier Award for Best Actor as Malvolio, which he subsequently won.

Julian Curry: Are you having fun playing Malvolio?

Derek Jacobi: Yes. I haven't had fun all the time, because I was very frightened by it at first. Not just Malvolio. Some time ago I had a bout of stage fright which kept me off the stage for about three years. And when I started rehearsing Malvolio, it sort of resurfaced vaguely – not badly, otherwise I couldn't have gone on. I think it was because Malvolio is such a lonely part to play. He doesn't have much contact with anybody else, and his two big scenes are mainly with the audience... to the audience. So I didn't really relax in it, I wasn't really enjoying it. I was doing it, but there was a certain amount of dread in me before I went on: 'What's going to happen tonight?', you know.

Outside the normal kind of dread?

Yes. Outside the normal apprehension of standing in the wings, thinking what a silly way to earn a living. That's taken for granted. But now, with only four weeks to go, I'm beginning to relax and I am enjoying it.

It must have helped to be nominated for an Olivier.

Actually, no, it put more pressure on. It has put people's expectations up, and that makes it worse.

I didn't know you'd had stage fright. Do you remember what brought it on?

Yes, I can remember exactly what started it. I talked myself into it. I put what I would call a worm of doubt in my head, quite fortuitously. I was on tour with *Hamlet* in 1979. We did a world tour finishing in Australia, in Sydney. Our interval came before the nunnery scene, so the first thing I had to do after the interval was 'To be or not to be...' On the last Saturday of the tour, the Saturday matinee, I was thinking to myself how strange it is when an actor says 'To be or not to be...' There is a kind of silence that you can actually touch when he says those words. What would happen if I forgot it? I went on and I was about two lines in, and had a total blank. Total blank. I'd played it nearly four hundred times, so automatic pilot took over, and I carried on talk-ing, but I didn't know what was coming out. It was all done absolutely automaton-like. Every pore in my body opened, the sweat poured off my face and my body. It stayed like that for the rest of that performance and for the evening performance. And I didn't go onstage again until 1982. All those silly questions that people ask you: 'How do you learn the lines?' I thought 'Yeah, how *do* I? How *do* you get up in front of a thousand people?' And I questioned my enjoyment of acting, my ability to act, everything. It went, totally. It was awful.

How very frightening. It's quite fashionable to call Malvolio a tragic part. Do you think there's anything in that?

I do think he makes an extraordinary journey, and is punished beyond his due. He puts himself in the firing line, but what they dish out to him is way over the top. They try to send him mad, it gets out of control. In that sense he's a tragic figure. And by the end when he talks of revenging himself, I think he really means it. His life has taken a very, very different course to what it would have done. And I think he'll be dedicated to ruining the marriages.

It's an interesting name. There's a Benvolio in Romeo and Juliet *who seems to be a well-wisher. Is Malvolio an ill-wisher, do you think?*

There are several interpretations. One that I like very much is Leslie Hotson's. He says that the name Malvolio may have been an in-joke, sending up Sir William Knollys, Comptroller of the Queen's Household. He fell in love with his seventeen-year-old ward Mary Fitton and wrote overblown letters to her. His passion for her was known at court and made him a figure of fun. Mal was short for Mary, so 'Mal Volio' could mean 'I want Mary!' That's what I like to think.

Malvolio is much described. All sorts of epithets are attached to him, from a 'rascally sheep-biter' to being 'sad and civil'. Did they help you as you were approaching the part?

And a Puritan. Yes, I think they did. We experimented at first with having him a class lower than anybody else, and an ex-military man. There are remnants of it still – my haircut is one of them. And we thought that he was newish to the household, he'd not been there for long, which made him even more of an outsider. We tried the military thing that when he spoke to people he tended to bark at them. I came on like a barking sergeant major, with 'Let's be 'aving yer' and so on. Well, that and being lower class didn't work. It lasted about three days, until Michael Grandage and I both decided at the same time that it wasn't working. So the upright-rod-down-the-back, rather remote, rather cut-off persona is the one that we went for.

How much were you able to imagine Malvolio's life outside the play, or what he might have been before?

Well, we stayed with the idea that he had been an army man. He'd been used to giving orders rather than receiving them. So it was an odd situation for him. It made him a bit introverted, and a little bit harsher than he would have been with those under him, because he had to take orders from Olivia. And Sir Toby, of course. So anybody like Maria or Feste would get it in the neck from him, as compensation.

He's an odd mix, isn't he, because he's got the efficiency of a military man, but his head's full of strange fantasies.

Yes. That moment when Maria says he's practising behaviour to his own shadow. That's very odd. He has fantasies of being Count Malvolio, of being above his station. So he's very class-conscious.

Very. Did you model your performance on anyone, or take it direct from the text?

Oh, from the text. I did have somebody in mind when we were rehearsing it, only because he sat like an elephant on my shoulder, and that was Donald Sinden. He was a famous Malvolio, especially for one particular bit of business, which we obviously couldn't do.

What was that?

It had to do with the set. You know the moment when he's fantasising about sending his men off to bring Sir Toby to him, and he says 'I frown the while, and perchance wind up my watch…' [2.5]. Sinden brought out his watch and started to wind it, then looked at the time. There was a sundial on the set. He looked at it and back at his watch, then went and altered the sundial. Huge laugh. That was the big moment, it made his Malvolio famous. I kept thinking of him in rehearsal, trying to get rid of him. Well, we did the first preview on the 5th of December, I was practically catatonic with terror, but we got through it. And round to the dressing room after the show came Sinden. I said 'Had I known you were out there I would never have gone on the stage.' I couldn't have done it. It's hard enough anyway, when you rehearse a comedy. 'Are they going to laugh, will there be stony silence…?' And he walked through the door. Quite by chance, he'd come up to London for a dinner party which had been cancelled; he thought 'I'll go to the theatre, I'll go and see *Twelfth Night*.'

Can you describe the setting and your appearance?

There are three main sets. At the back there are shutters, which first contain Orsino's house. They fly out, and there's another set behind, which reveals Olivia's household. That eventually flies out, and we're on the seashore with the sound of seagulls, and the lighting very golden. There are no pieces of stage furniture except a couch for Olivia. There is a windbreak on the beach area, that is all. Otherwise, it is a very open set. There is nothing for an actor to lean on, sit on or relax by. It is you, the text and your fellow actors. There are no safety nets at all.

A bit of a mixed blessing?

Yes. You feel very exposed. But as far as Malvolio's concerned, of course, he never is relaxed enough to sit down. He's too uptight. He is dressed in a rather tight-fitting black suit, black tie with a high starched collar and a watch chain. When he goes into the yellow stockings he adopts white shorts and a sailor's cap, looking as if he's just stepped off a yacht. And particoloured shoes, white and brown shoes. A rather large yellow handkerchief coming out of the top pocket of his double-breasted jacket. And a yellow cravat. He's a symphony of yellow.

When I was coming out of the theatre I overheard a lady talking about your shorts, saying 'Oh, I think he probably got that from Eric Morecambe.'

[*Burst of laughter.*] Oh dear! No, I got it from the designer Christopher Oram.

Let's talk about the text. You cut Fabian, didn't you?

Yes, Michael decided to cut Fabian. He comes from nowhere and goes to nowhere, so Michael portioned out most of Fabian's lines between Maria and Feste. I don't miss him actually. Some people do, I don't. I think it makes the narrative very clear. When Fabian comes on for the guying of Malvolio you wonder 'Well, who is that?' It's an odd, odd part, and I think the play works without him.

Otherwise the text is more or less as per, is it?

Yes, as per. He made a few internal cuts, but not many.

Since Michael Grandage took over the Donmar, he's had one huge success after another. What's his secret? How does he do it?

Simplicity. I think his secret is confidence, and relying on the text, and presenting it in narrative terms before you get to the emotional context. He tells a wonderful story in all his productions. He casts wonderfully well. He works in tandem with his partner, Christopher Oram, who does the sets. So the designer and the director are very much on the same plane, know what the other's thinking. But mainly Michael loves actors, was an actor himself, and knows actors' problems. In the rehearsal room he's a kind of benign dictator. You have fun, there's a lot of laughs, a lot of enjoyment, but a great deal of discipline too. He won't let anything pass that he disapproves of, or thinks is bad for you. So it's not as with many directors who think that an actor's creative juices only start flowing when he's in a state of abject terror. You don't end up acting for Michael, you end up acting for the play, with his encouragement and support. He surrounds you with amazing support. It was the same when he was running the Crucible Theatre in Sheffield.

What kind of support?

Everybody is part of what you're doing, it's not just the actors and the text. There is a meeting before anything happens. You know, the first day at school. Everybody's there, the usherettes, the ushers, the box office, the wardrobe, the electricians, the carpenters. You have this meet-and-greet. Then the actors are left to read the play. After that – this is typical of Michael's technique with *Twelfth Night* – he rehearses scene by scene, but the people who are not in any scene are not allowed in the room. This goes on for about two-and-a-half weeks. Then you do your first run-through and, of course, you're all in the room the whole time, so you see what everybody else has been doing. It's a wonderful moment. You haven't seen other scenes rehearsed, you don't know what people have been thinking of or making up. And then, as you run it more often, everybody else comes back in. The tea lady comes in, the ushers, the electricians. Everybody sees it. He also surrounds you with the best lighting, the best sound. They're allowed in all the time, and they're there a great deal. So it's a communal effort. There's nothing precious about it, nothing arty about it – that we're doing Shakespeare, doing High Art. No, we are creating a piece of entertainment, and everybody is involved in how the public eventually receives that entertainment. I think that's one of his great secrets, that he makes everybody part of a huge family for that time. And if you're having problems, not getting it, not finding it, he makes you feel that you *will* get it. Don't worry. It's how Sir Laurence was, all those years ago. He takes the anxiety from you. He says 'Give me your anxiety, trust me, and I will show you.' And it works.

In your first scene [1.5], what have you got against Feste? You obviously have it in for him.

Yes. Well, it's because he's allowed to be jokey and intimate with Olivia in a way that I can't. He has his freedom, and he can sit beside her and play to her. He's allowed to eyeball her, and even kind of flirt with her. I'm jealous. And when I voice my jealousy in that first speech, she immediately puts me down and is on his side, which makes it worse.

You say 'I take these wise men, that crow so at these set kind of fools, no better than the fools' zanies.' Have you any particular wise men in mind? Olivia's father, for instance?

No, I think it's general, I think it's still a class thing. He associates wisdom with nobility, people who can afford a fool, and think it's clever to have a fool, and will indulge their fool and laugh at them, however bad they are. And that upsets him dreadfully.

She says 'O, you are sick of self-love, Malvolio.' But that's the only time she's in any way harsh to you, isn't it. The rest of the time she's…

Yes, she's fine. Later she says 'He is sad and civil, / And suits well for a servant with my fortunes' [3.4].

And when she says 'There is… no railing in a known discreet man, though he do nothing but reprove,' it can perhaps read as her saying sorry that she was harsh to you a moment earlier. You are the known discreet man who has just railed. Does it work like that, do you think?

Yes, I think so.

So she's making it alright again with you?

Yes, she is.

At the end of the scene there's another piece of Sinden biz, when she says 'Run after that same peevish messenger.' And he mouthed, horrified, 'RUN?!'

Cheap, cheap. But Sinden did a lot of cheap gags, which were wonderful.

Were you ever tempted to go along those lines?

Yes, I was. I did start to walk off, and then burst into a run. But Grandage said 'Don't do that.' So I've never done it in performance. It came and it went in the rehearsal room. Like earlier, when Olivia says 'Tell him, he shall not speak with me.' And I say 'He's been told so; and he says he'll stand at your door like a sheriff's post, and be the supporter to a bench, but he'll speak with you.' I did that imitating his voice. But Michael, I think quite rightly, said 'No, don't give him a jokiness. The whole point about the smile is that he tries to smile, but we never want to see him smile. And if you make him jokey then we assume that he can smile.' That undercuts it.

The following short scene with Viola [2.2] lends itself to jokey 'ring biz', doesn't it. Getting it stuck on your finger, or…

Yes – which we eschewed. Once it rolled into the audience. That was wonderful, because it fell at a man's feet in the front row, who bent down and picked it up. Then I had my exit line 'be it his that finds it', which got a round!

I've seen a Malvolio who slid the ring down his very slender staff, onto the ground.

Yes, that's very good. But it's tempting with Malvolio to make him a turn. And I think he's more than that, he's more important than a turn. There are many opportunities to do turn-like things of that sort, which titillate an audience, and of course I was tempted. But part of the production was Grandage's refusal to let me do that, and teaching me to be just a little more tasteful. And right for the character. It's too easy to gag Malvolio to death.

There are a couple of lines that read strangely in that scene. 'She took the ring of me,' says Viola, but Olivia did no such thing. And when you say 'Come, sir, you peevishly threw it to her…'

Neither of them are true, no. It's inexplicable really. They're both talking rubbish. But you just have to go with it. In performance I don't think one notices.

Moving on to the night scene [2.3], he says 'My masters, are you mad? Or what are you?' How easy do you find it to attack Sir Toby?

Well, I have been sent, specifically. Maria says 'If my lady have not called up her steward Malvolio'… to come and sort you out. And to 'turn you out of doors…'

Including Sir Toby, although he's a knight.

Oh, I think so, yes. Well, already in that first scene [1.5] Maria comes in and says there's a young man outside. Olivia asks who's looking after him and Maria says Sir Toby. Olivia then says 'Oh, call him off, he's rubbish!'…'Go you, Malvolio.'

So you know his stock is already pretty low.

Very, very low. And by the end of the play, Toby himself says it's rock bottom now. But that 'My masters' [2.3] is another one of those moments. This time, it's Olivier. When he came on, Sir Andrew hid under the table. Olivier said 'My masters are you mad, or what?' Then pulled up the tablecloth and said 'ARE YOU?'

How are you dressed for the night scene?

I've got black silk pyjamas and a large black quilted dressing gown. And slippers.

You don't wear a nightcap.

No. In the design, and when we're having the fittings, I did have a hat with a tassel. But it looked gimmicky. At that time we were trying to get rid of all the gimmicks.

Toby says 'Go, sir, rub your chain with crumbs.'

Yes, he does. I said to Christopher 'Am I going to have a chain of office? Because it *is* referred to.' 'It's only referred to once,' said Christopher. And the little black suit he put me in didn't fit a chain. The chain was Elizabethan. So you assume he's got a chain of office, but he certainly wouldn't be wearing it in his nightclothes.

'Art any more than a steward?' That hurts, doesn't it. That stings.

It hurts very much. I try to show that, I do get very uptight. It's interesting, because when Malvolio reads the letter later on [2.5], and he comes to the phrase 'Let me see thee a steward still', it's a moment of great elation. Because it's confirmation that the letter is really for him.

That night scene [2.3] is extraordinary, but for Malvolio it's very short.

It really sets up the gulling scene. I think Malvolio's got to be deeply unpleasant. He has a torch and eyeballs Sir Toby, shining it full in his face, saying 'Look, unless you can separate yourself from your misdemeanours, you're out, mate, you're out.' Really getting at him.

You shone the torch at each of them individually, didn't you, one by one.

Yes. And then kept it on Toby, after he responds with 'Art any more than a steward?' and 'Go rub your chain with crumbs.' Toby then turns to Maria and tells her to fetch some more drink. And the confrontation then is palpable, because Malvolio says to Maria 'If you obey what Sir Toby's just said, I will see to it that Olivia knows not only about him, but about you too, Maria.' It's a great threat to all of them.

That gets her dander up as well. I was surprised there was no drink onstage.

They keep calling for it. Toby comes on at the beginning, shouting 'A stoup of wine!' I think they've been out, they're drunk already. They've come back home, everybody's asleep. They've got to get somebody to go to the pantry and get some wine, because they're not about to go to bed yet.

Shakespeare likes gulling scenes, doesn't he? You've played Benedick in Much Ado. *This is very different…*

Yes, but it's reminiscent of it.

'Get ye all three into the box-tree,' Maria normally says in Act 2, Scene 5…

We didn't have anything like a box-tree. So the line is cut. They hide behind the windbreak. We've gone to the seaside, which I like. I also like the way the play opens with a (slightly too loud) tremendous thunderclap. Viola later refers to tempests being kind, and they are in the middle of a tempest. Not only practically, with the supposed drownings, but the tempest in Orsino's head. It begins in a great fury, both emotionally and with the elements. So I like it when the stage opens up for the gulling scene, and we're on the shore, with the sea just over there. We're reminded that this is all taking place in a seaside resort.

Malvolio's said to be 'practising behaviour to his own shadow' before he comes on in the letter scene. What do you think you're doing?

Well, I think I'm doing exactly that. I'm making shapes. I'm seeing how I look at certain angles. I'm rather admiring my figure, which I've kept, however old I am. And my profile in shadow. I think I'm just admiring myself.

Before you come on, Maria says to the letter, 'Lie thou there.'

She wedges it between the slats of the stage.

What's in your mind when you come on and say ''Tis but fortune; all is fortune…'?

I'm fantasising about Olivia. I say 'Maria once told me she did affect me.' We had a problem with that line, because it's not quite clear whether Maria was saying that she, Maria, was in love with me; or saying as a joke 'You know, Olivia fancies you…' I think it must be the second of these, because the line is 'Maria once told me she did affect me, and I have heard herself come thus near, that should she fancy, it should be one of my complexion.' So Shakespeare is setting him up for the gulling by having him come on and say 'I've heard Olivia drop hints that if she ever had thoughts of hitching up with anybody, it would be me. And Maria is of the same mind.'

Do you see yourself as something of a ladies' man?

I think so. Yes.

How does a person become so deluded?

The word 'mad' occurs a great deal in the play, and I don't think it's accidental. There's a degree of… not mental aberration exactly, but certainly a mental twist in Malvolio. At times he seems hardly human. There's a strange mentality to the man that keeps him apart from other people, and shackles him into his own head. I don't think he's mad, ever, but he is highly eccentric.

Certainly prone to strange fantasies.

Oh, yes.

How about 'play with my…?'

Well, Michael let me do the cheap gag on that only because Christopher Oram, his partner, loved it when he saw the first run-through.

What is the gag?

Well, you know you call your genitals your 'crown jewels'. He says 'Or play with my... some rich jewel.' Rather than deflect the line onto something else, I imagine I'm going to masturbate while I'm waiting for Sir Toby.

'... Quenching my familiar smile with an austere regard of control.' That's a curious line, isn't it. It seems almost unhelpful.

It is, terribly unhelpful, given that we don't want him ever to smile. But I think, again, he's fantasising. He's fantasising that Olivia loves him, he's fantasising about himself, and he's fantasising about his smile – what he gives off, his look. He doesn't smile at all. He's absolutely deluding himself. He looks sullen and cross, and angry and disapproving all the time. The nearest he would get to a smile would be a smirk. However, in his mind, in this picture he has of himself, he has a dazzling smile. But it's in his head. It's not reality at all.

The moment when you find the letter can lend itself to all sorts of tricks and teasing of the audience – getting it stuck to the sole of your shoe, for instance.

I just walk over it. I ignore it...

Almost like Krapp with the banana skin.

...and then realise it's there and turn back.

What's your first reaction when you see the letter?

I pick it up and immediately see that it's in what I think is Olivia's handwriting. It's addressed 'To the unknown beloved'. Given the possibility that Olivia could fancy me... well! I find a letter written in her handwriting, which is obviously a love letter.

This is when you start a bit of by-play with the audience: 'These be her very C's, her U's, and her T's; and thus makes she her great P's.'

Yes. They laugh at 'her great P's'... and I just give them a little reproving look.

You tell us not to be so smutty. A touch of the George Robeys.

Yes.

Do you have any problem opening it? Because it's not addressed to you.

No, it's not addressed to me. I do have a slight problem opening it, which is why I do it behind my back, so that I can't see myself opening it. Oh, and suddenly it's open – but I didn't open it.

'M. O. A. I.' Have you any idea what that means?

No. I looked at every possible note, from the Arden to the Temple to the Variorum... None of them helped me at all. It might have had some significance four hundred years ago when the play was written. It may have been a huge joke at the time, but I'm afraid it's gone.

It's got to stay in.

Oh, it's got to stay in. Yes.

'If this fall into thy hand, revolve...'

Yes, that's another one.

Another tempting moment, that begs for a gag. What do you do?

Well, I look puzzled at the audience – what could this possibly mean? I look around to see if anybody's watching. I start to look as if I'm going to turn on the spot, and then give it all up as a bad job.

Oh dear, this is unfair. It's horrible to ask you to describe a visual gag. But it's terribly funny in performance, and we have to mention it. 'Remember who commended thy yellow stockings...'

Yes. Again it's a problem, because Maria says later that Olivia hates the colour yellow, and she also loathes the fashion of cross-gartering. So what I thought was that maybe there was a party before the brother died and she went into mourning. It was a fancy-dress party. And Malvolio had turned up in these things, and Olivia had said, politely, 'Oh!!! Oh, they're good, they're nice!'

So there could be a grain of truth in it. Not pure fantasy this time?

There could be a grain of truth, yes.

What else about the letter?

It's full of little moments, particularly 'some are born great, some achieve greatness, and some have greatness thrust upon 'em', which incidentally is going to come back twice more, in the yellow-stocking scene [3.4] and right at the end of the play, when Feste repeats it [5.1]. No, it's just the nice little clues in the letter that lead up to him finishing it, absolutely knowing that he is the subject of it.

So you get to the smile.

He has several attempts at smiling. When he eventually achieves a smile it's as if he's wrenched it up from his guts. It's come from somewhere deep inside him, and ended up on his mouth. And it sticks there. He's very proud of it and carries it off into the wings.

You're so proud of it that you give Jove a smile every time you thank him.

Yes, that's right.

I read that Olivier was so outrageously camp and hammy as Malvolio that he fell backwards off a bench in the letter scene. Gielgud, who was directing, hated it and begged him not to. Who would you sympathise with?

[*Without hesitation.*] Gielgud. As I said earlier, the danger with Malvolio is to make him into a turn. There are plenty of opportunities to do funny things. But if every time he appears, the audience think 'What's he gonna do now to make us laugh?', you lose more than half the person.

And much of the weight of the play.

Yes.

Moving on to the cross-gartered scene [3.4]. Again we get a report of you before you arrive. Maria says 'He does nothing but smile.' It's almost as if he's so pleased, once he's found the smile, that he's kept it going from the end of his last scene to the beginning of this.

Yes. He's been chuckling away whilst putting on the stockings. 'She's going to love this. She's going to go absolutely mad for me now. I've obeyed everything she said in the letter…'

So you're confident about the stockings and the garters. What is cross-gartering, by the way?

I think it was a fashion, literally, of garters that criss-crossed up and down one's leg. What we do is we have yellow stockings with a cross pattern on them, held up by black garters with little brooches on the front. They are obviously elastic garters, and are at one point twanged to show that they are elastic.

'Please one, and please all'; then 'Ay, sweetheart…' These are two lines that might be sung. A moment later you say 'Nightingales answer daws.'

Interesting. That never occurred to me.

They are from old songs, according to the notes I read.

Yes, because he mentioned 'the very true sonnet'.

Yes, but you don't sing them, do you?

No.

'Wilt thou go to bed, Malvolio?' How do you react to that? Christmas has come early!

Oh, absolutely. This is the final confirmation that I'm in like Flynn. She's inviting me to bed.

During the scene you quote the letter quite a lot.

Oh yes, I quote all the greatness stuff, and the commending of the yellow stockings and all that.

Are you carrying the letter or have you learnt it by heart?

I've learnt it. It's ingrained. No, I couldn't carry the letter because she might immediately say 'What have you got there? Can I see it?'

Of course, then the play would end rather abruptly.

Absolutely.

'A sad face, a reverend carriage… in the habit of some sir of note.' All these lines that you quote to yourself after she's gone off, they're not in the letter, are they?

I think they are. I think they are his interpretation of what she asks him to do. She asks him to 'Be opposite with a kinsman, surly with servants, let thy tongue tang with arguments of state, put thyself into the trick of singularity.' I think the 'sad face', the 'reverend carriage,' the 'slow tongue' and 'the habit of some sir of note' are all his interpretation of those instructions.

So half the time he's quoting the letter, and half the time he's extrapolating from it.

Yes.

Tell me what happens at the end of that scene. On the one hand, you're one hundred per cent convinced that she's in love with you, but on the other, Sir Toby and Maria start taunting you with the idea that you've got the devil inside you. Do you start to feel at all mad and disturbed?

I think he's gone onto another plane at that point. Their attempts to upset him, to rile him, to suggest that he's mad, have absolutely no effect on him at all. He calls them 'idle shallow things; I am not of your element'. And I think he believes that. He's gone somewhere they cannot possibly follow. And his exit line – 'You shall know more hereafter' – means 'I am going to be your master, for I am going to marry Olivia. Things around here are going to be very different.'

Then, after your exit, 'If this were played upon a stage now, I could condemn it as an improbable fiction.' Fabian's line originally, whose is it in your production?

Maria says it.

It's absolute gold dust, isn't it, because it means you can do whatever you want in that scene. Gives you carte blanche. And I suppose the more eccentric Malvolio is, the more plausible that he should be thought mad.

Yes, particularly in that scene. But really, from Maria and Toby's point of view, for him to even conceive that Olivia would write that letter and leave it where he would find it 'by chance' and fall for the whole set-up, is a sign of madness. The man is barking if he thinks that any of it is conceivable.

So they would half think 'Our trick is working really well', and they would half be thinking 'Hang on, perhaps he really is…'

Yes, I'm sure it's that. It started as a bit of fun, but he has displayed a degree of gullibility which encourages them to go that much further. 'Let's see if he *is* mad. Let's try and *make* him mad.'

On to the prison [4.2]. A very dark scene, isn't it.

Yes, very dark.

What started as a merry jape gets out of hand. Was it ever funny, that scene?

No.

The Elizabethans enjoyed bear-baiting. Maybe cruelty was funnier to them than it is to us today?

Well, yes, and they used to go and see people in Bedlam. I think for the plotters it's fun, up to a point. But then Sir Toby says 'My stock with Olivia now is so low that we'd better stop all this.' At which point Feste agrees to Malvolio's plea to let Olivia know what's happened to him, by giving him ink, pen and paper.

In the earlier scene [3.4] Toby said 'We'll have him in a dark room and bound.'

We've taken it that I am down under floor-level, with my legs chained to the wall.

Again, Shakespeare surprises you. It's unexpected, isn't it, to have your leading actor out of sight for one of his key scenes – just a voice!

Well, we try to help that by having my hands and arms visible. I'm standing behind the bars. My face is there, but not lit.

A sort of trapdoor opens about a foot, doesn't it, with a grille.

With my hands poking through it. I do a lot of hand acting.

Sir Topas talks complete gobbledegook. What do you make of that?

I would have cut it. Because it is just a lot of gobbledegook.

You say it's dark four times, as if you're clinging to the only certainty. I wonder whether there's a touch of King Lear's 'Let me not be mad!' Are you starting to feel perhaps…?

Well, yes. I think he is starting to feel a bit mad, which is why he has to keep protesting that he's not. Otherwise he might well go over the edge. Feste keeps saying 'It's not dark, you've got bay windows down there. You're mad, you're mad.' And Malvolio's saying 'No, I'm not, I'm not!' But he was gullible enough to believe all that had happened before, which suggested a mind that wasn't absolutely normal. Then he was chained and shut up in darkness, we don't quite know for how long, with presumably no hope of rescue until Sir Topas comes along. They might have left him there for ever.

Are you sobbing?

I do sob a bit, yes. It's a desperate situation. When Feste comes first in the guise of Sir Topas and then as himself, I have to convince him to help me. And he takes some convincing.

Do you remember how unpleasant you were to him at the beginning of the play?

No. I just keep saying 'Good fool… good fool… good fool' all the time. I think he's desperate.

Your last scene [5.1] could be subtitled 'Hell hath no fury like a Malvolio scorned'! But is it more in sorrow or in anger?

He comes on in a bad state. He cannot believe Olivia would be responsible for this, but she is the one he comes on to blame. He assumes it's all her fault for having written that letter. He cannot understand why she did so. He obeyed every part of it. And as a result she threw him into prison, into this dark room, and tried to drive him mad. Why? He's in a very bad state at that moment. He's tearful. He's outraged. He's incredibly deeply hurt. Then Olivia says 'It wasn't me, it was Maria.' And Maria (in our version) confesses that it was her and Sir Toby. Then Feste joins in, sending him up and saying 'Remember what you said about me a while back?' During that time I think he travels from this deep hurt, this deep embarrassment, this deep shame, to boiling fury. And when he says 'I'll be revenged on the whole pack of you', he means it.

This last scene is the only time Malvolio speaks in blank verse. Is that helpful? Shakespeare often goes into verse when he wants to heighten the emotional temperature, doesn't he?

Yes. But when you actually speak it, it doesn't sound like verse, it sounds like prose. And one of my theories about Shakespeare (because I'm so anti Peter Hall's 'dah-de-dah-de-dah' stuff) is to treat the prose as poetry and the poetry as prose. At least it works for me.

Maria isn't onstage in the original text. But with Fabian cut and Maria having his lines, it's very good for you, isn't it.

Yes, I can focus on her.

One of the chief malefactors is there in front of you. Definitely an improvement on Shakespeare!

Yes. She's trying to say sorry, but I'm not having it. And in fact I tear the letter up and throw it at her.

Most of Shakespeare's leading characters achieve some kind of resolution at the end of his plays, but I'm not sure that Malvolio does.

No, I don't think he does. You're left wondering. If he means his last line – 'I'll be revenged on the whole pack of you' – which presumably includes Olivia, then they'd better watch their backs, all of them.

Have you any idea what happens to him next? Does he stay there?

I don't think he can stay there. Olivia says 'He hath been most notoriously abused.' And Orsino says 'Someone go after him and calm him down', but I don't believe he's in the market for calming down. I think he will start playing his own game. Doing his own gulling. He will make those marriages hell if he can. He may even do something at the weddings. I don't know. He will plan something. I think there is life after, for Malvolio. I hope there is. I want him to be revenged, because what they did to him, although it came out of his own character faults, went too far. Punishment should be meted out to them.

Jude Law
on
Hamlet

Hamlet (1600–01)
Donmar Warehouse in the West End
Opened at the Wyndham's Theatre, London
on 3 June 2009

Directed by Michael Grandage
Designed by Christopher Oram
With Ron Cook as Polonius, Peter Eyre as the Player King and the Ghost,
Gugu Mbatha-Raw as Ophelia, Kevin R. McNally as Claudius,
Alex Waldmann as Laertes, and Penelope Wilton as Gertrude

Hamlet may or may not be the greatest play ever written, but it is certainly one of the most written about. It has been analysed, interpreted and argued over from countless perspectives. The old Arden edition had 152 pages of 'Longer Notes', devoted to the detailed examination of tricky passages of text. By contrast, *Antony and Cleopatra* had just three such pages.

Hamlet is Shakespeare's longest play. It is a jewel in the late Elizabethan crown. Hamlet is a man whose theatrical antecedents stretch back to the Middle Ages, yet whose thoughts echo timelessly through world culture. The play is a masterpiece: a thrilling drama of revenge, politics and inner turmoil, that has never been off the stage since it was written. In the past four hundred years Hamlet has been played by the leading actors, male and occasionally female, of each successive epoch. He is the most intriguing, yet ultimately unfathomable, of Shakespeare's creations. One can never know everything about him. As the critic Hazlitt commented: 'It is we who are Hamlet.' A university student, Hamlet is philosophical and contemplative. He is plagued with questions that cannot be answered with any certainty. It is through the play's five towering soliloquies that the audience gets closest to understanding the workings of Hamlet's mind and imagination. He is thoughtful to the point of obsession, yet on occasion he can behave rashly and with surprising rapidity, as when he impulsively kills the hidden Polonius.

The play investigates madness, both real and feigned. Hamlet appears effortlessly to assume the role of a madman, with erratic behaviour, wild speech and sudden sharp innuendo. Yet the audience is often left uncertain as to whether they are watching the genuine article or an accomplished fake. His mood ranges from overwhelming grief to seething rage, as the playwright explores themes of treachery, revenge, love, lust, incest and moral corruption. Shakespeare endows Hamlet with brilliant verbal dexterity. His words may mean several things at once, indicating his fragmented thoughts and disturbed emotions.

His melancholy and discontent are frequently counterpointed with wit, which is facilitated by chunks of the play being in prose, as for instance when he needles Polonius after the 'play-within-the-play' [3.2]:

—   Do you see yonder cloud that's almost in shape of a camel?
—   By th'mass and 'tis like a camel indeed.
—   Methinks it is like a weasel.
—   It is backed like a weasel.

—   Or like a whale?
—   Very like a whale.

Though not always funny, such repartee could only come from the lips of a person with a heightened sense of the absurd. His banter is often defensive/aggressive, as of a man on guard against real or imagined enemies. For all Hamlet's profundities, a nimble wit is never far below the surface. He repeatedly sees comedy in the bleakness of his situation. 'What news?' he asks Rosencrantz. 'None, my lord, but that the world's grown honest,' joshes his fellow student. To which Hamlet replies 'Then is doomsday near' [2.2]. It is a response worthy of Samuel Beckett.

There are Hamlets for every generation, often made memorable by a special quirk. David Warner wore an endless scarf, Mark Rylance was in pyjamas, and Jonathan Pryce startlingly ventriloquised the Ghost and spewed it up from his own entrails. When Ian McKellen played Hamlet in the West End, Mander and Mitchenson, a legendary pair of first-nighters, came backstage. 'Congratulations! You are our twenty-eighth Hamlet!' 'Twenty-eighth?' said Ian. 'How on earth do you remember them all?' 'Well, there's always something special, something that marks a performance out from the rest. For instance, John Neville, we'll never forget, had a tiny hole in his tights' – pointing to the crotch – 'right there!' I treasure this story, not only because it makes me laugh. It puts what we do into perspective. Imagine being cast as Hamlet, the great part, the pinnacle of an actor's ambition. You excitedly tell friends and relatives. You research and prepare, eager to put your own stamp on the part. You rehearse. The first night arrives. Your dressing room oozes with flowers and good-luck messages. At the post-show party champagne flows, you're embraced and told you were excellent. Next morning you run out to buy the papers and find your performance praised. You're over the moon. But wind the clock forward ten years, and what is your Hamlet remembered for? A tiny hole in the crotch of your tights.

I'd worked with Jude Law on the film *Sky Captain and the World of Tomorrow*, a movie shot entirely against blue screen, with everything except the actors computer-generated, and 'put in' afterwards. This involved unusual challenges. I remember, for instance, the astonishing spectacle of Jude fighting a robot that wasn't there yet. We met again in his dressing room during the run of *Hamlet* at the Wyndham's Theatre in 2009. In spite of doing eight shows a week, he was relaxed and seemed as fresh as a daisy. Of all the contributors to this book, he was one of the most genuinely thoughtful and spontaneous. My only regret was that our time was limited to an hour, which meant that I wasn't able to cover all the questions I had intended to ask. However, if one hour isn't long enough to do justice to a discussion of Hamlet, you could well say the same of ten hours.

Julian Curry: This is the first time you've played Hamlet. And your first Shakespeare as well. You dived straight in the deep end.

Jude Law: I guess I did.

You said during rehearsals that you were terrified. Are you enjoying it now?

Did I?

You said that to Charles Spencer when he came and interviewed you for the Telegraph.

I don't know, it's funny. When a theatre critic is in front of you asking how you feel, I suppose the terror comes simply from the side of the job which is offering it up to other people for their opinion, especially theatre critics. But the process of the work was phenomenal, so my overriding memory of that period of time was one of great joy. I loved the rehearsal process. I'm in an amazing cast, being led by a wonderful director who works with a very collaborative and incredibly efficient team. As you well know, you don't get a much better scenario than that. I think the terror, as I said, is when you realise you'll have to give it to the outside world, and all this joy and discovery could well be thrown back in your face. Fortunately we've been well received, and embraced somewhat by the theatre community. So now on the other side of the fence, having opened, I can finally relax and get on with the job at hand.

I thought there was a dynamism to the production, obviously coming largely from you, which was gold dust. Hamlet *is so familiar that it's easy to think 'Yes yes, alright, I've heard this bit before. Come on, get a move on!' But I never had that feeling with this production.*

Good. That was very much the idea, from several angles really. Michael Grandage always wanted the piece be told with a freshness, so that we didn't ever sit on the laurels, if you like, of so many famous set pieces. He liked the idea that we would almost trick those who knew the play well into suddenly thinking 'Oh my goodness, we're up to there, he's in that speech now', and not present them with too much air, or indeed, too many graces. He also wanted to motor it along as if going back to its origin as a thriller. There should be a thriller ride to it, an aspect of 'What will happen next?'

I wonder whether the terror in the article I quoted might have been in the context of however many famous actors had played the part before. Olivier said 'Actors are magpies, they steal from each other.' What did you steal for Hamlet?

There were all sorts of little things that I'd seen in film versions and on stage that inspired demonstrations or stresses on certain lines. But what I've tried to do with this part is to keep it as fresh as possible every night, I haven't really settled yet upon a particular blueprint of the performance. Something I learnt early on in the rehearsal process, as soon as we started running it, was that it's easier to live very much in the moment. If you step back and look at Hamlet's whole journey it's overwhelming, and there's no way of imagining for yourself, as the man you are at the beginning, where you will be at the end. So it's much better, I felt, to play every moment as it comes, and indeed as each person arrives on the set feeding you (because for huge chunks you don't leave the stage), using them as triggers to create new energy, and to respond off in the moment. And funnily enough that goes hand in hand with my sense of the huge amount of existentialism that Shakespeare, either knowingly or unknowingly, put into Hamlet. I found it a very helpful footnote to the act of playing him, to think of his journey existentially, trying to live in the moment and culminating in 'The readiness is all… let be' [5.2].

That applies to most acting though, doesn't it.

I suppose so, although it's easy to say that and hard to pull it off. It's hard to genuinely forget last night's show and start afresh. And the same applies, I suppose, with accumulating the influence of other people's work and keeping it, if you like, in your back pocket: you don't rely on it but let it come out at a given time – maybe subconsciously.

Do you mind if I mention your reviews – are you a review reader?

I haven't read any, but go ahead.

There were several phrases like 'an angry young Dane', 'a human time bomb', 'you hear his emotional short fuse sizzling'. Was that part of your performance that you cultivated intentionally?

No, not particularly. I just try to play each moment as it comes.

People say that Hamlet is an unusual part in that he becomes you, rather than you becoming him.

I would agree with that one hundred per cent. Going back to what I said before about it being a part that serves you best when you play it spontaneously, keeping yourself and the other actors guessing, as opposed to formulating a pattern that you lock in to, I suppose there's an element in that which demands of you to be yourself. But I would also say that the questions he raises are so vast – questions that none of us have answers to and yet we all have feelings on – that it's very easy to fuel them with your own take on life, the universe and everything. And of course, in each of us individually, that take is different. But also the part is so broad that it draws on many, many aspects of the person playing him, and certain aspects come out more in some actors than in others.

Hamlet has been called the 'wittiest tragic hero ever written'.

I think that's absolutely spot on.

Is his wit a defensive shield?

No, it's his brilliance. He's the cleverest person on the stage, and that's part of the problem.

The play's a revenge drama and it's a psychological thriller – very much so in your production. What else is it about?

You tell me. God, it's about everything, isn't it.

Charles Spencer also asked you that. I thought it was a rather cheeky question.

What else is it about? It's about many, many things. It's about life, it's about death, it's about love, it's about lost love. The answer's endless – how long is a piece of string! I think each person takes something different from it.

Is Hamlet mad or is he merely adopting an 'antic disposition'? Both, presumably, at different times. What's the balance?

My feeling is that he is deeply affected by finding himself in a very extraordinary situation, which begins with meeting his father's spirit. That encounter, and what he learns from it, alters him. I think he's also aware that it is going to produce in him a new way of behaving, which he assumes as a form of self-protection to allow himself freedom to think, freedom to work it all out, and to discover whether or not what he has learnt from the spirit is true. But moving on from that, I think that once he learns the truth and, so to speak, battles himself into a corner where he is a man capable of killing someone, and indeed *does* kill someone, he then touches on an area that is close to madness. From Polonius's death [3.4] to Hamlet being sent to England [4.3] I believe there are elements of hysteria, and to me that's about as close as he gets to true madness. The meaninglessness of life, the cycle of life, the pointlessness of matter really seem to overwhelm him. But I suspect that Ophelia's genuine madness and eventual suicide – possible suicide – are put in as a barometer to measure Hamlet's journey as opposed to her real descent.

This production opens with a brief tableau of you alone in a spotlight. I'm going to wave my magic wand and grant Hamlet one wish at that moment in the play. What would it be?

If you could give me a wish when the curtain goes up, of course it would be that my father were alive and I could get back to a normal existence. If you take the play on face value I think, as far as Hamlet was concerned, everything was alright when his father was alive, he was in Wittenberg studying, and life was normal. So I suppose he would want to go back a couple of months.

One of the first things you say is 'I have that within which passeth show' [1.2]. Can you define the pain?

I don't think I would ever bring myself to define any line of Shakespeare's because there are far too many opinions, far too many brilliant people. But of course what he's saying in general is that his feelings of sorrow go beyond the trappings of surface demonstrations, such as tears, facial expressions and, of course, mourning dress. He has been internally affected by this death.

Hamlet throws up smokescreens a lot of the time. But a soliloquy is always true, isn't it.

It is, but it's also thought in progress. He changes his mind, which is a bold and wonderful element of the part. It's like all of us, we all change our minds. And we also follow thoughts until we can follow them no further, and sometimes those thoughts split off and we will go one way rather than the other. What I think Shakespeare discovered with Hamlet's soliloquies in particular was a way of allowing the audience to follow a man's thought processes.

You do them direct to the audience. They're not inside yourself, they are conversations with us. Do you need us as allies, as confidants?

It's a really interesting question. I'd say that Hamlet needs the audience as allies within the realms of it being a play. If this story existed elsewhere and was really happening, then these dialogues would be going on inside Hamlet anyway. They are what's going on in his mind, they are conversations he's having with himself, is how I picture it. In the structure of a play the inside of his mind, if you like, is the audience. So in that sense, yes, he does need them; he needs them as allies to draw him through the play. If you were to cut all the soliloquies, Hamlet wouldn't be as interesting or as sympathetic a role, driving this story, as he is with them. It would be a fascinating exercise to cut all the soliloquies and just do the play, and see how Hamlet came over then.

I suppose it must have been done.

I wonder.

In the next scene [1.3], Laertes and Polonius forbid Ophelia to see you. They think you only want to get your leg over, don't they?

Yeah.

I find that surprising, because one would imagine that Hamlet would be a fine catch.

Indeed. Well, it's a seed, isn't it, the first seed sown for the theme of the play that is to do with love, affairs of the heart against affairs of the body. In the way they respond they're very, very protective of her, and very wary of him, and I guess they're right in that he *is* impulsive, emotional. Indeed you *would* have thought Hamlet was a good catch, but clearly not in their eyes. Jumping ahead for a moment, you could also look at it in the way Polonius evolves. Everything he thinks he understands is eventually incorrect. Initially he warns Ophelia, saying 'Hamlet just wants to fool with you,' then she comes back [2.1] and says 'He's come to me all frightened.' And he says 'Oh, these are the ecstasies of love. I thought he was only going to mess around with you, but he's obviously madly in love with you.' So he changes his mind. He convinces the King of this view, when in fact it's nothing to do with the real reason. Then after the play-within-the-play he persuades him again [3.3]. He says 'Let me go and spy on Hamlet', when Claudius (who's more astute) wants to get rid of him. So Polonius sells himself as being this great mind, but he is in fact wrong on every single count, and changes the goalposts on every single occasion so that they suit him. He also lies to Claudius about what he said to Ophelia. He says he told her that 'Lord Hamlet is a prince out of thy star' [2.2], which is not what he said. So he isn't quite to be trusted.

The Ghost calls Claudius 'that incestuous, that adulterate beast' [1.5]. Do you think that Claudius and Gertrude were having an affair before the murder?

Yes, it's a very good question. I'll say this first, incidentally: in my opinion there's no evidence that Gertrude knew about the murder. But I think they probably were, yes. But as someone (I think it was Michael Bogdanov) said, no man would murder another man and have to take on the role of king, simply to get a woman. It's far too much responsibility. You've got to run a country, you've got to assume all sorts of responsibility, and your only perk is to sleep with her. I think the affair was happening anyway, but the murder and his assumption of the role of power was motivated from within a different part of him. It wasn't because of Gertrude.

It's after the Ghost's exit that you talk about putting on an 'antic disposition'. Where does the thought come from? Does it just occur to you there and then?

Well, I can only speak for myself. I play it off seeing Marcellus and Horatio's reaction to the Ghost's voice. He's making us run all over the castle swearing here, swearing there, saying 'swear by his sword', we keep hearing this voice [1.5]. Hamlet's in a sort of strange, playful communication with the Ghost – he calls it 'True Penny' and 'Old Mole' and 'Boy', like a little dog almost. He's made ecstatic by it, almost high off it, whereas the other two men, because they haven't seen or spoken to the Ghost, are clearly in a very different emotional state. Horatio says how strange this is, and Hamlet's reaction is:

> as a stranger give it welcome.
> There are more things in heaven and earth, Horatio,
> Than are dreamt of in your philosophy.

I think it's off their reaction that he says 'Okay, swear on this. However strangely you see me behaving, this is why. But you must never *ever* let anyone know the reason for my odd behaviour.' So I think it comes off their shock and perplexity. He sees in them an inability to cope with what's happened, as against his ability to cope. He recognises that he has to quash, there and then, any possibility that they'll talk about it.

Hamlet's relationship with Rosencrantz and Guildenstern is interesting, and in this production the journey is especially vivid. When you first meet you have a laddish, joshing greeting – you seem to be really pleased to see them.

I think they're genuinely good friends. When he first sees them it's a great surprise and he keeps saying 'How are you, what are you doing, wow, how long have you been here?' And even when he learns that they've been called by the King and Queen he's not overly suspicious. He keeps them a little at arm's length, but why would he be suspicious? He knows he's been behaving strangely, so it's not a great surprise that the Queen has probably asked for friends to come and cheer him up and sort him out. There's nothing dodgy about that. It becomes suspicious when he realises that they keep cornering him, and question him constantly about what he's doing. And then when they come after the play and say 'You must come and speak to your mother. Stop behaving like this.' He suddenly realises 'They're here for my mother, not for me!' And that, to me, is when it turns. But earlier on there's a contrasting beat with Horatio that I think puts the Rosencrantz and Guildenstern relationship into perspective. We made a choice in our production that when Horatio first arrives, whilst Hamlet's pleased to see him, we didn't want it to be hugs and cuddles and 'Oh, it's so great to see you!' It's more formal. He says 'My lord… your poor servant ever,' and Hamlet says 'Sir, my good friend, I'll change that name with you' [1.2]. I think they know each other from Wittenberg, but they're not great mates. So what you get then is a developing relationship that is founded on trust. Horatio never speaks a word of what he knows, and he's always there for Hamlet. And as Hamlet says to him later on [3.2], you have been:

> As one in suffering all that suffers nothing,
> A man that Fortune's buffets and rewards
> Hast ta'en with equal thanks…
> Give me that man
> That is not passion's slave and I will wear him
> In my heart's core.

Horatio, right through to the end, is very much the proof of true friendship, whereas Rosencrantz and Guildenstern are old buddies who eventually descend into being traitors.

Hamlet never suspects Horatio of having been sent for, does he?

No.

Your next soliloquy – 'rogue and peasant slave' [2.2] – after the arrival of the players, seems to be the one that most moves the plot onwards. You plan to stage the murder of Gonzago. It looks like the turning point from Hamlet being a passive character into being an active one.

It's a huge turning point, yes. The arrival of the players provokes something in him. There's a certain amount of self-hatred at the beginning of 'O, what a rogue and peasant slave am I' because of his inability to show his feelings, to act, and to carry out his revenge. But you're right in that, once the idea has been planted, it moves the speech forwards. It motors him towards a position that will hopefully give him a solid sense of whether Claudius is guilty or not.

'To be or not to be' [3.1] seems rather an oddly placed soliloquy, just when Hamlet has become newly energised.

Well, I think it's very different. The soliloquies up to then have come at moments when he is struggling with circumstances involving other people – his own situation too, of course, but mainly how to resolve matters to do with everyone else around him. He has just come up with a firm idea of how to move onward and find out whether Claudius is guilty or not, to get some sense of peace in his life, or at least some sense of order. You then suddenly have an opportunity to see much deeper inside Hamlet, what he really feels about life itself, away from the madness of the story. So it's more reflective. It's a window into his soul, his heart and head.

Is it about suicide?

I don't believe it's as simple as that. I think it's about living or dying, not about whether to take your own life or not. To me he's saying 'To be alive or not to be alive.' That's what it's all about: you live fully or you die. I would never say that he was suicidal. In the very first speech he mentions self-slaughter, but I think that's the closest he comes to it. Since then he's made a promise to his father's Ghost.

You do the speech in a blizzard [see the front cover of this book]. Why is that?

Well, you'd have to ask Michael Grandage really, it's not just my decision. As any actor will tell you, the journey is a mutual one that you go on with the director, it wasn't me saying 'I want snow' or him saying 'You're in snow'. We looked at rain, we looked at all sorts of ideas. Hamlet wanders the corridors. We liked the idea that they were sometimes outside, around the ramparts. He spends a lot of time barefoot, and we thought it would add to the oddity that he was out in the elements, in the cold. There are references to it being freezing and bitterly cold, and it just seemed to set him apart, helped to establish his isolation and loneliness and desperation.

You meet Ophelia for the first time after the speech. Is it underwritten, that relationship?

Well, it is what it is. Who are we to say? Are we going to tell Shakespeare he underwrote?

You can do.

It's become a legendary relationship for a reason. What surprises people is that it's incredibly short. In fact they have just one scene really – well, one and a half scenes together, and that's about it [3.1 and 3.2]. But I discussed this with many people who have seen it or been in it, and with Gugu [Mbatha-Raw] who plays Ophelia, and obviously Michael and I have talked a lot about it. I think the reason it's become such a legendary love story, or emblem of love, is the promise. Everyone talked about the possibility of what might have happened. Hamlet says 'I did love you once,' and then doesn't allow himself to go on. He sort of pushes her away because of his dismay at women and the way women can behave, dismay at love and the way love behaves – the way his mother behaved as a wife to his father.

What's all that based on? Apart from his mother's 'o'er hasty marriage' [2.2], what's all this 'Frailty thy name is woman' [3.1]?

Exactly that.

It's rather a sweeping statement though, isn't it. What else is it based on?

It's obviously heartfelt. His father's died, his mother's remarried within a couple of months, she hasn't spoken to him about it, and he's furious.

Let's talk about Hamlet's sex life, or lack of it. You do a vivid kind of energetic shagging mime at one point…

Yes, with Polonius. He says 'Do you know me, my lord?' and I reply 'Excellent well. You are a fishmonger' [2.2]. Fishmonger also meant *flesh*monger, or pimp. He's been talked about for quite a while as being mad, and I wanted to demonstrate something to the audience that was fearless and inappropriate, something that immediately gave them another sense of who Hamlet was. Up till then all you've seen of him is this despairing, grieving, dark, woeful figure, whether on the battlements or inside the castle at the very beginning of the play. It feels to me like a very different energy when he comes back on with Polonius. After that you get Rosencrantz and Guildenstern, and then the Players. I wanted to start that new section with something really weird and unexpected, for the audience to either laugh at or be shocked by – just to make them go 'Good Lord, what's he doing?' And I took that line because of the double meaning of 'fishmonger'.

He seems strange, sexually. He hasn't been to bed with Ophelia, has he?

We decided that he hadn't, no. Well, he makes references to living in Fortune's private parts, and Fortune being a strumpet [2.2], so who's to say? He's a young guy. You'd have to go back to an Elizabethan to find out what would be expected of a man in his early thirties, which is about the correct age. Yorick was twenty-three years in the ground, and Hamlet would have had to be around seven to remember him, which makes him about thirty. Therefore I'd say he's probably slept with people, whether it was whores or who knows what.

So you wouldn't say he is particularly hung up?

I think he's certainly hung up because of his mother's behaviour. She has upset him deeply. In my opinion everything was fine beforehand. He probably knew nothing about the affair, he loved his father, loved his mother, he was off at school, no problems. And suddenly his whole world fell apart and no one has really spoken to him about it. His father's gone, his mother is completely involved in moving forward with her new life, and it's thrown everything into turmoil.

In the play scene [3.2], the dumbshow starts with the King and Queen getting married. You're quite a busy stage manager, as well as a spectator. Is that confetti or snow you sprinkle over them?

I don't know… confetti, I guess. Sort of symbolic of snow too.

Following on with Rosencrantz and Guildenstern: 'Will you play upon this pipe?' You play that scene with blazing anger. It's the end of any friendship, isn't it. You completely lose your rag with them.

Yes.

It's very strong, and it charts the huge change we talked about.

When those two come back after the play, they are very much on the side of the King and Queen. The way they talk to me, it's suddenly quite evident what they want to get from me and why they're doing it. I question them about it, and they won't give any answer. So, to me, that's when he decides to wash his hands of them.

I'm moving on to the closet scene [3.4], which was wonderful, very raw emotionally. It lifted off after the first couple of lines when Penelope [Wilton, as Gertrude] gave you a violent slap across the face, and the scene immediately became highly charged. That led rapidly into the killing of Polonius. But Hamlet shows no remorse, does he? You said he goes a bit mad after that.

I think there is some remorse, actually. Towards the end he says 'For this same lord / I do repent,' but then again he figures it out and says:

> but heaven hath pleas'd it so
> To punish me with this, and this with me,
> That I must be their scourge and minister.
> I will bestow him, and will answer well
> The death I gave him.

So there is repentance of sorts. But he's suddenly in a state of flux and he's so alive at that moment, I think, that he can answer anything and give anything a reason. Also, he's dealing with everything so quickly, and that's why he's so acerbic and quick-witted with Rosencrantz and Guildenstern when they come to get him, and then again with the King before being sent away. It's like he's on a high of adrenalin.

He has actually committed an assassination, after much talking about it. The wrong man, but he has killed someone.

Yes, he's killed someone.

'Look here upon this picture, and on this.' Normally there's a locket or a portrait, or something to refer to. But you didn't have anything.

No. Well, as with the snow, this is just as much a question for Michael and Chris Oram. But Hamlet is presumably talking about large pictures somewhere in the room, because he mentions how his father stands, his station. And unless they are big you can't see 'Hyperion's curls, the front of Jove himself... A station like the herald Mercury / New-lighted on a heaven-kissing hill.' But it was evident from the design that they couldn't suddenly fly in two big pictures, so the alternative was to use miniatures in lockets. However, we didn't really want to get all fussy with having to pull them off our necks, so it was my idea actually. I suggested it should all be inside our heads. What he can't believe is her inability to grasp what he's trying to get her to see. She keeps saying 'What are you talking about?' 'What have I done?... Ay me, what act?' So to me it made sense to be able to grab her and say 'Look in there, this is what I'm talking to you about!' A lot of the books I read said that this is very much the pinnacle of the play for Hamlet. This is what he's wanted from the beginning, to be able to sit down with his mother and talk and say to her 'Fuck you! The way you've behaved is appalling, and here is what I know about this man.' And I adore what Penelope found, which in fact married what I found, and that is the way they come together at the end. She comes round to him and says 'Oh my God, you've split me in two, but I won't tell anyone I'm on your side.' And in another way they come back together because, as Penelope realised, after that she hardly ever talks to Claudius again throughout the play. She seems to avoid him. That must be the result of what happens in this scene, where Hamlet wins her back and makes her understand what she's done.

At one point you're having a tussle and you pinion her down on the ground and sit astride her, in a suggestive-looking manner. Is it in any way an Oedipal relationship?

No, I think that's a modern addition to this play. People are always desperately trying to find something new and twisted and cool to add. In my opinion there's no indication in any of the text that Hamlet wants to sleep with his mother. I think he has a problem with her having a sex life, and with her immediately moving on to another man after his father. An awful lot of young people have a problem imagining their sixty-something-year-old mother sleeping with someone. But to him it's brought to a head because this man happens to be what he now feels sure is a murderer and a villain. The reason we do that in our production is because he needs to hold her down and make her listen to his true feelings.

At the end you say 'Goodnight, mother' four times, one way or another. How has your relationship changed during that scene?

The way we play it, I think it's opened up again. I certainly don't think it's completely healed, but it feels, if you want, healthier just for having had a good airing. Unfortunately it's such a screwy situation – there's a man he knows to be the murderer of his father, married to his mother. He dashes from the room with a dead body in his arms. So I certainly wouldn't say it's entirely healthy or healed, but there's an element of openness that's been achieved.

You have an odd little scene with Fortinbras's Captain [4.4], which always seems to me a bit contrived, followed by 'How all occasions do inform against me'. I think if one had to cut any of Hamlet's soliloquies, it would be that one.

I don't know. For one thing, it's necessary to conclude his relationship with the audience. He's been talking about taking his own life, taking someone else's life, the worth of life. Suddenly he *has* actually taken someone's life, but he's still not achieved what he wanted to achieve. To me that speech is a vital turning point because he's saying, 'Good God, if I look around me the world is giving a demonstration of men dying all the time, thousands of them for no reason': 'for a fantasy and trick of fame'. And it's an important realisation when he says:

> Rightly to be great
> Is not to stir without great argument,
> But greatly to find quarrel in a straw
> When honour's at the stake.

To me it's a real step onwards, a return to his mettle. He goes to England vowing that his thoughts will 'be bloody or be nothing worth', which signifies, I think, the loss of the innocent Hamlet. It's the end of a man who thought before he acted, and the transition to someone who will act with impulsive violence. Indeed you hear about that when he comes back – how he sent Rosencrantz and Guildenstern to a really conniving manipulative death – and he then proceeds to kill two more people. So he's a dangerous man. There's a loss of innocence demonstrated in that scene.

After that you have a long gap, and you indeed return in Act 5 very much a changed man.

Well, he never talks to the audience again.

He doesn't need any more soliloquies, does he?

He doesn't. I always laugh at the way he comes back in heroic mode. He has a great sword fight and sorts everything out and kills everyone and dies heroically, whereas when he went away he was always 'Oh God... !' He kept talking, he was thinking and talking about doing it – will he ever actually do it? Then he returns in the boots of a hero.

The gravedigger scene is an orgy of morbidity [5.1]. But he meets his match, doesn't he, chop-logic wise.

Yes, he does. It's a wonderful Shakespearean meeting of a prince and a pauper, so to speak, who are of like minds in the wit stakes. It's also a continuation of something he started after Polonius's death. One of my favourite lines is where he talks about the cycle of a man being eaten by a worm: 'We fat all creatures else to fat us, and we fat ourselves for maggots... a king may go a progress through the guts of a beggar' [4.3]. And then of course in this scene with Yorick it's the same. This is what we return to. This is it.

'Thou wouldst not think how ill all's here about my heart' [5.2]. Can you expand on that?

Having agreed to fight Laertes, he then feels a sense of foreboding in his heart that perhaps his death is imminent, that this situation he's got himself into has been manipulated. You could say it's something that in the past he would perhaps have talked to us about, philosophised about, asked 'What does this mean?' But in this situation he passes on it, he says 'No, no, no, I'm not going to think about it, it doesn't mean anything, it's foolery': 'There is special providence in the fall of a sparrow,' and we must be ready for anything. 'I'm going to ignore that, I'm going to step in and let life come to me as it comes. There's nothing to quantify what we leave behind, so what is it to die in a moment, anyway?' And he draws a line under it, if you like, when he says 'Let be.'

In the context of a highly dynamic, pacy performance on your part, that passage is unusually drawn out and slow. You give it an extra-strong focus.

To me it's another real turning point.

Do you believe at that moment he's achieved spiritual enlightenment, or is he just being fatalistic?

I think fatalism *is* a form of spiritual enlightenment.

You have a brilliant sword fight – long, fast and dangerous. There is an excellent shift of focus between the fencers downstage and the poisoned Gertrude vomiting, upstage. Your death scene took me by surprise, because having spent much of the play on the ground, crouching or kneeling, you died standing up until the very last minute. I enjoyed that. Finally, you make Horatio live to tell your story.

Yes.

I don't believe he can. Your story's far too private, I don't think even Horatio knows the half of it.

No, indeed. Well, Russell Jackson, the prof who worked with us during rehearsals, and wrote the foreword in the programme, said that Horatio proceeds to *not* say what happened. And you're right – how can he? There are several little moments that volunteer, I think, a sense of what Shakespeare wants you to think about. Just before he dies [5.2], Hamlet turns and says to those watching:

> You that look pale and tremble at this chance,
> That are but mutes or audience to this act,
> Had I but time – as this fell sergeant, Death,
> Is strict in his arrest – O, I could tell you –

and then chooses not to say anything except 'But let it be'. It's an unfinished sentence. And in that moment, to me it's almost as if he is saying 'I've talked too much, I'm going to leave it up to this man.' He turns to his friend and there seems to be a choice dramatically, with Shakespeare saying 'It's up to you now, how you take this.' And as Hamlet dies, once again he doesn't finish his sentence, he just says 'The rest is silence.' It's silence, everything is silence, the end is silence. 'Arrest' means stop. So there's a play on words, perhaps. 'Arrest is silence' – the stop is silence. In a way he's saying this is unfinished. Then, as you rightly said, Horatio proceeds to report it, but in a very crude way – a beautiful but crude way – which makes you think 'God, but that's not what happened!' Then Fortinbras says 'Bear Hamlet... to the stage', and I always think that means not only 'Put him up there', but also 'Let's tell this story again. This story must be told, and that's why we're doing the play.' There is a sense at the end of 'How do we summarise this?' Well, the play's the thing. And it concludes a wonderful theme that runs throughout *Hamlet*, which is that the play *is* the thing.

Hamlet is an actor through and through, isn't he?

He is an actor. He's a believer in the performances we all put on. It's a wonderful theme – he's an actor talking to us about an actor putting on an act, and being amazed at how he does it. It's a very odd part of the night when I say:

> Is it not monstrous that this player here,
> But in a fiction, in a dream of passion,
> Could force his soul... *etc.* [2.2]

And I think 'Well, *I'm* a player here in a fiction, in a dream of passion. And I'm putting all this on, and reporting it to you!' It has extraordinary resonance and it runs throughout. So I think there are moments towards the end where Shakespeare is saying 'Come back and see this play again', or 'Look, this play holds the key to all that Hamlet wanted you to hear.'

Can you summarise his journey?

Oh, I wish it was so simple!

Do you want to have a go?

I'll give it a go. I think there are different strands to his journey. One I would pick out is indeed the journey of allowing what happens to happen, to be ready for it, whatever it may be. But the way he gets there unfortunately also involves losing a sense of his humanity, his exuberant poetic love for life, and enables him to kill. There are those elements to him at the beginning of the play that eventually, in order to achieve his revenge, he has to dull.

Are you saying that, rather than achieving serenity, perhaps he ends up coarser?

I think he is a little coarser, yeah, but serene also.

An interesting mix.

Well, you could say that's life, isn't it. We all start with great optimism and exuberance and belief, then we end up realising actually that life can be fucking hard and brutal – a grunting, sweating, weary life – but we choose to bear it. What's the choice? But then while we're bearing it and while it can be brutal, and not as shining and joyful as perhaps it was when we were six or seven years old, we also have to be ready for anything, and that in itself makes it extraordinary. The rest is silence.

Adrian Lester
on
Henry V

Henry V (1599)
National Theatre
Opened at the Olivier Theatre, London
on 13 May 2003

Directed by Nicholas Hytner
Designed by Tim Hatley
With Peter Blythe as Exeter, Robert Blythe as Fluellen, Penny Downie as the Chorus,
Ian Hogg as the King of France, Félicité du Jeu as Princess Katherine,
and Adam Levy as the Dauphin

The play covers events surrounding King Henry V's victory over France at the Battle of Agincourt in 1415. It is the fourth in Shakespeare's cycle of eight history plays spanning the Wars of the Roses. A tradition holds that *Henry V* inaugurated the newly built Globe Theatre in 1599 – hence the 'wooden O' mentioned in the opening Chorus.

Shakespeare had already introduced Henry V in his *Henry IV* plays as Prince Hal, the freewheeling teenager who lived it up with Falstaff's gang in the tavern at Eastcheap. Since then, following his painful rejection of Falstaff at the end of *Henry IV, Part 2*, Henry has matured almost beyond recognition. He now has a pragmatism, focus and charisma rarely glimpsed before. As King he shows great resolve, and at times an unscrupulous determination to achieve his ends. He displays brilliant rhetorical skills, which he employs in a variety of different modes. He terrifies the Governor of Harfleur into surrender with threats of carnage, while contriving to foist responsibility onto him should the butchery actually take place. He is passionate and inspiring to his outnumbered soldiers before battle. And in Act 5 we see him charm the French Princess Katherine into marriage. A king for all seasons.

The play's attitude to warfare has been variously interpreted. On the one hand as a piece of tub-thumping patriotism, a celebration of English valour leading to a miraculous triumph. In Shakespeare's time it would have reflected nationalistic pride at recent conquests in Spain and Ireland. The most stirring passages have been widely adopted. *Henry V* is a favourite of politicians, and an urgent rallying cry is often referred to as a 'St Crispin's Day Speech'. It has been quoted, adapted and parodied on numerous occasions. Conversely, however, *Henry V* can be seen as an anti-war allegory. The play pulls no punches in depicting the savagery of conflict. In the twenty-first century, many people are made uncomfortable by a celebration of martial glory. Henry is at times devious, seemingly sincere but willing to resort to any form of compulsion and deceit in order to achieve his objectives. And his constant invoking of God can seem disingenuous. The play has the capacity, in common with many great works of art, to be understood and interpreted in radically different ways.

I'd never met Adrian Lester before, and sad to say, I didn't see him play Henry V, so had to rely on his excellent reviews. But I was very well aware of his talent and remarkable versatility. If in doubt, talk to anyone who saw him play Rosalind in Cheek by Jowl's all-male *As You Like It* in the 1990s. In terms of the demands made of an actor, there can't be many characters further from Henry V. I was especially pleased when he agreed to discuss *Henry V* in view of the production's strong contemporary resonances, being played in modern dress at the time of the invasion of Iraq. We met in February 2009 for lunch at a restaurant near his home in Dulwich, and he was generous with his time. We talked before the food arrived and again afterwards, and went on until interrupted by a call from his wife to remind him that he was late at home for babysitting duty.

Julian Curry: You played the lead in what was described as an 'urgently topical' production of Henry V, *at the time of the invasion of Iraq. Here's part of a review: 'This production will make you think deeply and disturbingly about the nature of war, of war leadership, with a shocking portrait of what war does to the souls of those engaged in it. It's about national pride and the damage done to a politician's soul in pursuing it.' Does that ring a bell with you?*

Adrian Lester: Yes, it does. I think the situation we found ourselves in as a country, at the time we did the play, helped to scrape off a kind of romantic veneer that the play can sometimes have. Performances can get lost in poetry and the beauty of the language. The deeper and uglier the emotions involved in any of Shakespeare's plays, I think, the more vibrant the production will be. I have to admit that before we started work on it, I had a slightly removed sense of *Henry V*. I felt that it was about the higher end of human thought and endeavour, bravery and patriotism. But when we put the play on its feet in that particular climate, we saw that there was so much more in there.

For many people, Olivier's film is the iconic Henry V. *He made it in 1944 when heroes were hot and the validity of war was not an issue, and Churchill was Prime Minister. But by the time you played the part sixty years later, heroes were no longer fashionable, the war in Iraq was widely thought to be unjustified, and Tony Blair was Prime Minister. Each production reflected its time, but each was only partially true to Shakespeare's text. Olivier expurgated the most gruesome aspects of war, but Nick Hytner maybe overemphasised them.*

I don't think so. We were very careful not to use the play to make a political statement. We wanted to make sure that it correctly reflected what we knew of modern-day politics. In the opening scene where Henry asks the Archbishop to make a case for war [1.2], there's the understanding that if he does not make it convincing, Henry will take the money he needs from the Church. Once you put that in a Cabinet setting, with suits, ties, glasses of water, files and laptops, people thought we were being cynical. But actually it's exactly the situation that Shakespeare created, and it's one that people felt they were watching on BBC News 24. We were being told we have to go to war, and these are the reasons. But people were thinking 'We're not being given the whole story here, there's something else happening.'

So if I asked if you were an anti-hero, you'd say no, would you?

Some people felt that Henry was still heroic because the country comes before the individual, the public good comes before considerations of whether he as a leader can sleep at night.

You're making him sound a more selfless person than he sometimes seems.

Sometimes, yes.

He's worried about his grave having a 'tongueless mouth', isn't he, not even having 'a waxen epitaph'. He's concerned about his own legacy.

Well, there was a reflection of that in 'History will be my judge', that Blair kept saying. And again, everyone went 'Whoo, you're being cynical.' But no, Shakespeare wrote it.

I have the impression that it was a brilliantly powerful account of the play, but some people felt it was not sufficiently equivocal.

Maybe they did. But we felt we were riding the middle ground. We were trying to be quite exact, with the information we have now on the conditions and the psychological effects of war. We had a paratrooper and an ex-SAS sergeant who did drill with us, and taught us how to run and fall and use weaponry, look like soldiers. These guys described how, in the middle of battle when bombs have fallen and fires are burning, you have to navigate through dust and smoke, with this very strange orange light being your guide. It's impossible to see, there's the smell of burning wood or flesh, and it's completely disorientating. Nick wanted to reflect that. A lot of dry ice was used. We had speakers around the auditorium, under seats and behind the public, so that when bombs went off we could turn up the volume and say 'Look, it is this loud.'

So the audience really felt they were in the middle of it.

The earth moves when ordnance goes up. It's terrifying. When we think of people suffering from the psychological effects of war, it's hard to imagine the noise, eardrums popping, the sting of heat. You can't see properly. A commander is shouting out commands: 'Drop!', 'To the left!', 'Move forward, GO NOW!' That's all you have to hold on to. We tried to represent that. We tried to say 'Listen, this is how difficult it gets. It's not all clean.'

The setting was completely modern. Tell me about it.

We used videos.

For what?

We found two particular moments where Henry seemed to be addressing the public at large. We had those up on a big screen, filmed with a hand-held camera.

You were performing live and being seen on-screen at the same time?

At various moments. You got strong resonances of the situation in Iraq, where commanders in full fatigues would talk on camera: 'We've taken this section here and we're about to move on to such-and-such.' But every time we did that, people said we were being opportunistic, exploiting the current climate.

Isn't that what putting on a play's about?

Well, yeah. But when Nick first decided to do *Henry V*, he didn't know whether it would be a modern or a classic production. He chose the play because it had never been done at the National. It was his first show as Artistic Director. As he started talking to me about it, the situation in Iraq began to heat up. But we still didn't know if we were going to war or not.

What stage was the build-up to war in Iraq when you started rehearsal?

At that stage the invasion was going ahead. It had just started. But at the time of casting, we didn't know. Then as the situation escalated he said 'Because of all the talk of soldiers preparing themselves, and the weapons inspectors going in and all of that, I don't think we can get away with a classic production set in the past. I think we have to do a modern production.'

You were overtaken by events.

Suddenly the country went to war, as we were in rehearsal. We responded to the situation.

Can you say something about Nick Hytner's rehearsal methods?

Straight up on its feet. Books in hand.

He's not a sitter-around and talker.

We had a read-through as usual. And he talked a bit about acting Shakespeare, what he didn't like, what he thought was 'dead' Shakespeare. He didn't want to see that.

What was the result?

The result was that everyone freed up completely. At the beginning of rehearsal actors tend to worry whether their ideas about character and performance will fit in with the director's, so that everything gels and they won't be working at odds with each other. So they look to the director for the direction the play's going in, which way they are pointing. Once they know that, all these experienced actors just take off. Nick stood up and said he wanted the Shakespeare to sound like modern language, like squaddies and officers on a battlefield, but without pausing and going 'um' and 'ah' in between, or saying 'fuck' and all the rest of it.

So you didn't worry a lot about the blank verse.

We didn't worry that every syllable was absolutely correct. But there were times when he said 'No, no, no. Come on, stick to the metre here, make sure you honour the text.'

How much did you refer backwards in your thinking about King Henry, in the sense of him being a sequel to Prince Hal? At the end of Henry IV, Part 2 he renounces his old self, doesn't he, when he says to Falstaff 'I know thee not, old man' [5.5].

Early, in *Henry IV, Part 1* [1.2], Hal says:

> I know you all, and will awhile uphold
> The unyok'd humour of your idleness.
> Yet herein will I imitate the sun,
> Who doth permit the base contagious clouds
> To smother up his beauty from the world...

And you see a massive ego. He knows what's going to be asked of him, and he has a plan. The way in which he's going to be remarkable is to seem unremarkable, seem sullied and a wrong'un, as it were. So that when he then adopts the mantle of the King he will be 'more wonder'd at' (his words) and held in higher esteem than those who had become kings before him.

Does that make him a hypocrite?

Well, yes. Except... here's a story. A mate of mine did a radio interview, representing Labour on some topic, and the Conservative he was up against was a friend he'd known at college. He was terrified because this guy was very witty and quite strong. They met beforehand, and the Tory went 'Oh, you'll be fine, don't be nervous.' On the radio my mate suddenly goes for his old friend on certain policy details, and rips him to shreds, embarrasses him on the radio. And he thinks 'Oh my God, now I've done it, he's gonna hate me.' Afterwards they're walking out of the studio, and the Tory says 'There you are, I told you it would be fine. I loved that lashing you gave me – ooh, very good, I've got to watch you!' And he said he felt really disheartened. He said it's just like some big game.

Water off a duck's back.

My mate said 'That's what you do. You make believe there are two opposing points of view, and you just play the game, you score points.' And I thought to myself 'Well, Hal is a bit hypocritical.' But actually doesn't that make him a really good leader, understanding what is leadership?

A brilliant leader but perhaps not a brilliant man.

Perhaps not. But if you *are* a brilliant man, can you also be a great leader? That's the area in which his character exists in this play. I think we oscillate between his conscience as a man and his conscience as King, and we bounce between the two as we go through the story.

Tell me about the preparation you did before rehearsal.

I did a bit of reading on the real Henry V, and of course on Shakespeare's Henry and the Protestant nature of his beliefs, rather than the Catholic that Henry was. And then a lot of research on the conflict and what Blair was saying – how he was sounding, his intonations, his patterns – and what was happening in the field. As we were rehearsing, some British commander used Henry's St Crispin's Day speech to his soldiers before they went into a town. He took elements of it: 'The war hinges on this moment... it's going to be remembered... we wear the uniform and take up arms not for self-preservation, but for the preservation of those who are not with us', and so on. It was reported in the paper. And we went 'Oh my God. Life imitating art, imitating life!' So the research had three different strands.

Here are a couple more quotes from notices: 'The great heart of this performance beats in its combination of humanity and ruthlessness.'

The duality, that's great.

'More flashes of anger and impetuosity than the text invites.' Any response to that?

I thought of him earlier as Prince Hal hanging out with Falstaff, Nym and Pistol, the gang – the old days in the tavern. Bringing it up to the modern day, our Henry would have been mixing with that kind of crowd. He'd spent a bit of time on the street, he knew proper hard men. He knew the flick-knife brigade, people who had been cut or scarred because they'd crossed the wrong man. I imagined him being able to hold his own in that territory, and then becoming King. He had to cover all of that up. But now and again the surface cracked and you saw a flash of him wanting to deal with things in a much more direct manner – like receiving the tennis balls from the Dauphin [1.2]. I felt it was much more interesting to make sure the diplomatic choice was the final choice.

How do you mean?

Rather than be completely in control, what he wanted to do was grab the guy by the throat and drag him out over the table and hit him or snap a bottle. I felt that was his impulse. But he chose to speak instead. And I think that happened throughout the play.

You playing Henry V was called 'a triumph of colour-blind casting'. Did it worry some people?

It's strange, because as I carry out my job I don't see the performance. But I know that some people will make judgements in connection with my skin colour, and for them the performance will become something new. For every individual it depends what references they make.

You've played Rosalind in As You Like It, *who's traditionally not only white but female. So you're no stranger to adventurous casting. However, she's fictional, whereas Henry V is a famous historical character.*

You have to think 'It's not real, it's not a documentary.' In the theatre you sit beside strangers watching a stage, we are telling you a story. Nowadays, people say 'Oh, that's fine, that's great, yeah, tell us a story.' But earlier on it was 'You can't really tell us that story cos you're not white.' When I was fifteen, doing *Sweeney Todd* in Birmingham, a couple of reviews said 'It's wonderful, but they wouldn't have that guy in London. It just wouldn't happen.' In those days everybody could tell the story and become different characters apart from the black guy: 'He's black, so he can't be anything other than black.' But that doesn't happen any longer.

Tell me about the Chorus.

That was Penny Downie. It wasn't easy for her at first. She began with the notion of being a war correspondent. Then she got introduced to the idea of playing it like a lecturer trying to reimagine the play for the audience. So she came on with books. 'Now, imagine, if you will...' at times referring to the action onstage. I don't think she was quite happy with the Chorus as a three-dimensional character. But in the end she was both in the play and completely separate from it, which is what the Chorus is. It's an interesting path to walk. She was in love with what this guy did. In her eyes he was brilliant, a great king. She was caught right up in the excitement of the heroism and the sacrifice.

Wasn't she sometimes undercut by a counterpoint? For instance, when she said, at the outset of Act 2, 'Now all youth of England are on fire', you got Bardolph and Nym watching the telly and staring gloomily into their pints.

Yes. I remember at one point her coming on and choosing not to see what was happening onstage. She just looked the other way: 'Well, we won't say anything about that, will we? We'll just talk about his wonderful deeds.'

Before the battle in Act 3, the Chorus says that England is 'Guarded with grandsires, babies and old men.' But later on [4.3], Westmorland wishes for 'But one ten thousand of those men in England.' Would you say that was Chorus spin or Shakespeare inconsistency?

Chorus inconsistency. Because in our production the Chorus was played as though her understanding of what happened was from books, and she loved it. But the reality was different. She didn't quite get it.

Launching into the play. At the beginning, the Archbishop of Canterbury says your body is 'a paradise / T'envelop and contain celestial spirits' [1.1]. That's a rather rose-tinted view, isn't it.

Yeah.

In your first scene you tell him 'Take heed... How you awake our sleeping sword of war' [1.2]. How much does Henry genuinely want advice, and how much is he guiding the discussion towards the end that he's already decided upon?

Oh, he knows what he wants. It's a warning. He's saying 'I want everyone to know that I have the right to go to war with France. Just make sure you do this correctly.' Then you have an endless, convoluted speech from the Archbishop. And we didn't cut that. He went right through it.

Really? It's full of all this pedantic and repetitive stuff about the Salic law and why it is invalid, but I'm not sure that he ever actually explains why you do have a right and title to the throne of France.

Well, he says the French argue that my claim is barred by Salic law, which decrees that no child born of woman shall succeed in Salic land. Then he goes on 'But that's irrelevant, because Salic land is in Germany. So your claim is correct and just.'

And in any case the French themselves had inherited through the female line.

But what was great about that long speech was that as he pulled up all the names and dates and facts to justify his argument, people sat in the audience laughing, with pain actually, because he sounded exactly like the news we were watching. 'We have the right to walk into Iraq and ensure that they don't have weapons of mass destruction…' 'Well, but Hans Blix says the inspectors have found nothing…' 'That's because trucks are moving them around…' 'How do you know they're moving them around?' 'Because we've got intelligence from MI6 who say so.' All of this was going on to justify the invasion. It was incredible. During this convoluted speech the nobles (i.e. Henry's 'Cabinet') were flicking to and fro in the pamphlets and documents that the Archbishop had handed out, trying to find the page that he was referencing as he spoke. They were getting more and more confused. Some were putting them down and just listening, giving up. I think the audience recognised the reality in what Shakespeare had written.

How did you listen? Did you take it seriously?

Henry's chief concern was what everyone else thought around the table. He wants war, and the man of the cloth is making a case for it. He wants to see whether they swallow it, whether they go for it. And they all slowly agree, they fall in line. 'Good, that's done.'

When you finally say the single line – 'May I with right and conscience make this claim?' – after his endless speech, it can get a big laugh.

No, I think it was an interruption. We had TV images on-screen at the time with squadrons of kids, twenty-year-olds, about to be sent over to do active service.

From real life?

From real life. A lot of laughs were pushed to one side, because the reality was so immediate for the audience. The seriousness of the situation was felt anew. Current affairs brought a lot of stuff in the play into sharp focus. Some people felt we'd done that to the play, we'd sharpened it, given it an extra dig. Well, actually, Shakespeare had written it. And we simply chose not to fudge those realities, not to slip over them. So when Henry says 'May I with right and conscience make this claim?', it's 'All bullshit aside, tell me here while everyone's listening: *May* I?' 'You may.' 'Right, call in the Ambassador.'

He enters with tennis balls, and the Dauphin's joke seriously backfires. You talked about wanting to bash the Ambassador up.

Some nights, as I stood up sharply and leaned across to him, the table moved and a couple of glasses fell and smashed. And people thought 'Oh shit, here he goes!' But Exeter, in our production, very much held Henry in line. Every now and then he would just give me a look, or touch my shoulder, to remind me that we need the King and not the brawling youth. And that was one of those moments. So I then walked around the table, and breathed deeply.

You used words instead of violence. But I imagine it provoked a lot of adrenalin. Got you going.

Yeah. And, just technically, we had to create distance at that point. I had to get away from him, think for a moment, and then begin the speech from the other side. That way the words could sail across the Olivier stage like stripes of a whip.

Later on in that speech you say:

> We never valued this poor seat of England,
> And therefore, living hence, did give ourself
> To barbarous licence.

I don't remember anything about him 'living hence'.

I think it's just a reference to him spending his time as I described. Clubbing, being out of it.

Away from court, but not living abroad.

Away from court.

Moving on to Act 2, with Scroop and the other two conspirators. A lot of cat-and-mouse goes on, doesn't it, before the unmasking occurs.

Yes, he takes his time about that. He lets them sit, and watches them open the envelopes and read, and then they're apprehended.

It's almost vindictive. But Scroop is obviously a close friend. The speech to him about his betrayal [2.2] is full of personal hurt.

Absolutely. Onstage they were forced down on their knees, with hands behind their backs, automatic weapons at the back of their heads, and they're stripped. We didn't only do it for the image, although of course everyone felt 'I know this.' But Henry does publicly what could easily have been done in private, to show everyone around him, who still have Hal in their mind, that this is now the King. He's about to lead these men into war and say 'Do or die under my command.' And he shows them what that command is. 'This is the person I have now become.' It's not just to say 'You've hurt me and I'm upset about it.' It's also to show who they were trying to betray. They had no idea what he was capable of.

So it's a public-relations exercise.

It is. Every commander would understand why a soldier might lose his temper, be insubordinate or have a fight, but still an example has to be made because you have to keep the others in line. Every active soldier has to be kept with enough adrenalin to kill or risk being killed, but with enough technical ability and discipline to follow commands when they're given. And a good leader keeps them just in that narrow bandwidth. It sounds like animals: you don't give them their head, but also you don't subdue them so much that they have no idea what to do unless they're told. It's just keeping them in their place. And I think by the end of that scene, everyone around Henry thinks 'I'm glad I'm with him, we're gonna be okay with him at the front.' Finally, after I said 'Bear them hence…'

You didn't kill them onstage, did you?

No, they were taken offstage for that. I gave myself a moment to put my hat back on and fix myself up. Then the cameras came on, and I turned around and said:

> Now, lords, for France; the enterprise whereof
> Shall be to you, as us, like glorious.
> We doubt not of a fair and lucky war.

In the scene reporting the death of Falstaff that follows [2.3], they showed a video with you as the young Hal, dreadlocked, having a merry time with Falstaff and your old mates.

That's it, yeah. We shot that in a pub in the East End. You got the accents and the pub atmos. 'Remember that night after the match… we drank the place dry… remember that bloke that came in… !!' That was the nature of it. They were re-showing it to look back on the old days. And you saw the King looking very different.

'Once more unto the breach, dear friends…' [3.1]. You got a groan from the army, you were made to work.

That was brilliant. The noise was deafening, there was dust in the air, we were at war. Henry comes on to rouse his army. I had to use every molecule of what I learned at RADA, every vestige of my lung power. My diaphragm ached, my voice was sore. With automatic weapons you may have to sprint five hundred yards to get into firing range. We imagined we had been blasted out, there'd been grenades, we'd been sprayed with automatic weapons. Men had been dropping left, right and centre. We'd called a retreat, run all the way, half a mile back again from that position. As we came onstage guys threw their packs off, took their helmets off, grabbed drinks of water, collapsed onto their backs, were sick. That was the state they were in when I started the speech. They would fire lines back at me, whatever came into their heads. They'd had enough.

That was a rehearsal exercise?

A rehearsal exercise. But we tried to keep a sense of it in performance. It really made me need Henry's changes of gear.

> Once more unto the breach, dear friends, once more,
> Or close the wall up with our English dead.
> In peace there's nothing so becomes a man
> As modest stillness and humility.
> But when –

(And they're still going at me)

> BUT WHEN the blast of war blows in our ears,
> Then imitate the action of the tiger.

They forced me to find that energy to convince them, to kick them up the arse and say 'We can do this, we've got to go back.' That made me be a great leader.

As the speech goes on it becomes quite surreal, almost cartoon-like: 'Then lend the eye a terrible aspect; / Let it pry through the portage of the head / Like the brass cannon...' and he goes off on a riff about how a soldier's head, when he's really fierce, resembles an overhanging cliff. What's he on?!

Well, as I said, they were breathing hard, sweating and coughing, their limbs had gone soft, there was no energy left, their legs felt like lead. The ordnance was going off all around. So he's getting them to dig really deep. 'Get yourself ready, get your breath back, get your blood ready, tighten the jaw. Summon your last resource. Knit the brow, fix the eye, secure your target.' Somebody was crying – a younger actor was snivelling and we had to slap him about the face: 'Come on, pull yourself together. You're embarrassing us, and yourself, and your dad, and your grandfather who died before him. You're embarrassing your line, get yourself on your feet.' I was hitting backs, stiffening chests, slapping helmets and saying 'Put it on your fucking head, COME ON!' And gradually, so they did. There would be snotting and spitting and then 'Right, I'm ready!' Towards the end I referenced my weapon:

> I see you stand like greyhounds in the slips,
> Straining upon the start.

Then it was ckk-ckk with my rifle, which they all did, checking their weapons. 'The game's afoot.' By then they were up for it. 'Okay, okay!' gulping huge lungfuls of oxygen, then it was like 'GO!' And we ran in. So the speech came together. Nick didn't spend a long time talking about metre and meaning, we just bounced off each other.

I don't think it can avoid being a glamorous and virile and thrilling speech, can it?

If you have shining metal, armour, swords and shields, it can have glamour. Fighting like that can be romanticised, and the appalling hacking that went on can be forgotten. But as we used automatic weapons, and we were tightening the straps and checking grenades and getting ready to run, it was more immediate. So it wasn't glamorous at all, I don't think. But it was definitely rousing. And because of the noise and so on, it wasn't like St Crispin's Day, when you could hear the language.

I believe Henry's speech to the Governor of Harfleur [3.3] was televised except for the really savage bits: 'Your naked infants spitted upon pikes', etc. You had the camera on half the time?

Yes. The army couldn't make another attack. There was sickness, they weren't in the position, the town was proving impregnable. And he addresses the Governor like a poker player, saying 'If you want us to come again, we will. And if we attack again, there will be no mercy.' Up to then the camera's on him, he pushes it away, and they turn it off. Then he begins to describe the frightful things that will happen to their daughters, their infants and old men. And the Governor says 'Our expectation hath this day an end.' 'The Dauphin hasn't sent reinforcements, therefore we lay ourselves open to your mercy and your honour...' And Henry says 'Open your gates.' He puts the loudhailer away. And only when his men have left the stage to go into Harfleur does he show what he's been through. It's how the men were feeling during 'Once more unto the breach', which he's kept under wraps right the way through to taking Harfleur. Finally at that point, when only Exeter is beside him, you see what it's cost him. He's the one now who's about to throw up. He's coughing, can't breathe, feels faint. Exeter hands him his helmet and gives him a little 'come on'.

That speech looks like another instance of Henry's ability to pass the buck. He did it with Canterbury at the beginning: 'Give me my justification for war,' he said. And now he's saying to the Governor 'If we commit atrocities, it'll be your fault.' Isn't that right?

Yeah. 'On your head be it.'

Next, a shocking moment. Your old mate Bardolph is executed. Not as in Shakespeare, hanged offstage. But shot by you in full view.

We knew we were deviating from correct procedure, of course. But the conspirators had been executed offstage, and Nick felt strongly that he wanted Henry to do this himself. So we took the medieval law of war and put it into our modern production. Bardolph was shot onstage by Henry with a gun to the head. We felt that everyone would know he was an old mucker, so this was a real test. Henry has already shown that his former life is forgotten, he's above board. Bardolph has been caught stealing from a church. He is a criminal, a common thief. So, as a supreme example to his people, Henry executes him.

I wrestled with it for a moment, then walked up very quickly and BANG. He dropped. And as everyone's thinking 'Bloody hell!', Henry jumps on top of their reaction with 'We would have all such offenders so cut off' [3.6]. He shows in that act that there is no weakness, no sentimentality. Henry's pissed off. 'If I do this to him, what will I do to anybody else who doesn't know me as well?' It's cold, and we took a slight liberty. But it worked to great effect.

That'll be the ruthlessness we talked about.

I remember one performance – I went to do it, and the gun just clicked, didn't shoot. The actor was waiting to drop, I started swearing, did it again. Luckily the tech guy was watching. So they put the sound cue in, we got the bang, and he drops. At which point I threw the gun halfway across the stage, and it just missed another actor. The anger was real.

I didn't quite understand that.

When I pulled the trigger on the gun it was like pushing a button on the sound desk to cue gunfire, which would normally come through the speakers. But what happened was that when I pulled the trigger there was no sound, nothing.

So it was the sound cue that went wrong, not the gun?

Yes. But when I did it again the guy up there hit the button.

Even at the National Theatre, such things can happen! The end of Act 3 is a big contrast to Harfleur. Did it feel odd to be quite so downbeat with Montjoy?

He's just executed his friend, they've taken Harfleur. I think the fatigue speaks in him. There's no bravado, no rousing speech, he tells the truth. 'I'm not gonna pay you': 'My ransom is this frail and worthless trunk' [3.6]. 'If you want payment, you'll have to kill me':

> Though 'tis no wisdom to confess so much
> Unto an enemy of craft and vantage,
> My people are with sickness much enfeebled.

He's telling Montjoy they have the advantage.

> My numbers lessen'd, and those few I have
> Almost no better than so many French.

To the soldiers listening, he's lost faith in them. They look at him thinking 'What is he doing?' It's a weird card to play.

He's shot his load for the moment, bravado-wise.

In a way, yes. He certainly chooses another tack. He's saying 'We're down to the bare bones. But if you want to bring your army here, we will fight':

> Go, bid thy master well advise himself.
> If we may pass, we will; if we be hinder'd,
> We shall your tawny ground with your red blood
> Discolour.

After Montjoy goes, Henry says:

> Beyond the river we'll encamp ourselves,
> And on tomorrow...

– and I pause there. The ragtag army are still looking at me uncertainly. Then '...bid them march away' is a snap: 'Go! Leave me alone!!' And they leave. The effects of war are starting to take a toll.

Act 4. You borrow Erpingham's cloak and put on a disguise. The first person you meet is Pistol, from the old gang, and you seem to have a fond exchange with him. Are you still thinking about Bardolph and perhaps making amends, or is it just a relief to see an old friend?

Pistol meets this stranger in the middle of a field and tells him 'The King's a bawcock and a heart of gold... I kiss his dirty shoe' [4.1]. Pistol knows about Bardolph. Nonetheless, he states his allegiance not only to Hal the boy but to Harry the King. So it's a very positive exchange. Henry even plays a little game, calling himself Harry le Roy.

Shakespeare loves disguise. His characters often get released by it. Did it have any particular effect on Henry? Did you want to be one of the lads again and seek communion with them, or was there something else?

His conscience eats at him now, because he's led his men up to this point, and they are going to be slaughtered. That's his belief. I don't think you can go through that area of Act 4 without believing that you all are going to die in the morning. Nothing you do or say can change that. He borrows the cloak because it's cold, and puts the hood up. Then he walks among his men to get the true measure of them. Rather than see the face they wish to show to the King, more importantly he sees the face they show to each other, and can tell how they're doing. But he doesn't seek the chat with Williams and Bates. He's alone with his thoughts when he bumps into these guys. And they start having a discussion. It wasn't forethought, not planned.

It's a wonderful scene. Very strong stuff from Williams about the cost of war.

That's what he's worried about, the reason he's out on his own. He will die, but what's on his soul when he goes? Williams says it for him.

Your 'flashes of anger' – maybe one was with Williams in this exchange? Because what he's saying gets to you?

Yeah, it really does. We've heard the justification for the war from Canterbury. But aside from that, his concern is that all these young lads have followed him, and will die for him, because they believed the cause was right. What if it wasn't? He's face to face with his own vanity. Here, he questions whether the cause is right, because he doesn't know. And that will sit on his conscience. He'll take that to hell with him.

So he's questioning the justification for the war itself at that point?

Purely selfishly. It's what he'll have on his soul when he dies. He tries to shake it off, saying 'I think the King is but a man, as I am' [4.1]. He's dethroning himself, absolving himself from responsibility, as he does throughout the play. He's trying to say 'On your head be it. If you die, well, it's not my fault, it's yours.' But these men, not knowing who he is, are saying 'No, it's the King's fault.' He says 'No, no, no, it's the war, it's circumstance.' They go 'No, but we followed him. If we die and it's not a good death, it's not us, it's *his* fault.' And he has trouble dealing with that.

Do you think there's a conclusion to that debate? Does anybody win?

I don't think so. Williams says:

> If the cause be not good, the King himself hath a heavy reckoning to make when all those legs and arms and heads chopped off in a battle shall join together at the latter day and cry all 'We died at such a place' – some swearing, some crying for a surgeon, some upon their wives left poor behind them, some upon the debts they owe, some upon their children rawly left.

That's terrible to hear. The King responds:

> So, if a son that is by his father sent about merchandise do sinfully miscarry upon the sea, the imputation of his wickedness, by your rule, should be imposed upon his father that sent him. Or if a servant, under his master's command…

And he rattles on, trying to reason it out. I did this speech incensed at the fact that they're blaming the King. But toward the end I realised they'd walked away, thinking 'Fucking hell, this bloke!… What's up with you, mate?' So I was left briefly on my own. Then I turned and went 'No, no, no, but I haven't finished, I haven't finished, because the point is – the point is that you can't say that, you can't…' It was that vehement. 'You can't say it's my fault – you can't, none of you can, you can't. You came here because you were being paid, you're being paid to come here, and you are doing it for honour and your country, and that's good…' But he couldn't quite wrestle himself out of it.

Do you think he almost forgets he's in disguise?

At times. The hood stayed up, he wouldn't show his face, accent changed, went very Birmingham. But there were moments where they'd look at him oddly... Then the quarrel ('Give me any gage of thine'), which is picked up later on.

How was the soliloquy 'Upon the King'?

It's bitter. 'O poor we that have to rule and tell others what to do. If they get it wrong it's our fault because we told them.' It's very bitter –

> What infinite heart's ease
> Must kings neglect, that private men enjoy!
> And what have kings that privates have not too,
> Save ceremony, save general ceremony?

'In all this power there's nothing except that I don't sleep as easy as you lot!' It was amazing, delivering that speech at the time of the invasion, to the National Theatre audience. I liked to leave the house lights up a little bit so I could look in the eye of the audience, we could see each other and interact. Even now, six years later, I can remember faces, people sitting in the front three or four rows, often nodding in agreement. But when I mentioned the wretched slave who sleeps easiest, someone went 'Hmmph!'

What was that noise you just made?

It was a derisive snort. So I took my next line to them, as if to say 'What? You disagree? You don't think it's true?' If an audience is feeling tired, it's one kind of speech, and if they're feeling active and engaged with the play, then it's very different. It changes from night to night. I was never locked behind the fourth wall with the audience in a black space. I have to see their faces. Everything's positive. If someone's bored and they're not really watching the play, I can engage them: 'You're not listening. I've got to say this to you. Listen, *understand* this...'

Henry invokes God a lot, often wearing his Christianity very publicly. But the prayer 'O God of battles...' at the end of this long scene is genuinely private and vulnerable, isn't it.

Yeah, it's for no one but himself. The end of that last speech was beautiful, describing the life that he doesn't have and never will have:

> the wretched slave...
> Sweats in the eye of Phoebus, and all night
> Sleeps in Elysium; next day after dawn
> Doth rise and help Hyperion to his horse,
> And follows so the ever-running year

With profitable labour, to his grave.
And, but for ceremony…

– which is what's made his life such a hell. As he finishes, Erpingham comes in and says 'Time to go, got to go. They're all ready.' Henry tells him 'Collect them all together, it's now time to think of war.' Suddenly it's brisk, he doesn't have much time. He has ten seconds to himself before going to his death, so what does he say before God? Until then he uses God rhetorically: 'God be my witness' or 'God be praised', those kinds of things. He never sits and calls upon God, imploring help, seeking guidance or forgiveness. He does here:

> Steel my soldiers' hearts…
> Take from them now
> The sense of reckoning…
> Not today, O Lord,
> O not today, think not upon the fault
> My father made in compassing the crown.

That comes out of side field, doesn't it, the first reference to your father usurping the crown. Has it been much in your mind?

Well, maybe. The scene, as I said, started with guilt and reckoning. Now it's not considered, it comes tumbling out, I have to get this off my chest: 'PLEASE… make my soldiers unable to count, so they're not frightened by the size of the French army. And don't think about the fact that my dad stole the crown' –

> I Richard's body have interred new,
> And on it have bestow'd more contrite tears
> Than from it issued forced drops of blood…

(I've reburied him, I've done this, I've done that…)

> More will I do…

But then he realises:

> Though all that I can do is nothing worth,
> Since that my penitence comes after all,
> Imploring pardon.

Nonetheless, at the end of the scene you say 'The day, my friends and all things stay for me.' You sound refreshed. It seems as though the meditation and prayer have been beneficial.

Not really. He's taken off the mask of the King, the mask of confidence, and engaged with the soldiers. By the end of this scene he's simply this young man who feels he's about to die with stuff on his conscience. It was quite measured, not upbeat. I put an extra comma in that line, so it went 'The day… my friends... and all things stay for me.' Nothing will happen, the play does not continue, unless I move. It's almost as if the sun won't rise. So that moment where I get off my knees and walk is the beginning of the battle.

Looking at the text of the St Crispin's Day speech [4.3], so easy and unforced, you do seem to come back on blistering form. You've even got a nice, relaxed joke later with Montjoy: 'There's not a piece of feather in our host – / Good argument, I hope, we will not fly...' How did you play it?

I drove onto the stage in a jeep. The army's brittle, they're worried. Someone says:

> O that we now had here
> But one ten thousand of those men in England
> That do no work today!

Henry says 'What's he that wishes so?' Nobody says anything. Silence. Then Westmorland puts his hand up. Henry's face is straight and stern, and they all think 'Oh my God, is he going to take him out and have *him* shot?' Because that's what they know of this new King: you do not want to mess with him. He gets out of the jeep and walks right up, face to face, and says 'My cousin Westmorland?' Then he slaps his helmet – BANG! And they all start laughing. And he says 'No, no, no, my fair cousin.' Then a wonderful line:

> If we are mark'd to die, we are enough
> To do our country loss. And if to live,
> The fewer men, the greater share of honour.

And they all start to smile and laugh. 'God's will, I pray thee wish not one man more.' And he says 'I'm not a covetous man. But if we have one man more and we win, then we're going to have to share our glory with him. No, I want it all for us!'

> But if it be a sin to covet honour
> I am the most offending soul alive.

And so they start smiling and thinking beyond death: 'It's *our honour* that we're fighting for now. It's gone beyond winning or losing, it's the quality of the fight. It's making sure that we do ourselves and our forebears justice in how we fight. No fear.' Then the King says 'O do not wish one more.' And he climbs up onto the jeep and he says:

> Rather proclaim it, Westmorland, through my host...

– and with full voice:

> That he which hath no stomach to this fight,
> LET... HIM... DEPART.

Big pause.

Bit risky that, wasn't it.

Risky.

Again, he's a poker player.

Yeah, we can see that he is. They're looking at each other, wondering 'Does he *mean* it? He *can't* do. He'll shoot anyone who tries to move...' And Henry says:

> His passport shall be made,
> And crowns for convoy put into his purse.

And just as a couple of feet shift, thinking 'Well, if that's really what you mean, sir...' he says:

> We would not die in that man's company
> That fears his fellowship to die with us.

He's talking freely about death, which he hasn't done before. He's saying 'I'd rather die with people who have the British mettle about them.' After that, no one moves. It's honour. He has them.

The bluff worked.

The bluff worked. Then 'Oh, and by the way, did you know today is called the Feast of Crispian?':

> He that outlives this day and comes safe home
> Will stand a-tiptoe when this day is nam'd...

– moving into:

> We few, we happy few, we band of brothers.
> For he today that sheds his blood with me
> Shall be my brother, be he ne'er so vile.

Honour, honour, honour, honour. It's momentous. 'We're making history. Your names, the names of your loved ones, they'll be famous. Think of what you're doing, simply by standing here.' They are absolutely in awe of this. They love the idea. He enters a degree of politicking and leadership that was beyond the earlier Henry, before the dark night of the soul. He's come to a new sense of leadership, which is, if you like, Dalai Lama-ish. It's not reaching the destination that's the point, it's the journey. It's not 'Am I going to die?', it's who I die with, and how I die. It's 'Will I be remembered, and how will they remember me?' That's what we should all be thinking about.

It comes right back to the 'waxen epitaph', doesn't it.

The waxen epitaph, yes. But oh my God, it was brilliant. Delivering that in the Olivier auditorium, it makes you glad to be an actor. Some of the things you get to do… Sitting on top of a jeep, in fatigues, speaking those lines about honour and duty and how you'll be remembered, at a point where people were risking their lives in another country where the British flag was flying, for a just or an unjust cause – who knew? – and feeling that speech just go through you, I'll never forget it. You could sense different reactions in the audience. The young ones loved it, because they didn't think Shakespeare would *be* like that. Others who had seen many productions were looking at us thinking 'This is opportunistic, and oh, it's a bit brutal…' And then there were people who were much older, watching us push each other around and hold guns to heads, spitting and cursing – and they loved it. You could sense the gap between people who didn't know conflict and the generation above them who knew it only too well. It was weird.

Don't get too pleased with yourself! During the battle that follows we have Exeter's very moving account of York and Suffolk's death [4.6], and then there's a real shocker. You say 'The French have reinforc'd their scattered men. / Then every soldier kill his prisoners!' How could you do that? It's a war crime. It's not revenge, because we don't know about the boys being killed until the following scene [4.7].

He needs the numbers. He doesn't want to waste good men guarding prisoners when he needs them to fight the enemy. It's also a symbol to the French – that we are not fucking about here. Ideas of war and rules of engagement get pushed to one side.

What did your military adviser have to say about that?

He said what you believe happens in battle, and *should* happen, often *doesn't* happen.

So the business made sense to him.

He understood it. Another ex-soldier was talking to me about killing four-year-olds, shooting toddlers who are sent out to walk towards your army with bombs strapped to them. If you have to take a village, you have to take it. It's total war. Notions of fair fighting, he said, are naive. You beat your enemy, the soldiers rape the women, leaving as many pregnant as possible, and you move on. The Vikings did that kind of thing. Nowadays we call it 'shock and awe'. Take away the will to fight, and you've won half the battle. That's what the solar-plexus punch in boxing is all about. If you hit that correctly and the insides go jittery, they're not going to want to fight, regardless of whether they could. It's all in Shakespeare's text.

How did you stage the Battle of Agincourt?

There was masses of choreography. We had dry ice, lighting effects, bombs and so on. People were running, turning, firing, being fired upon, falling. Some had to get into French costume, shoot, fire, whatever, and then run off, change back into British costume, run back on again. It was a bit like *Black Hawk Down* – have you seen that film? It's harrowing. Mogadishu, urban warfare. People are running for their lives and shooting, firing, being fired upon, hiding round corners and going through buildings, it just keeps going. You think there must be a rest from this, and there just isn't, it keeps going for two-plus hours. That's what we wanted to try and touch on.

'Henry's post-Agincourt tears are preserved on tape, as video merchandise.' Tell me about that.

That must have been after the death of the Duke of York [4.6]. We didn't tape the herald saying 'The day is yours' [4.7], and Henry's relief, weak at the knees, helmet off. But at the end of that scene, we marched off carrying the flag and singing a hymn, and that was videotaped. It was like an advert for fighting for your country.

You had a rap soundtrack?

It wasn't really rap, more speaking in rhythm. Do you remember The Art of Noise? They were around in the 1990s – it was a bit like that. A choirboy singing, rhythm going through a spoken rhyme, and harmony. It was a rather portentous song that Nick Hytner wanted. He said 'What would happen if we came back victorious, and wanted to tell the world?'

'A stink of sanctimony pollutes the victory celebration.' Does that sound accurate?

Completely.

Act 5. I think you cut out the Pistol and Fluellen leek-eating scene [5.1]?

Yes, we did.

The French King's first line is 'Right joyous are we to behold your royal face' [5.2]. But he's just lost the battle and his daughter is being forced to marry the conqueror. He can't have been 'right joyous' at all, surely. Can you describe that scene, their attitudes?

We were in Officers' Number Twos.

What's that?

It's not ceremonial army dress, but it's green, brass buttons, khaki and tie. Henry starts with 'Peace to this meeting, wherefore we are met'. The French King is crying, he's holding his wife's hand, his son's dead. They're destroyed and demoralised, wearing black. We offer a military presence rather than a political one. So Henry's first word to the French, 'Peace', really rubs their noses in it. Then 'We do *salute* you, Duke of Burgundy', not 'We *greet* you.' It's military. The French King tries to make a formal response:

> Right joyous are we to behold your face,
> Most worthy brother England; fairly met.
> So are you… princes English… every one…

But he didn't finish, he trailed off, couldn't look us in the eye. The Queen took his hand and came in with 'So happy be the issue, brother England…', but you felt the acute sense of loss. It wasn't clean.

In the wooing scene that follows you're suddenly revealed as a dazzling ladies' man. You're full of compliments and self-deprecation, and you're very witty. It's a long scene. It must have been a joy to play – a total contrast to what went before.

It was. Félicité du Jeu [as Katherine] was amazing. At first the scene wasn't really taking off, so we got together and reworked it. Henry wants this marriage. He needs an heir that is both French and English to create a line, and to bring both countries together. At first he tries to be charming, but she doesn't respond. Then he uses comedy. He uses everything at his disposal. He understands French perfectly well, but he disarms her by pretending not to. I tapped a comic vein and became an actor. I wanted to do everything I possibly could to make Katherine smile – speak bad French, use different voices. Finally he tells her that a marriage made out of duty and honour is much better than one made out of love. 'Looks fade, and the heat of the blood will pass. But you must know this: I'm an honourable man. I'm true to my word, I will stay with you, I will love you for ever as your husband, I will honour you, and you will not get a better offer than that: the King!'

But he does also flirt with her, doesn't he?

Completely, completely. Different tacks are tried at different times. That's typical Shakespeare. People sometimes approach Shakespeare with the thought that they should occupy one emotional space at a time. But Henry's a reckless youth and a king, a guilty son and a witty man, all rolled into one. And if he knows what to say to his army under different circumstances, then when presented with another problem, namely this young lady, he'll tackle it in the same way. 'Which way will work with you?' Once I've found the right vein, I'll mine that.

Pragmatic.

At one point the pragmatism went so far that when she wouldn't kiss him, he ordered her to. By the end of the scene he's saying 'Put off your maiden blushes. (Come on, let's stop fucking about.) Wilt thou have me?' And she, eventually, steps forward and kisses him.

The final scene looks relatively upbeat on the page, and quite merry. You get the girl, the treaty is concluded, end of play. Looking back on the production after six years, do you still think that was a good way to do it? Or was the text distorted?

No, I think it was a good way. But these plays have to be re-evaluated for every generation, and in each new production.

Ian McKellen
on
Macbeth

Macbeth (1599)
Royal Shakespeare Company
Opened at The Other Place, Stratford-upon-Avon
on 9 September 1976

Directed by Trevor Nunn
Designed by John Napier
With Judi Dench as Lady Macbeth, Ian McDiarmid as Ross,
Bob Peck as Macduff, Roger Rees as Malcolm, and John Woodvine as Banquo

Macbeth, Shakespeare's shortest tragedy, is about killing a king and what happens afterwards. The play has powerful supernatural elements, which have contributed to the tradition of its carrying a curse. Theatre lore is rich in examples. Laurence Olivier's 1937 performance was blighted by ill-fitting sets, the director was badly injured in a car crash and had to be replaced, Olivier himself narrowly avoided death by falling stage-weight, and, to cap it all, the theatre's founder Lilian Baylis died during the dress rehearsals. Many theatre people refuse to quote from *Macbeth* or even name it backstage, preferring to call it 'The Scottish Play'.

The role of Macbeth has always been a Mount Everest for leading actors. It contains some of the most thrilling verse in the Shakespearean canon. The character has a stunning poetic imagination – but also a challenging blend of soldierly ruggedness with hypersensitivity, and vaulting ambition with fear. It is a murky play, with key scenes often being staged in gloom. The audience cannot easily find any point of identification. Many actors attempt the ascent but few, in critical terms, reach the summit. Ian McKellen was one who did. The production, directed by Trevor Nunn and co-starring Judi Dench, is considered iconic. It opened in Stratford-upon-Avon in 1976 in the RSC's smallest theatre, The Other Place, and subsequently played on the RSC main stage, the Gulbenkian studio theatre in Newcastle, the Donmar Warehouse and the Young Vic in London, before being filmed by Thames Television.

I saw the production over thirty years ago at the Donmar, and remember its impact vividly. It ran for two hours, fifteen minutes without an interval, and was an unforgettable example of 'chamber Shakespeare', of less being more. The confined space, the small bare stage, the muted colours and minimal props provided a perfect setting for performances that were as true and intense as they were unhistrionic. An attic full of theatrical clutter had been thrown out, and the play swept clean and fresh. It was a revelation.

I've been in *Macbeth* three times myself, including playing the lead at a Shakespeare festival in California. I couldn't resist having a go at it, but I should have been more wary. Not only did I fail to reach the summit, I fell to the bottom of a deep ravine, swept away in an avalanche of miscasting, poor direction and my own lousy acting. So I speak from experience. I've been friends with Ian McKellen since we were at university together, and have worked with him on several occasions. As well as being a brilliant actor, he has rare theatrical intelligence. Ian's the best I know at talking about theatre and the craft of acting. Consequently I was as pleased as Punch when he agreed to discuss *Macbeth*. We met in 2006 at his riverside home in Southwark.

Julian Curry: There have been countless unmemorable Macbeths, but yours was a triumph. You've also had huge successes with Iago and Richard III. Why do you suppose you have such an affinity with these Shakespearean villains?

Ian McKellen: Well, I suspect it's because those are the parts that Shakespeare wrote best, or made most entertaining or of most interest to the audience. It's unexpected, isn't it, that the greatest playwright who ever lived should have written about monsters as successfully as he wrote about heroes and heroines. *Macbeth* is an extremely popular play. In fact it was the first Shakespeare play I saw, in an amateur production at the Wigan Little Theatre when I was pre-teens. It's short, which I think helps the audience. The story doesn't have a subplot, so it's relatively easy to realise what's going on. Particularly as Macbeth keeps telling the audience what's going on, at least inside his head. And if the actor can convincingly convey, with the immediacy of Shakespeare's language, what he's thinking and worrying about and suffering, agonising over, then the audience can't help being engaged. The result of his decisions is appalling, and one has the privilege of being inside the head of someone whose behaviour, if read about in the newspaper, would be dismissed as that of an 'Evil Monster'. But I think Shakespeare's message is that those sort of words aren't helpful in explaining human behaviour, because they don't explain it, they just give it a label. Therefore I didn't think of Macbeth as a terrible man, any more than I did Iago. I thought of each of them as a man with a problem, and in both cases that problem is shared with the audience.

It was enormously helpful that our production was first put on in The Other Place, which only seated a hundred people. I'd seen *King Lear* done there very successfully, in a Buzz Goodbody production. It's riveting to be so close to the actors when they're not having to project their performance, either vocally or emotionally. Or indeed to select from it what they want the audience to receive. It's part of our job to let them know what's going on, but if you're working in a big theatre you can't let them know everything, and they're not close enough to glimpse it for themselves. So they're relying on the actor carrying the character on his back, as it were. But in The Other Place, the actor and the character can become much closer together. The level of speaking can be conversational and the audience can see not only the eyes, but perhaps what's behind the eyes. A play like *Macbeth* is about the psychology of the person. You have to be very close to the subject to be of any help. So that was all set up in my favour: (a) it's a popular play, it's one that people want to see; and (b) we had the right circumstances for plugging into what is special about the play, what's needed if it's going to come across. And whilst we're on the subject of the play being popular, I believe the reason why it's thought of as an unlucky play is that when your stock touring company was in trouble and you heard they're going to take off a less popular play and substitute *Macbeth*, it would probably mean that there wasn't enough in the coffers to pay the salaries by the end of the week. So... don't even mention *Macbeth*!

Another reason given for the superstition is the play often being minimally lit, and you get actors falling off the stage in the dark and breaking a leg.

That may well contribute. People also talk about there being supernaturals in the play, but it's nothing to do with that. There are many more in *Doctor Faustus*. Indeed, there's a wonderful story about *Doctor Faustus* on tour in its original production when the actors suddenly realised that there were *eight* deadly sins onstage, and the performance was disrupted and ended abruptly. The actors didn't dare go to bed – they stayed up all night drinking and playing cards. Isn't it a wonderful notion? I can believe that: that the devil was summoned up in that play. But in *Macbeth*, well, there's Hecate and the witches, and are the witches *really* supernaturals? So I would go for the practical reason that *Macbeth* is very popular. But it's odd, isn't it, that being so popular, it should so rarely be thought of as being well done.

Exactly.

I think it's often because the play is in the wrong sort of theatre. And what we know about Elizabethan playhouses from the discovery of the Rose (much more telling information than from any supposed recreation of the Globe) is that those playhouses were small. Imagine Lear's 'Pray undo this button' with a button that can be seen! When Hamlet says 'Speak the speech, I pray you, as I pronounced it to you, trippingly on the tongue,' Shakespeare is advising his players in a wonderful bit of rolling prose, to speak naturalistically. Once you put *Macbeth* into a large theatre, a Victorian theatre, let's say, the actors get betrayed into doing things that are just not helpful to the play. And the designer too: 'Oh God, where *is* Scotland?' Scotland is the least interesting feature of *Macbeth*, I think, the real Scotland. In John Napier's design for our production there was no sense of Scotland. We were actors on a stage, and the play began with us coming in and sitting on fruit boxes, round a rough white circle painted on the floor of the stage. We could be seen doing the sound effects. At one point I was in charge of the thunder machine. You could see Macbeth and Lady Macbeth putting the blood on their hands in the wings. I don't think this was an attempt to be Brechtian in any sense, but just to say this is a group of people telling a story, and it'll be just as riveting and frightening and exciting as if we were in a large theatre trying to convince you that we were in medieval Scotland, which is no help whatsoever. That's one thing that Trevor Nunn solved. The second thing he solved, which again can go wrong in a big theatre, is the magic. What do you do about heads coming... not the heads... the, er...

Apparitions?

The apparitions. In an earlier production with Nicol Williamson, Trevor had a puppet show of some sort, and we were left over with a couple of the puppets. But ours was happening inside Macbeth's head, where, as I said, so much of the play takes place. So the idea was that he had been drugged and laid on the floor and told these things were happening to him, even though they weren't. I thought that was much more plausible in the twentieth century. The witches were very clearly ordinary – well, not *ordinary* but they were, believably, people going about their business. And they had a relationship that Trevor worked out between the grandmother, the daughter and her daughter. They were a little family of people who were in touch with things beyond themselves. Hecate was cut. So the magic was solved. And the third difficulty of *Macbeth*, which is, I think, the least understood, is that the fifth act isn't very good. Well, it's not very good if you're telling the story of the leading part, because so much of it is about other characters. You've had the long scene with Macduff and Malcolm in England [4.3] – very welcome! – as a result of which they decide to come back and invade Scotland where Macbeth's holed up in his castle. But you've no sooner got to Macbeth in his castle, and he's saying something riveting about how he feels, than Shakespeare cuts to the boring old English troops with their rhododendron leaves and all that. And when you stage that, as you feel you have to in a big theatre, the audience is constantly frustrated. And time and again in the reviews you will see 'The amazing Mr So-and-So as Macbeth unfortunately couldn't bring off the fifth act.' But it's not his fault, it's the play's fault. And what Trevor did brilliantly was to cut down the number of lines of the invading army, which are much less interesting than Macbeth's dilemma. He kept Macbeth in the centre of the magic circle the whole time, while the words of the invading army were spoken by the actors standing round observing Macbeth, so the focus never left him. So that was Trevor giving me the chance to bring off the fifth act. It was his awareness that there was a weakness there.

Is there a problem – maybe another reason why a lot of actors fail – in that this extraordinary person, with such a hyperactive mind and a head full of stunning poetic imagery, is also an expert killer? Is that hard to reconcile?

What, the soldier-poet? Well, there have been plenty of them. I don't think you can say of Shakespeare's characters that because they're speaking poetry, they are themselves poetic.

If you listen to Caliban talking about his plans to commit murder he uses very different terms from Macbeth.

Alright, yes. Well, *I* didn't find it a problem. One related problem, which may be an answer to playing the part, is what is Macbeth like before the play begins? Normally I wouldn't be very interested in that. 'How many children had Lady Macbeth?' might be something for actors and literary critics to worry about, but not for the audience. But Shakespeare sets Macbeth up to fall from a great height. He's described as the most amazing warrior, who almost single-handedly saved the country. He couldn't be at a higher peak of his physical and professional activity. But we don't actually ever see him like that. He comes in and the first thing he says is 'So foul and fair a day I have not seen' [1.3]. Already there are two things going on in his mind: 'Is it good, is it bad?' Whereas the man who kills like that surely has nothing in his mind but killing.

When he says 'So foul and fair a day', what do you think he's referring to?

Well, they won the battle – that's fair. And it's pissing down – that's foul.

So it's not the gore that he's created by winning the battle, the carnage?

I thought it was lighter than that. He doesn't seem to care how many people he's killed, does he? He's a brilliant professional commander and man of action. You're right, the starting point of interest in the play is 'My goodness, that man has a startling inside which is nothing like what he appears to be, he's seriously ambitious.' Ambitious? But you can't get any better than he is! He's the favourite of the King. He's the great commander. People bow down in front of him. He's happily married… but that's not enough for him. Not enough. And so the story progresses. I think he has the wonderful imagery not only to show the complexity of his imagination, and then his conscience. But also, how else can you explain the insides of a man who is prepared to kill the King, kill a god in a sense, unless the language is dense and complicated and full of imagery? We mortals who don't want to kill anybody can only wonder at such language, open-mouthed and open-eared, and thank our lucky stars it's not our dilemma.

So you think it's all part of his adrenalin, do you?

Yes. I must say I didn't look beyond the imagery for some other information. I didn't think when I was saying 'blow the horrid deed in every eye, / That tears shall drown the wind…' [1.7] What's before that?

'And Pity, like a naked new-born babe…'

'Like a babe…' I didn't, as I said that, imagine the new-born child lying on Lady Macbeth's teat. I just thought of a child. I think that's the only image it was meant to convey to the audience, I don't think it's further information about him. You see what I mean? We've all seen a new-born child and therefore know exactly what he's talking about. This imagery is very colourful and precise and pictorial.

Stunning. There are various possible reasons for the murder of Duncan. No doubt there's ambition. The witches egg him on, and his wife certainly works on him very effectively. Also, it seems to me, there may be a mountaineer's need to court danger, a need for that kind of adrenalin rush. Do you think that contributes?

Certainly the first three things, yes. His ambition is supported by his wife, it's confirmed as a possibility by the witches, but he only hears what he wants to hear. But as for him courting danger, I think rather than that, he wants to know what it feels like to be King, to be supreme boss. He's one of many very successful warriors in Shakespeare who want to go into civilian politics. It's the same story for Macbeth, as I observed later when I was doing Richard III, exactly the same story. With Richard, Shakespeare is beginning to imagine Macbeth – it's astonishing. They both come back hugely successful, they've both been germane in bringing about the end of a civil war. (Well, in Macbeth's case, it's fighting the Norwegian sledded somebody or other.) And it's not enough for them. Similarly, it's not enough to be Coriolanus, single-handedly defeating a town. By his breeding and his temperament, he wants to run the country. Richard III wants to *own* the country and will do anything to get it. He's totally conscienceless until that last amazing speech after his nightmare in which he asks himself, is he doing the right thing? Is he a monster or not? And he speaks in language worthy of Beckett, it's quite extraordinary. It's more modern than even you get in *Macbeth*. Then he writes *Macbeth*, and instead of bringing the conscience in right at the end of the play, he thinks, 'Of course, I must put it in at the beginning!' And that's what he's exploring – that Macbeth should be ambitious for civilian power, wants to be King. As I say, he shares that with a lot of other characters in Shakespeare. Shakespeare's always writing about soldiers.

Titus Andronicus is another, a great soldier who later comes unstuck.

Yeah, it's the same part. And all those conspirators in *Julius Caesar*. *Troilus and Cressida*'s all about soldiers, soldiers off duty. *Much Ado* is also about soldiers off duty – a comedy version. There's something about them that Shakespeare just can't stop writing about. I don't know if there were a lot of them around in the 1600s, but there were certainly wars going on. But it's almost as if Shakespeare thought that to be a warrior was to be fulfilled as a man, and yet he realises that the warriors themselves don't feel fulfilled, they want more. I think he's saying if you're prepared to kill somebody, well, you've gone off the rails. And they make dreadful kings, all of them, these soldiers.

Tell me some more about the production. How much was it preconceived and how much did it evolve as it went along?

I think Trevor has increasingly become a director who pre-imagines more than perhaps he would ideally like to do. It's not surprising, given the amount of work he does, and the responsibility at that time of running the RSC. I can understand it. It's a dreadfully dangerous, nerve-racking situation to be doing all the work in rehearsal. If you're running a building with bills to be paid and tickets to be sold and other plays to be cast, you might think 'I'll just jot down a few ideas about this play in advance.' But the big, crucial pre-decision with *Macbeth* was to do it in that particular theatre. All the strengths of the production, I believe, flow from that. And from the easy way in which Trevor, I think for the first time, was working in such a small space. Likewise his renowned designer John Napier, who later went on to build some of the biggest and most complicated sets ever seen in the British theatre – but loved the idea of not having to do that at all. The look of the production was something that was devised during rehearsal. I can remember quite clearly, John didn't know what the set was going to look like, although he knew there probably wasn't going to be one. And such as there was kept getting more and more minimal, as suited a tin hut where the audience were looking at each other across the stage on three sides. It was restricted by the size of the theatre, and then released by the size of the theatre. And restricted by the size of the budget. That production cost £250. Sets and costumes. The set for *The Alchemist*, which we did in the same theatre shortly afterwards, was built out of old bits of wood that were hanging around Stratford. Some of the costumes were bought from second-hand shops in Birmingham. I wore an officer's uniform from the Birmingham Fire Department. It had buttons all the way down. And the leather overcoats that John Woodvine as Banquo and I rather fetchingly hung on our shoulders, were worn like that because they were too small for us to get into.

This wasn't because the RSC couldn't afford...

Well, who knows. Perhaps with the other big productions in that season, including a musical of *The Comedy of Errors*...

They ran out of cash?

It's possible, isn't it. *The Winter's Tale, Romeo and Juliet, Much Ado About Nothing*, these were big, big productions. And I don't think The Other Place had a budget, or much of a budget. Directors were told 'Look, just be glad the audience can see and hear, and therefore they won't need much help.' I think it was also 'Let's see what happens when you do that.' 'Rough theatre' is it called? Peter Brook was still knocking around Stratford. I think he'd already moved into the distressed Bouffes du Nord in Paris. And of course we all know that in rehearsal, without costume or make-up or scenery or lights, with just close attention on what's going on, a play is often revealed more excitingly than when it's dolled up and put into the theatre. And The Other Place was easily able to tap into that. At one point there was nothing but a sixty-watt bulb lighting the action. Or a candle. Directors must long for Lady Macbeth to come on with just a candle. You can't do it in the main Stratford theatre, but you can in The Other Place. It may have been done in the small theatre where the play was originally performed. I think it was one of the first shows that was staged indoors at Blackfriars. So maybe that's how the first Lady Macbeth sleep-walking was illuminated, with nothing but a candle.

One of the few less-than-ecstatic reviews says 'So much of the production is subdued that emotion seems banished by efficiency... not exactly conducive to the nightmare gigantism that is in the text.'

Well, that was one reaction – I can't help that, can I? I've seen the video, which still stands up as a production. But if that audience member detected in my performance someone who was being very efficient, and had his performance organised, he'd be quite right! There was another man, a priest, who saw the production at least three times from the front row of the audience, who used to carry his crucifix in front of him. He said to protect us from the evil in the production.

But he kept coming back?

To protect us! The doors were banged shut. And the play didn't stop until the end. No interval. People were trapped in there, whether they wanted to pee or whatever. It was a very hot summer. Baking in there. Baking! The Other Place audience never missed out. I wonder if that person didn't see it there, but saw it in its next port of call. The production was such a success that they made the disastrous mistake of transferring it the following season into the Royal Shakespeare Theatre itself. Our little acting area was put on the front of the main stage at Stratford. And more people saw it under those unfortunate circumstances than ever saw it in the intimate spaces of the Gulbenkian in Newcastle, or the Donmar or the Young Vic. Maybe he saw it there, and if so I couldn't blame him for not thinking much of it.

One reviewer, talking about you and Judi, describes you as 'an ostensibly nice and reasonable pair'. He also talks about you as having 'a certain courtliness, even wit. He can regard his downfall as an inexorable joke.'

Yes, I cottoned on to that early on – that Macbeth's got a very good sense of humour and is always cracking gags. I think his first line indicates that: 'So foul and fair a day I have not seen.' Isn't that a witty thing to say? And yet isn't it totally germane to his problem? He sees both sides. Anybody who sees both sides can laugh. And 'If it were done when 'tis done…'[1.7] – you know ? 'If I do this, then that… If I do that, then the other.' There's almost a chuckle as he's saying it. It's funny. And laughter releases you. Later he gets more and more bound up. But even 'She should have died hereafter…' [5.5] is within calling distance of wit. And the courtliness, yes, he's a warrior whom everybody loves and admires. He's clearly 'a man's man', they all adore him, everybody thinks he's fantastic. And it's a great shock as it dawns on them that he's dreadful. Lady Macbeth too, she's the perfect hostess. When we were rehearsing it was not long after Watergate, and I said 'Well, of course, they're the Nixons, aren't they?' And Trevor Nunn said 'No, no, they're not the Nixons, they're the Kennedys.' They're the golden couple, the couple everybody wants to be with, whose house everybody wants to visit, including the King. A couple we all admire. There the comparison with the Kennedys ends, presumably. But that's the sort they are. We're privileged to see inside their lives, and when we do we find they are dissatisfied, and want more. I should imagine they have great parties. It's against that background of people with social graces and great strengths that people admire, that the horror of the banquet is even more intense [3.4]. Because normally these people do it superbly.

When does he first think of the murder? Is it preconceived? Does the witch's comment 'shalt be king hereafter' [1.3] strike an immediate chord, or does it take a while for him to make that real inside himself? Is he completely a golden boy at the beginning, inside and out, who then falls from great height? Or is there a corner of him that's already thinking in those terms?

I'll go out on a limb and say, without really being able to remember, that Macbeth lives entirely in the moment and what happens is happening to him as it happens. I think Shakespeare would say that anyone who is riding as high as Macbeth at the beginning, might well think himself invincible. So if at that point when you've just won a BAFTA and an Emmy and an Olivier, someone comes along and says 'You're going to win the Oscar,' you say 'Of *course* I'm going to win the Oscar! Of *course* I'm going to be King, I can do anything!' He feels invincible. So the witches arrive at just the right moment, is what I'd say. I wouldn't put it any more clearly than that. And I can't think, when I was playing him, that I needed to come on saying to myself 'I want to be King, I want to be King, I want to be King.' He's with his best mate, they're coming back from the battle, they're going to see the King. Everything is just unbelievable – they've won! He must be so high that if someone says 'You can go higher still', dreaming as he does, he responds to that. Now, when he gets back to Lady Macbeth, they do seem perhaps to have talked about it in the past, but he's had other things on his mind. She's been thinking a little bit more about it than he has, left at home with nothing much to do but think. He's a man of action.

When she says 'What beast was't, then, / That made you break this enterprise to me?'
[1.7], she could be referring to his letter, after talking to the witches. It doesn't neces-
sarily mean they've talked about it before the play begins, does it.

No, no. I think they're highly attuned in their marriage, deeply in love and
dependent upon each other, or have been in the past. It's later on that they get
rather out of sync. Macbeth behaves like a general who says 'We have to plot
this out, we have to write these things down. Now, "if it were done when 'tis
done", we have to do it quickly...' But Lady Macbeth says 'God, what's the
matter with you? Get on with it! I thought you were the man who just went out
and killed people!' But no. He's a commander who works out the best place –
'What would happen if I do that?' He *thinks*. He works things through in his
mind, Macbeth, as well as his imagination. She can't see any problems, she's
not a man of action, she's not a great organiser of armies... she's a hostess.

What was your physicality like with Judi?

As far as possible we were never out of each other's arms. Certainly what she
can give him, which nobody else in the world can, is her love and her passion
and her sex. I always felt that I was a husband coming back to my beloved, to
my wife, my sweetheart, the only woman that I cared about in the world, coming back from the long, desperate life elsewhere and hardship with the men.
And she immediately wants to talk about killing the King. No wonder he's a
bit put off. And yes, I think the story of their progression is of them getting
separated from the bliss of that union.

It can be played, can't it, with her emasculating him – diminishing his manhood at sev-
eral moments in those scenes early on, in order to challenge him.

Well, she thinks that's how to get at him. And she's right, because he's very
proud. So she says 'You're not being yourself.' It's not that she wants to be
Queen and have a consort at her side, she wants him to be King. He's her man.
These are very, very private conversations. She's not trying to change Macbeth, but make him more like himself. She can't understand, she doesn't
understand the problems. That's why quite soon afterwards, she's not privy to
the problems. He doesn't include her because she doesn't understand. He's on
his own. And of course he's not at his best when he's on his own.

When you do soliloquies as Macbeth, do you talk to yourself or to the audience?

To the audience. It's the most wonderful release an actor can have. It's both-
ering me a bit with King Lear [which Ian was about to start rehearsing] that he
doesn't seem to have any soliloquies. Any more than Othello. It's interesting
in *Othello*, that the villain is the only one who talks to the audience. No wonder everybody likes Iago. Everyone likes Richard III, of course. He comes in

and tells them what's going on in his mind. Macbeth too. Lady Macbeth does-n't have any soliloquies. You have a special relationship with the audience. Some actors worry about 'Who is the audience?' I remember asking Tony Sher who he thought he was talking to in the first speech in *Richard III* and he said 'Oh, I imagined they were all cadet Richard IIIs, they were all going to grow up to be Richard III, and I was telling them how to behave.' And I said 'Well, I just think of them as the audience.' They are there, here, now. There's an immediacy about soliloquies, which I think should always contain the possi-bility of the slight pause, the question mark, the raised eyebrow, inviting the audience to give their response.

I've heard it suggested that the audience consists entirely of your very best friends.

I think they are friends, and they're going to give you the time of day and the benefit of the doubt. And in exchange for that you will give them, as the char-acter, total honesty always. Now you can puzzle about what the characters think and feel and have done in the past, and what they really want to do. And of course that's a very twentieth-century preoccupation, isn't it? 'What's really going on? Yeah, I know what he said, I know how he looks, but what's *really* going on inside?' Well, in the soliloquies, you are told and it's true. It's as true as the character can be. They may have got it wrong, but that is how it seems to them.

There's no subtext.

No subtext. And when people say Iago is a motiveless character, it's absolute bollocks, he gives his motives one after another. And Macbeth too. It's a won-derful gift to have.

He talks a lot about being fearful.

Every soldier you ever meet will tell you he's scared stiff. That's what a sol-dier's whole training is about, to cover up the fact and handle the fear.

Were there any especially difficult bits that you found problematic?

I don't think so, but it was a very worked-out performance. There were things I could always hold on to. The shaking hands with the clinking daggers. I had strings going through the performance which connected everything in my mind and made sense, so there was never a passage when I thought 'I just don't know what this is doing in the play, or what I'm meant to be doing.' I always knew what I was doing and why it was there for me. That had come of course from talking to Trevor about it. But there's usually a problem scene, isn't there? I think Act 5 would have been a problem if Trevor hadn't solved it.

When we see Lady Macbeth for the first time, with the letter, and she says 'Yet do I fear thy nature; / It is too full o'th' milk of human kindness' [1.5]. Do you think that's accurate?

Well, there's nothing wrong with the milk of human kindness. But for that to be the dominant feature of your personality, to be *too* full, would be a drawback.

One of the editors has a footnote suggesting that it should be humankindness, all one word, not human kindness. So she's saying he's too much of a human being as opposed to a beast.

Oh, I see. Well, you know… these… Oh God! How does Shakespeare's language work? I don't know. Do the characters know as much about what they're saying as editors do when they've analysed it? I don't know. We betray things, don't we, in the way we speak because we're not listening to ourselves, we're just speaking. I don't remember our rehearsals being a constant puzzle over 'What does this mean?' It all seemed to mean what it meant in the moment. I like to present what I know about the character, but I think the trick of it is not to let the audience know that you know, so you don't get in the way. And, to repeat the question, how does Shakespeare's language work on an audience? It's almost enough for them just to hear it. Because we know so much about it (as when you do a play at the RSC), if you try to tell the audience, as you're speaking, all that you know about the way it's written and what it means and its complications, you end… up… speaking… so… SLOWLY… that every word is exaggerated and you probably end on a rising inflection because you can never get to the end of the sentence! To be avoided, if at all possible. It's an odd thing to claim as an actor, that really you shouldn't do much more than just speak the lines. And I don't really mean that, of course, but there's something there.

Less is more.

Yes, yes. I try to be a little bit more cunning about knowledge than was sometimes the case. I mean, when you're acting with Judi Dench, you're not up against a great analytic mind that has sourced everything within herself and within the other works of Shakespeare, in order to speak his lines exactly as they were meant to be delivered. What you get with Judi, and with the best actors, is a pumping heart and blood coursing through the veins, living in the moment, terrified or ecstatic, whatever is required. And able to turn on the emotions as easily as a tap. That's not given to many of us. What she doesn't do is give a running commentary on the character, as I tended to do in the past. That *Hamlet* that we did – I've heard or seen bits of it and had to turn it off in horror because that's all I'm doing. I'm just saying 'You note this, you note that, listen to this!'

Tell me about this astonishing speech: 'If it were done when 'tis done, then 'twere well / It were done quickly' [1.7]. It seems he doesn't care about the afterlife. Do you agree?

That speech is not so much about the afterlife, I think, as what will happen politically if you assassinate the king.

     If it were done when 'tis done

(Those two *dones* mean different things, and in meaning different things there's a pun, and a pun is fun, it's another example of his wittiness)

     If it were done

(If it were over and done with)

               when 'tis done

(When the dagger's gone in, when the murder's committed '…then I should do it quickly')

     If the assassination

(Because that's what it will be, killing the King)

                  could trammel up the consequence

(Could put it in a net and secure it)

                                and catch
     With his surcease success

(And there you go again, the wit: 'surcease' and 'success' should sound the same. Meaning his death and my achievement. Surcease/success – of course he's got a sense of humour!)

                  that but this blow

(On his head or to his stomach)

     Might be the be-all and end-all

(If it were all over, that was the end of it)

                  here,
     But here, upon this bank and shoal of time

(In this life, this sandbank of time that we're living in)

     We'd jump the life to come

(Then it'd be *FANTASTIC!*)

                But in these cases
     We still have judgement here

(But when we commit an assassination, we are going to be judged by people)

> that we but teach
> Bloody instructions, which, being taught, return
> To plague the inventor.

(When we kill somebody, we could be teaching somebody else who will then come along and kill us.)

That's fine. But this idea of being prepared to 'jump the life to come', it's like Faust, isn't it. He'll sell his immortal soul for a reward on this earth?

Well, I don't think that is at the heart of the speech. What I think he's saying is that 'If I could do it with the certainty that nothing would happen as a result, other than my achieving success, fuck heaven, fuck hell, fuck the world, fuck everything, that's all I want in life.' In 'jump the life to come' he's not really talking about the hereafter, he brings in the hereafter as an extreme example of how wonderful it would be 'if it were done when 'tis done'.

Hmmm.

You can disagree but I think the speech is very much about the practicalities of what will happen if I assassinate the King. And although he uses apocalyptic imagery:

> his virtues
> Will plead like angels, trumpet-tongued against
> The deep damnation of his taking-off

All he's really referring to are those leading articles in the newspapers which will analyse how fantastic Duncan was. Everybody will be talking about him like an angel, but he's not. The listener might detect that he's worrying about heaven and hell and the future and God's sending him with the goats. But what he's actually talking about at this point is 'Will I get away with it?'

Where is his conscience?

His conscience is not relating to a moral code set by a far distant invisible God. It is how do we behave in society? Does the commander of the armed forces kill the King because he thinks he'll be a better king? What do I think? How do I see it? Is it just my ambition? It's the practicalities of surviving in the present-day life. I don't think you ever find in Shakespeare the mighty hand of God and scales of the ultimate day of justice. I don't think they feature. They're used as an image but not as a reality. Otherwise the play would be boring as hell, wouldn't it. There's no mention of God in *King Lear* that we can find, a Christian god. That it's written by a supposed Catholic seems to me extraordinary.

He carries on:

And pity, like a naked new-born babe,
Striding the blast, or heaven's cherubim, hors'd
Upon the sightless couriers of the air,
Shall blow the horrid deed in every eye,
That tears shall drown the wind.

It is quite extraordinary. How on earth did those images come to his head?

I suppose he's thinking of the most innocent, and therefore most honest creature imaginable, the new-born babe. Pity as a total innocent. Heaven's cherubim,
heaven's little babes. They're going through the ether, around the world on
horseback, 'striding the blast', and they'll 'blow the horrid deed in every eye'.
These innocents, these children, will tell everyone the truth. And at that moment
he's feeling, I suppose, anything but innocent, anything but childlike. So Shakespeare's talking about the difficulty of being a grown-up human being. It's an
argument with himself for the audience's benefit, which concludes:

> I have no spur
> To prick the sides of my intent, but only
> Vaulting ambition, which o'er leaps itself
> And falls on th'other.

'It's totally wrong to do this, because it's impractical. Not because God tells
me I mustn't do it' – although of course that's in his conscience – 'But I won't
get away with it.' 'I have no spur / To prick the sides of my intent.' 'I'm not
really the man for this job.'

And then the spur walks in the door.

Indeed. And she reminds him how he's felt on other occasions when, of
course, it was no problem. 'What's the matter?' she says. 'We'll buy out the
media! We'll kill Rupert Murdoch! We'll have a reign of terror!' And that's
the only way he copes – he has a reign of terror.

Do you remember how she said 'We fail' – factual or incredulous?

I think she just said 'We fail' – plain fact. 'If we should fail, we fail.' 'But screw
your courage to the sticking-place, / And we'll not fail.'

What about 'Is this a dagger which I see before me?' [2.1] What was your reaction?
Excitement? Terror?

Well, confusion as to what the fuck was going on. Just to go back to the first
scene with the witches [1.3] when Banquo, looking at Macbeth, says:

> My noble partner
> You greet with present grace and great prediction
> Of noble having and of royal hope,
> That he seems rapt withal.

Macbeth's just standing there, thinking, imagining, wondering. And so I thought it was in his temperament to see the dagger. His imagination was so alert and alive, and he was so used to imagining 'If I do this, what will happen? If I send my forces down here, what will they do? Oh yes, they'll come... I see them coming over the hill.' When this man sees the dagger it freaks him out, but it also sums up everything he wants to do, it makes concrete what he intends to do. But of course he's puzzled as to whether it's there or not, and whether it's a good sign or a bad sign. 'Remember the witches? They vanished. Is this going to vanish? What does it all mean?' This is the same man who later sees Banquo's ghost. It's all of a piece. So I think when I came to this I didn't think 'How am I going to be frightened and what are my reactions going to be?' I just thought this is the sort of thing that happens to Macbeth. You asked was he terrified, was he excited, what was his reaction to the dagger? His reaction to the dagger is 'Is it really there?' That's what he's talking about. 'Is it there? Why is it there? What's the significance of it being there?' And of course it's upsetting to him... Is my 'heat-oppressed brain' making a fool of all the other senses...? It starts to freak him out... 'I'm not thinking properly... I'm not... *uuuhhhHHH!!!*' Finally he gets on top of it with '*There's no such thing!!!*' He banishes it and he's in control. Phew! He's himself again. 'Now I'm up for it! Now this part of the world is dead. The world's dead, yeah, and I'm gonna kill.' And he psychs himself up as he must have done any number of times before going into battle. And you know, the pity of Macbeth is that he spends his life killing people – that's his job and he's brilliant at it. It's what the state employs him to do. Is it any wonder that he can't cope with being a civilian? He knows you can't be a civilian and behave like a soldier. He's trying to reconcile those two things. Soldiers kill. It's what they are obliged to do. And the more they kill, the more successful they are, the more heroic. In civilian life, one mistaken murder can bring down horror and terror on a whole society. And he knows it, that's what's playing on his conscience. But it isn't an outward conscience of a god saying 'Thou shalt not kill', it's about what is practical in the world. If we start killing each other it would be mayhem.

But you do the deed. What about the change in Macbeth after killing Duncan? One of your reviews mentioned 'McKellen's study of evil bursting through a mask like a clown through a paper hoop'.

Blimey! Well, that was his or her reaction.

It's a positive thing to have said about you, isn't it.

As I said earlier, I'm not a great believer in evil, and I don't think Shakespeare is either, he spends his time in another place. He analyses what evil is, and discovers that 'evil' doesn't sum it up by any means. One word can't.

Is that when paranoia sets in?

He's spent a long time puzzling over whether or not to do it; he's listened to the advice of the witches and his own conscience and his wife, encouraging him to do it. But as he finally does it he knows that this is not his kind of killing. He's acting out of character. This is not the great guy who shouts 'COME ON!' and saves the nation. He's going in the middle of the night, nobody knows, he's not doing it with an army following him, he's on his own. He's behaving like the lowest of the low.

Killing an old sleeping king.

There you go, that's right. The man to whom he owed allegiance, the man on whose behalf he has done all these amazing deeds. Lady Macbeth is innocent of all these things, and is just caught up with the thought that 'All we've got to do is kill him! Slip him an aspirin, and it's ours!' It seems so simple because she's got no imagination. When later on she does have imagination, when she realises what's gone on, she goes mad. She's much more frail than Macbeth. Lady Macbeth as the strong woman is not what you think once you've seen the play all the way through.

So he realises that it's not his way of killing. You mentioned how the daggers rattled in your hands when you came out of Duncan's bedroom, having killed him [2.2]. He's hugely distressed, paranoid, he's not himself at all. Was that something which set in at that moment?

Well, he anticipated it when he talked about an 'assassination'. Macbeth is not an assassin. He is a professional soldier, warrior, athlete, who kills. It's his job. This is not of that sort. And he is as conscience-stricken as any of us would be if we were killing somebody, not because they deserve to be killed but because we wanted them out of the way. What's remarkable about this great man (and it is, as I said, a problem of the play) is that you don't see him on the battlefield doing these things. You see him going in and causing the easiest death he's ever accomplished in his life. The guy's asleep. Put a hand over his mouth, he can't speak, you kill him. What could be easier, you'd think, for the professional soldier? But no, it's the worst thing he's ever done in his life and he immediately knows it. She can't understand that. 'Come on! Be a man!!!' Well, he *is* being, of course. He's being totally a man.

Humankind.

Humankind. I always felt as I was playing it: 'I've never done this before. I've done all sorts of other dreadful things which society has sanctioned. But this...' Then suddenly 'Whence is that knocking?' No wonder it freaks him out. 'How is't with me, when every noise appals me?' *Me*, Macbeth! Oh, he knows he's betrayed himself. He already knows he's on his own. She can help clear up the muck, the mess. But from there on their relationship is over. The idea that Lady Macbeth has a scene missing, I don't know where that's come from. Judi was adamant that there is nothing missing. It's all there. You only have to add the dots together.

Shortly afterwards they all come back on and he says 'Had I but died an hour before this chance, / I had liv'd a blessed time' [2.3]. Does he mean it?

Yes.

Why does Lady Macbeth faint? Is he not doing very well? Is he overacting by any chance?

She thinks he is. He's getting a bit carried away with how well he's covering up. It's probably for her a mixture of things. He's going into it in far too much detail, he's indulging himself. 'Here lay Duncan, / His silver skin lac'd with his golden blood…' She knows what he's like, he's going to start saying '…and I killed him!' People who've been listening to this description will be thinking 'Why is the man not just crying? Why is he describing it all in such detail?' And as he describes it, maybe her own stomach is beginning to retch as she realises quite what she's done, at which point she faints. She probably takes advantage of her own feelings, which otherwise she'd keep in control, knowing that she'll become the centre of attention. So it's a mixture of things. But I suspect Judi would see that very much as the start of Lady Macbeth's inability to cope.

And they drift apart. Can you say a bit about the changing balance, of who needs whom?

He's got to get on with being King. He has to sort out his friends and colleagues in government, he has to make decisions. She's only the consort. What did she think was going to happen when they were King and Queen? They were going to go on royal processions around the place and go to premieres? What did she think was going to happen?

So he leaves her out.

Well, what time has he got? She's no help in a man's world, the royal world of being a king. Also he's got secrets from her that he isn't going to share. 'Our fears in Banquo stick deep' [3.1]. And the people he's now depending on for help are not his gorgeous, wonderful, loving wife but two fucking people who are labelled as murderers. That's what they do – they're not soldiers, they're murderers. I remember Olivier in this scene. He was all done up in horns and furs and stuff, but in this scene he was walking up and down with his hands behind his back. I'd never seen that done in a Shakespeare play, someone walking as if they were thinking! He was just walking up and down between these murderers, who were in the presence of the King. He was demeaning himself to their level. That's what his life's like now. He says to the murderers: 'Your spirits shine through you' – 'You're my sort of men!' But they're *not* his sort of men, they're murderers, they're the scum of the earth.

So he's a good actor?

He's sinking down to their level. Is it good acting, or is it just that's where he now knows he belongs. He's one of them. How could he talk about that to Lady Macbeth, who says 'Oh, we've made it, we've done it! My man!' She doesn't understand. The only people who understand Macbeth are the audience.

Did you get laughs in that scene?

I dare say, I can't remember.

Because it's fun to play.

Yes, lovely scene to play.

Less stressful than some.

Yeah. You're covering up the whole time. 'All the world's a stage, and all the men and women merely players.' Macbeth is an actor. But with soliloquies he doesn't act.

Were you the mysterious third murderer in the scene where Banquo is killed?

I was not.

It's sometimes done, isn't it. But it doesn't make sense, because later on he's not supposed to know, is he, that Fleance has fled.

That's right, yes.

How was Banquo's ghost done in the banquet scene [3.4]?

It was done the right way, the only way that makes sense, which is that he didn't exist. The text says: '*Enter the ghost of Banquo.*' Well, maybe that's how it was done originally, but the only person who sees the ghost is Macbeth. Nobody else does. If you want to have the ghost appearing onstage, everybody has to act that they can't see him. But we in the audience can see him, so what's wrong with all those people, are they mad? Macbeth then becomes the only sane, sensible person in the room. It's the absolute reverse of the situation. In fact there's no ghost, just as there was no dagger, they're in his imagination. Poor old Tony Hopkins had to have a dagger, there was one floating round the stage in that Michael Blakemore production. It was projected onto the scenery, and he followed it around trying to catch it. Well, there you go, how far can you get from the reality of the situation! No, the ghost is not there.

I read that you played the banquet scene with 'excellent mobility'.

Ha ha! Well, I knew exactly where the ghost was, and I could see what he was doing – scaring the shit out of me! Probably in that little space with the audience on three sides, Trevor encouraged me to keep on the move so they could all see my reactions. It was very extraordinary. I think I was smoking at the time, but there wasn't a single performance when at the climax of the epileptic fit, as it were (that's what it appears to be), snot wouldn't pour out of my nose. It was wonderful. I don't know how it happened. I've never been able to cry at will onstage, but I effortlessly, as in the video, couldn't stop snot coming down. I think that was pretty riveting to the audience.

Tasty!

It was probably something to do with the mobility and running around and deep breathing and stuff like that.

At the end of the banquet scene you say 'I am in blood / Stepp'd in so far that, should I wade no more, / Returning were as tedious as go o'er.' What was your attitude? Were you feeling regret or loss, a hardening, or what?

That's almost a direct quote from *Richard III*. It's just a great river of blood, and I'm halfway across, so I might as well go on. I think he tries to get some strength, some moral purpose out of saying 'I'm going to go on. Because frankly if I were to go back it would be just as bad as going on, therefore I'll go on.' He's just defining what his new situation is. He's on an inevitable path. It'll be painful and difficult, but he's going to do it and he's still dogged. Then Lady Macbeth says 'You lack the season of all natures, sleep,' which Judi used to do wonderfully, because clearly there was nothing *she* wanted more than a good night's sleep! She knew all about 'the season of all natures'. Macbeth replies:

> Come, we'll to sleep. My strange and self-abuse
> Is the initiate fear that wants hard use

'I can do this' – and finally, 'We are yet but young in deed' (meaning bad deeds). But that's not a completed blank-verse line, incidentally, it just ends dot-dot-dot-dot. And in the dots I dragged her on my arm, forward into the light. Next time you saw her she was going bananas.

Very dark.

'Oh, Macbeth,' you keep saying, 'Oh, don't, don't. Pull back, pull back, admit. Don't try and do more, you can't do it, you're not up to it, Macbeth. Nobody's up to it. Your wife's had it, all she wants to do is go to sleep.' But 'We are yet but young in deed' makes him feel a little bit more heroic, a little bit more man-of-action.

A friend of mine remembered a bit of business when you did up a whole lot of buttons down the front of your tunic. It seemed like a symbol of exclusion, wrapping something round yourself to exclude Lady Macbeth.

Oh yes, I hadn't remembered that.

Do you know when that was?

It was probably at the end of that scene. Yes, I think he'd undone it during the fit, and was getting himself back together. In case anybody saw him.

Almost like putting a plate of armour around yourself.

That's right, yeah. It's very interesting. The Birmingham fireman's jacket. I did a similar bit of business in *Richard III*.

Then you've got the next scene with the witches [4.1].

There's a wonderful speech which is full of his poetic imagination, apocalyptic again:

> I conjure you, by that which you profess,
> Howe'er you come to know it, answer me:
> Though you untie the winds and let them fight
> Against the churches; though the yeasty waves
> Confound and swallow navigation up

(Drown all those sailors)

> Though bladed corn be lodg'd and trees blown down;
> Though castles topple on their warders' heads

(People who are looking after them are going to be killed by the structures they are meant to be taking care of)

> Though palaces and pyramids do slope
> Their heads to their foundations

(And how difficult is it to pull a pyramid down?)

>   though the treasure
> Of nature's germens tumble all together
> Even till destruction sicken

(He imagines something even worse than destruction, which sickens it)

> answer me
>
> To what I ask you.

So now he's taking on the universe. But again there isn't a God up there. He's a man who can imagine the end of the world and say 'Let it come, but just tell the truth, just answer me. I will swap the end of human life in exchange for the answer to the question I'm going to ask.' Is it any wonder that seconds later he's seeing visions of past kings and all that? You don't need a whole Loudon Sainthill set with props and fancy costumes to convince you of what he's seeing. What he's seeing, he sees. But we don't see it. Any more than we see the dagger, any more than we see the ghost.

Then you have a long gap with Macduff's family being butchered [4.2], the England scene [4.3] and Lady Macbeth sleepwalking [5.1]. You come back [5.3], and again I'm quoting, 'a hollow man, empty, weary, flaccid, all hope gone'. Has he gone mad, is he mad yet? He says 'I have liv'd long enough.' Is he close to suicide?

I don't think he's up for suicide. The last time we saw him, after the witches, he hears that Macduff has fled to England [4.1]. Trotsky has gone to America. 'WHAT!!! Get him back! Kill his wife!':

> The castle of Macduff I will surprise;
> Seize upon Fife; give to th'edge o'th' sword
> His wife, his babes, and all unfortunate souls
> That trace him in his line. No boasting like a fool,
> This deed I'll do before this purpose cool.
> But no more sights.

Oh yeah, this is Macbeth! You think maybe he's going to be alright. Maybe just issuing orders and making commands, he won't have any more nightmares. Now he's a soldier again. Right out of character, he depends on what the witches told him, not on his own ability. But then later [5.3] he learns that ten thousand English soldiers are on the march. 'I have liv'd long enough' is almost thrown away. Then:

> my way of life
> Is fallen into the sear, the yellow leaf

(I'm in autumn)

> And that which should accompany old age,
> As honour, love, obedience, troops of friends

(Grandchildren and days out at the seaside)

> I must not look to have; but in their stead,
> Curses not loud but deep, mouth-honour, breath.

(Nobody respects me any more. I'm King but nobody honours me.) The next minute he's saying:

> I'll fight till from my bones my flesh be hack'd.
> Give me my armour.

So he's up and down.

He's volatile!

Yes yes, he's feeling it, he's feeling it. And he overcomes it, that's partly why we like Macbeth, because he does keep trying to call up his strength. And then he asks the Doctor to help him, like a shrink:

> Canst thou not minister to a mind diseas'd

(He seems to be asking about his wife, but he's asking about himself.)

> Pluck from the memory a rooted sorrow

(Four centuries before Freud, Shakespeare knew that the 'rooted sorrow' was the problem.)

> Raze out the written troubles of the brain,
> And with some sweet oblivious antidote
> Cleanse the stuff'd bosom

(Not the stuffed nose, the stuffed bosom!)

>   of that perilous stuff
> Which weighs upon the heart?

'Therein the patient,' says the shrink, 'Must minister to himself.' But Macbeth's reaction is 'Oh, fuck medicine, fuck you!' ['Throw physic to the dogs']:

>   I'll none of it.
> Come, put mine armour on.

So he keeps getting close to a sort of salvation, and gets good advice from the Doctor – and what a fantastic part the Doctor is. Have you played the Doctor?

Me? Not yet.

Later [5.5] he says:

> Hang out our banners on the outward walls;
> The cry is still, 'They come.' Our castle's strength
> Will laugh a siege to scorn

(It's going to be alright)

>   Here let them lie
> Till famine and the ague eat them up.

Were they not forc'd with those that should be ours,
We might have met them dareful, beard to beard,
And beat them backward home.

(That's what I used to do, that's what I can do! But then –)

— What is that noise?
— The Queen, my lord, is dead.

'Oh, I see, oh, I see. It's all over. She's died, I'm going to die, we're all going to die. This is nuts, this is nuts...' And, I don't know, he's almost waiting for it to happen. He's volatile. In our version he was besieged, surrounded by the armies.

Then 'Tomorrow and tomorrow...' Does 'She should have died hereafter' mean that she would have died anyway later on, or that she should have delayed it?

Oh, I don't know. A mixture of both. It could be either, couldn't it. It's 'Oh, she really ought to have died later on', or it's 'Well, if she hadn't died now, she would have died some time.' Hereafter, it's inevitable.

There would have been a time for such a word.

I don't know... 'Tomorrow'... maybe that's the word. 'Tomorrow, and tomorrow, and – ' (oh, fucking hell!) ' – tomorrow, / Creeps in...' and he's off!

Where does that all come from?

Well, that's his future. What is the future? It's 'Tomorrow and tomorrow and tomorrow'. I used to think when I was saying it, if you repeat a word often enough – 'tomorrow, tomorrow, tomorrow, tomorrow, tomorrow' – does it stop having any meaning? It must have been the first rap song! It 'creeps in this petty pace from day to day...' and I used to think 'Tomorrow, today, and all our yesterdays'. So it's about the future and the present and the past. And all our *future* tomorrows, todays and yesterdays – all in advance of the certainty that we're going to die. And the poor players strutting and fretting our hour upon the stage. I've analysed it into the ground, this speech. But the way I think it actually hits home to the audience, which makes it such an unbelievable speech, is this: what other writer would dare, at the moment of trying to understand the complexity of the character's fictional life, to remind the audience that there are such things as poor players that strut and fret their hour upon the stage? You'd think that's the last thing we should be considering. But no, because the actor can say it with total conviction. He knows what it's like to strut and fret his hour upon the stage and then be heard no more. And talking to the audience, I can say that with total conviction as Ian McKellen. If they're not buying the story of Macbeth, at least they cannot avoid the certainty that the man who's speaking these lines knows and feels what he's talking about. It's a complicated thing going on. It just seems that with her death (the woman he loved, who's been his prop and best friend and everything), he can't cope with life. Life is death. That's what it seems like at that point.

On 'I 'gin to be a-weary of the sun' you had a naked light bulb which swung around your head.

It was just on a wire, and I used to tap it so it would go to and fro, or sometimes it went round, depending on how I tapped it. That being the only light, it sent shadows and flashed into the audience's eyes as it did in Macbeth's eyes, so they had the sort of experience he was having.

You had a talisman from the witches that you re-examined in the light of the bulb.

Did I?

That's what I read. One of Nicol Williamson's puppets, perhaps?

I may have kept a doll, I can't remember.

What about the fight at the end? They didn't bring your head back onstage I imagine, did they?

I don't know. By then I was getting ready for the curtain call. But the death takes place offstage, which is presumably because Shakespeare wants the head brought back on. It's not an easy thing to achieve, but in an ideal production it's important. Macbeth has lived entirely *through* his head, or has tried to. It's that head that's been exploding, full of all these dreadful images and certainties and worries. And all he is at the end is the head. 'Look at that, look at that! That's where it all happened, that's what the play has been about.' I think that's why Shakespeare wants the head brought on.

Can you summarise Macbeth's journey? What does he lose?

I think his journey is of a man who starts at the height of success and achievement and morality, and his purpose gets distorted. His ambition betrays his better nature. There is a constant tension of trying to be like the man he was, in circumstances which don't allow him to be. And his fatal flaw, if you want to put it in practical terms, is that he shouldn't ever have wanted to be King, he should have stuck with being a soldier. He shouldn't have gone into civilian politics. I think that's as much the message of the play as anything to do with conscience. Because it's in so many of the plays, once those soldiers go into politics, they've had it. And the rest of us have had it. So it's a mighty cautionary tale. But as a study in evil, or whatever word critics might care to use, I think it begs the question of what *is* evil.

Was there anything in particular that you were most proud of in your performance?

I don't think so. But I haven't yet had any reason to change my view that one of the most important qualities a Macbeth can have is that he is a believable warrior and soldier, and at my age of thirty-seven that was just credible. It wasn't credible that I could be Romeo in the same season! But there have been other Macbeths whose soldierly qualities have been non-existent and ludicrous, and consequently you missed the plot. We start with the plot.

Would you like to say more?

Well, you know, I'm just giving a partial review of the whole production. What was good about it was not my performance, it was *everybody's* performances – and the fact that Harold Wilson could come and see the production and be most riveted by the character of Ross, played by Ian McDiarmid. He said 'I knew a man exactly like you in the civil service.' It's wonderful that one can make those connections. Shakespeare's writing about a believable society of civil servants and soldiers and royalty, and if you think it's just about a man in a kilt who doesn't get on with his wife, you're missing the point. The play is much more resonant than that. Imagine the despair at the end when young Malcolm stood there and said what he was going to do, with such clarity and lack of passion. This was the man who lied so convincingly to Macduff in the England scene, when he said he was acquainted with all the evils of the flesh [4.3]. He could describe them, he could imagine them vividly. And you think 'Oh gosh, here he comes, Mr Innocent, what are *his* demons like? What's the inside of *his* head like?' Macbeth is no more, but Malcolm's going to replace him. I think you feel that at the end of *Richard III*, in a way you don't feel at the end of *King Lear*. At the end of *King Lear* something has happened to those people. 'We that are young / Shall never see so much, nor live so long' [5.3]. A suffering has taken place which is beneficial somehow. I don't think there's an optimistic ending to *Macbeth* at all. It's chilling. There's a chilling pause while you're just invited to look at these frail human beings and think 'Oh Christ…'

Helen Mirren
on
Cleopatra

Antony and Cleopatra (1606–7)
National Youth Theatre
Opened at the Old Vic Theatre, London, in September 1965
Directed by Michael Croft, *Designed by* Christopher Lawrence
With Clive Emsley as Enobarbus, Timothy Meats as Octavius Caesar,
and John Nightingale as Mark Antony

Royal Shakespeare Company
Opened at The Other Place, Stratford-upon-Avon, on 13 October 1982
Directed by Adrian Noble, *Designed by* Nadine Baylis
With Sorcha Cusack as Charmian, Michael Gambon as Mark Antony,
Jonathan Hyde as Octavius Caesar, and Bob Peck as Enobarbus

National Theatre (pictured above)
Opened at the Olivier Theatre, London, on 20 October 1998
Directed by Sean Mathias, *Designed by* Tim Hatley
With Finbar Lynch as Enobarbus, Trevyn McDowell as Charmian,
Alan Rickman as Mark Antony, and Samuel West as Octavius Caesar

Antony and Cleopatra is Shakespeare's late tragedy, first performed circa 1607. The play is in part a sequel to *Julius Caesar*, charting the break-up of the Antony–Octavius–Lepidus triumvirate that ruled Rome following Caesar's assassination. However, the main focus is on Cleopatra's Egyptian court, where the central pair act out their tempestuous relationship. Admirers of *Antony and Cleopatra* praise its sublimity, its rich characterisation and gorgeous language. Shakespeare, typically, shows the mighty conflict between Egypt and Rome revolving around the relationship of two lovers at the heart of the action. Despite its epic plot, much of the play is domestic in scale. With their all-too-human tiffs and hysterics, the middle-aged couple represent a touching fragility at the centre of world politics.

Cleopatra is one of Shakespeare's most complex heroines. She has political nous, charisma, and an indomitable will. Her self-obsessed histrionics can provoke an audience to laughter, even to scorn. Yet both she and Mark Antony carry tragic grandeur. The doting Antony tells her she is a woman 'Whom everything becomes – to chide, to laugh, / To weep' [1.1]. She is described as a lustful gypsy, a slave and a whore. She is resented by Rome as the enchantress who has made Antony neglect his duties and become 'the noble ruin of her magic' [3.10]. She can, as Enobarbus describes [2.2], be awe-inspiring. When Cleopatra takes the stage she does so as a diva, likely to elevate any colour of emotion to the most dramatic and captivating level. At the end of the play the victorious Octavius Caesar intends to lead her in triumph through Rome. Her determination to thwart him by applying a serpent to her breast is perfectly in character.

I first worked with Helen Mirren when she was starting out at the RSC, and later as her Cardinal brother in *The Duchess of Malfi*. She has progressed spectacularly from 1960's free spirit to Oscar-winning Dame of the British Empire. Every other interview in this book focuses on a specific production. But in Helen's case it was more open-ended, as she has played Cleopatra three times. The last occasion was at the National Theatre opposite Alan Rickman. This was considered dream casting and the show sold out before it opened. But, strangely, the production didn't amount to the sum of its parts. They were described by one critic as resembling 'a pair of glumly non-mating pandas at London Zoo, coaxed to do their duty'. So it didn't seem a good idea to dwell on that version. Nonetheless, Helen is superb casting as Cleopatra, and it's impossible to imagine anyone better suited to discuss the part. We met in August 2009 in her dressing room at the National Theatre during her run as Phaedra.

Julian Curry: You've played Cleopatra three times. First for the National Youth Theatre, I think, when you were nineteen years old, fresh out of convent school.

Helen Mirren: Well, I was at college already. But yes, pretty soon after school.

It's a wonderful part, one of the great tragic roles. She's also dead sexy and she's funny, she's ruthless and vulnerable. It must be a treat to play.

Not necessarily because *Antony and Cleopatra* is, as someone called it, 'a sprawling whore of a play'. It's a great role in not a great play. It's a flawed play with some very great roles in it, Cleopatra being one, and Enobarbus being another. Antony's not such a good role. Octavius Caesar is another great role. But it's very, very difficult to make the play work. So it's not a great role in a great play, which is the ideal scenario.

Somebody wrote about your performance 'All the shifts from teasing tart to imperial rage, she makes clear, are evasions of the truth.' Does that ring a bell with you?

In terms of the performance?

Yes, what Cleopatra's playing at.

I think there are three different Cleopatras. There's the Cleopatra of real history, there's the Cleopatra of Roman history, and then there's the Cleopatra of Shakespeare. I was interested in marrying up the Cleopatra of real history with Shakespeare's Cleopatra. However, Shakespeare's Cleopatra does seem to owe a lot to the Roman version of history, probably more than to the absolute truth of who she was. But of course the real Cleopatra is so much more interesting than either Shakespeare's or the Roman Cleopatra. So I was always looking for ways to bring the real person into this rather fake person that Shakespeare presents.

He certainly seems to focus on the whore, the strumpet, Antony's 'Egyptian dish' [2.6]. These things keep being said about Cleopatra. Whereas in fact she was extremely erudite, wasn't she, and a very astute politician.

Yes, enormously. And not very beautiful at all, but incredibly clever. My sense from history was that in order to save Egypt she had to suck up to Rome, because she knew that Rome could annihilate Egypt, and had its eyes on Egypt because it was the breadbasket of the East. It was incredibly wealthy, especially I think in agricultural terms. So Rome wanted it, they wanted control of it. To try and maintain both her own power and Egypt's autonomy, I guess, she knew she had to kowtow to Rome to a certain extent, and seduce Rome – not necessarily sexually, but in every way possible. That was my sense about her. So she uses Rome, she used Julius Caesar as far as she possibly could, and then she used Mark Antony as far as she possibly could.

Enobarbus's famous speech 'The barge she sat in…' [2.2] describes an amazing piece of stage management, it seems – an absolutely dazzling set-up that she created.

And that she did do.

But that was before she first met Antony.

Yes.

So she set out to seduce him without knowing the man?

No, it's much more than that, much more than a seduction. It was a power struggle, that was the way I saw it. The whole point of that particular episode was Antony had gone to the marketplace or wherever. He'd turned up as the big powerful guy from Rome, to have a huge public meeting, expecting every-one to be there, and they didn't turn up because Cleopatra put on a parallel performance and said 'Guess who is the most powerful person in this coun-try? It's not you, it's me. I'm the person that people want to see, not you.' So it seemed to me, that was much more to do with power than seduction. And then of course, the power play continued because she – I don't like the word 'seduce' but I can't think of a different one – the following evening she showed her unbelievable wealth. She put on this incredible evening for Antony and his crew. And that also seems to be historically accurate.

You're talking a lot about the history that Shakespeare would have referred to. As far as the play itself is concerned, I like Enobarbus's line 'I saw her once / Hop forty paces through the public street' [2.2]. It sounds quite unqueenly, doesn't it, unregal. Did you enjoy playing that aspect of the character?

Obviously you try to act Shakespeare's Cleopatra because you're in his play, so you have to pay attention to his version of the character.

Was it a problem to act 'queenliness' – if you'll forgive the expression – when most of her scenes are domestic and intimate, and also when she's always being described as a strumpet, or words to that effect?

Well, whenever you play a queen you should never act queenliness anyway.

Where does the queenliness come from then?

It comes from how other people treat you. You never play it. It's everyone around you who plays it, and then that leaves you free to be whatever you want to be. The regality of the characters – or the *power* of the character, forget regality, you could be a Mafia chief or whatever – the power of the character is created by the way they're treated by people around them. You don't have to play it.

One of the alterations Shakespeare made from history, apparently, was to change her age. I gather she was twenty-nine in reality, but Shakespeare made her older. Do you know why that would have been?

Well, she wasn't twenty-nine when she died.

I'm talking about when the play started.

Yes, but when she died, she was in her late forties, maybe even in her early fifties, so I guess Shakespeare telescoped twenty years.

The play relies on strong sexual chemistry between the actors playing Antony and Cleopatra, doesn't it.

I don't know that that's true.

Do you mean it can just work with good acting?

No, it's not that. I don't know that their relationship is about sexuality anyway.

Don't you? Early on in the play, when he's away and she's pining, it seems that she can't think of anything apart from his cock.

I don't get the sense that the beginning of the play is about sex at all, it's beyond that.

Hmmm. Well, she's certainly listless and all she wants is news of Antony.

Yes, because when he's around, it's fun. She wants someone to play with. And I think it's, again, about power. Certainly, it's about a kind of love, which is different from sex. It's about a kind of a love, or a kind of respect, or a kind of mythologisation – loving the myth image in the other person. They love each other's myths as much as they love each other. They love the *idea* of each other as much as they love each other. So I don't think it has anything much to do with sexuality. I don't think they need a sexual chemistry. Antony's myth is very much involved with the whole Bacchus legend, in the real story of Antony and Cleopatra. It is hard for us to grasp, and I still don't really understand it. But at one point I think Antony declared himself to be a god in Egypt. He identified with the bacchanalian cult, and claimed the god Bacchus was his protector. And you remember when his power leaves him, and everything starts going pear-shaped, in Shakespeare it's Hercules, but originally it was Bacchus who was leaving him. That whole mythological side of it is very hard for us to get our heads around. But I do think it's the key to both of those characters.

And she identified with Isis, didn't she?

Yes, she did, and I believe she declared herself a goddess as well.

How serious was that?

It was possibly a necessary political move, in that Egyptian world, in order to keep control of the people. Maybe at some point you have to declare yourself to be a god, because otherwise they might rebel. I don't know enough about that. But I do think it's so much higher and more complex than sexual chemistry.

Antony is another towering legendary figure, seen in the play warts and all. It's a big-ger part than Cleopatra and a much more complicated character, but you hardly ever get a successful performance, do you?

No, it's so difficult, the language is so difficult.

Just that?

Mmm. Cleopatra's language is so simple. She's very, very accessible. She has moments of poetry, and when she does, the poetry's quite beautiful. But a lot of it is vernacular, which is very accessible. Antony, on the other hand, has these long and rather linguistically complicated speeches – it's a far more difficult role. And also he's a strong man, but he's a weak man. He's set up as a strong, great big hero, but all you ever see him do is behave in a weak manner.

And often quite a foolish manner.

And sometimes a foolish manner, so it's an horrendously difficult role, and I've never seen it successfully played.

Can you imagine ideal casting for Antony?

No, I can't. But it's not a question of casting really, is it. It's a question of an actor who can just somehow reimagine the role.

On the subject of staging and design, your second Cleopatra was for the RSC at The Other Place in the early 1980s.

Yes. That was terrific because it is a chamber play with a lot of small, intimate scenes and the battles happening offstage. So it was really great to do it in a small space and very simply. But at the same time it was maybe a little too limiting, because although you have all of these small, intimate scenes, the landscape is huge.

Then the third time, at the National, couldn't have been more of a contrast.

It was very, very decorative in the Olivier. And yes, it was the opposite.

From what you've been saying, I guess you reckon that the simpler staging is preferable.

Not necessarily, no, it depends how it's realised. In my experience it was just great to be able to play it so intimately. It's always much easier to work in an intimate space, especially with Shakespeare, because the physical and vocal requirements of filling a huge stage are massive, and then to try and make it believable and naturalistic on top of that is sometimes just too much. At least you could play the realism of it in a small space.

In The Other Place you were barefoot in a rather tatty lurex smock.

The costumes are always a problem with *Antony and Cleopatra* because the iconic look is such a cliché… the white pleaty dress…

False Egyptian wigs and hairstyles…

Yeah. And the minute that walks on the stage you go 'Oh God!' But then if anything else walks on the stage it's like 'That's weird!' So that's another problem with the play, trying to get it away from that sort of *Carry On Up the Nile* or *Carry on Cleo* look, but with something that's authentic and real. I think that's what the costume designer at The Other Place was trying to do.

So does it perhaps need a timeless setting that's neither quite then nor now?

Well, that's the other problem. It's a history play. It's about Antony and Cleopatra in Egypt, and the Battle of Actium, and Octavius Caesar. It can't be about anything else. It can be about power, and it can be about love. But you can't say this is about twentieth-century Britain, or Germany between the two wars or whatever, you can't do that. And that, I think, also makes it a very difficult play to do.

Somebody described the story of the play as 'the fall of a great general betrayed in his dotage by a treacherous strumpet'. But I don't suppose you'd agree with that, would you?

Well, I wish it was about that. But the betrayal is very ambivalent, as it is in history. No one quite knows why she fled during the Battle of Actium [3.10]. It wasn't a calculated betrayal, that's for sure. If it was some incredibly manipulative and clever game she was playing, there's no evidence of it. She doesn't betray him up to then, and that's the only moment you could call betrayal. Shakespeare's explanation was that she was scared and ran away. If you look at history there are lots of different explanations. One is that she didn't flee at all, another is that the wind changed and her ships were forced away. No one really quite knows what went down at that moment. But I think that's not what the play's about.

The very first line you speak is interesting: 'If it be love indeed, tell me how much' [1.1]. *For one thing, are you doubtful that it's love? And for another, it's quite steely, like the* *marketplace.*

Yes. It's very practical, so unromantic, that's what I love about that line. It's cynical, if you like, and it's clever. She says 'If this really is love – I'm not too sure it is – but if it is, how much do you love me?' He says 'There's beggary in the love that can be reckon'd.' And she says 'I'll set a bourn how far to be belov'd.' In other words, 'I'm gonna make a rule about how much one can be loved.' And then he replies 'Then must thou needs find out new heaven, new earth.' He's the romantic and she's the cynical one.

In the next scene, Antony says 'She is cunning past man's thought.' Enobarbus replies *'Alack, sir, no; her passions are made of nothing but the finest part of pure love' [1.2].* *Who's right?*

Oh, Antony, definitely... Actually I'm not sure... You know what? They're both right. And that's not a contradiction. She *is* cunning, and I think both in Shakespeare's play and probably also in real life, she *does* love him.

You certainly get that impression from reading the play.

Yes. She loves him. She knows him and understands him and loves him. She doesn't love him in a foolish, romantic way. It's a very wide-open, all-seeing love. Shakespeare doesn't go a lot into the myth-making that they both indulged in, the mythologising of themselves and then loving the myth in the other person, but there is a feeling of it in the play. However, I certainly think they did that a lot in real life.

How about this trickery that she gets up to in the next scene? 'If you find him sad, / *Say I am dancing', and then the reverse [1.3]. And then when Antony arrives: 'Help me* *away, dear Charmian! I shall fall!' She sounds more like a teenage brat than a mature* *woman at that moment. What's she playing at, do you think?*

She's just being Rosalind, who says 'When you are happy, I'll be sad. When you feel sad, I'll be happy.' I'll be totally contradictory. It's the only way to keep him interested in me. She's simply being Shakespeare's Rosalind.

She's more grown-up than Rosalind, isn't she? She's a good ten years older.

Rosalind is talking about the future, how she is going to behave if they ever get married. But I think that's Shakespeare's idea of how to have a successful relationship: to be completely contrary and difficult.

A bit of a tease.

Just very difficult.

After Antony gives her the news of Fulvia's death, Cleopatra was a widow by then, but there's never any mention of her marrying Antony, is there?

No. I don't think marriage was ever on the cards.

I'm curious to know why not.

I'm not sure.

Perhaps she could only marry one of her own brothers – that was the Ptolemaic tradition, wasn't it.

Yes, maybe that was it.

Going back to the famous speech, 'The barge she sat in…' [2.2]. You explained about the set-up and her appearance being more a political tactic than anything else. But I'm amused by the contrast with Shaw's Caesar and Cleopatra, *when she presents herself to Julius Caesar rolled up in a carpet, which couldn't be more unlike this.*

Historically, you're talking about, or Shaw's play?

Both.

Yes, absolutely. But she didn't present herself as such. Again, the history was complicated. It seems what happened was that there had been a coup by her brother/husband Ptolemy, her life was in danger, and she'd had to escape from Alexandria. Then Julius Caesar arrived with his army and threw out Ptolemy, and there were riots. She needed to re-enter the palace and meet Caesar but she couldn't do so openly for fear of her brother's spies, so she had to disguise herself, which is why she arrived in some sort of pile of carpets. I think that was the truth of it. Well, then they became lovers and Caesar helped murder her sister Arsinoe, and put Cleopatra on the throne.

I see. Interestingly different techniques, nonetheless.

But it wasn't different techniques, it was different circumstances, totally different circumstances.

Pragmatic.

Yeah.

'Age cannot wither her, nor custom stale / Her infinite variety' is another of Enobarbus's famous lines about Cleopatra. Does the 'infinite variety' make the core of the part at all elusive?

On the contrary, that's what makes it infinitely playable.

So you never felt 'Where is the centre of this character who is constantly kaleidoscopic?'

No. I felt her centre was pragmatic and practical. Everything is either a performance or a calculation of some sort. A manipulation of some sort. Again, I was always attempting to marry what I felt the real person was like and Shakespeare's version which, as I said, is kind of a fake thing.

Jumping on to the messenger scene, Act 2 Scene 5. He gets a rough ride. Seemingly you pampered him with cushions and drinks, before flying at his eyes with outstretched nails. Do you remember that?

Which production was that in?

The Other Place.

No, I don't remember that.

It's important that Cleopatra is really dangerous in that scene, would you agree?

When she hears that he's married thingamajig [Octavia], yes.

It's quite funny, I suppose, but also very dangerous at the same time.

Yes, absolutely. She's completely devastated, out of control. If there's any point where she's truly out of control it's in that scene.

From what you're saying, it isn't a lover's jealousy, but rather because she sees it as a political disaster – is that correct?

I think so, yes. Well, it's also lover's jealousy, because I believe she does love him. Certainly in Shakespeare's version she does. So it's a combination of everything: emotional jealousy and a panic about politics and power as well.

So you go through Antony's defeat in the sea battle at Actium in Act 3, and we talked about the mystery of why she ran away. Then they reach an extremely low ebb. They're very vulnerable, very raw. She says 'Pardon, pardon!' [3.11], and Antony replies 'Fall not a tear... Give me a kiss.' That's touching, isn't it.

Yes, it's lovely. After she's run away. Yes, absolutely. He understands. They know that they're screwed at that point.

Octavius attempts to drive a wedge between you and Antony, and sends the messenger Thidias [3.13]. You're invited to betray Antony, and the deal is that if you do so you can save yourself. Cleopatra says everything Thidias wants to hear. She's compliant, she says 'Oh, well, whatever you want, I'll do whatever you want.' Antony then comes in and finds the messenger kissing your hand and flies into a jealous rage.

Yes, right.

So again, is she being a lying pragmatist or is she being genuine, I wonder?

Well, I wonder too.

Eventually she manages to calm Antony down, and she's got a very interesting line: 'Not know me yet?', as if to say 'Can you really believe that I would betray you?' Do you, Helen, think she would betray him?

Yes, I think she would. If Egypt was at stake she would betray him. I think our country and our culture takes precedence over Antony. I do believe that. But who knows. With Thidias she's probably playing for time and using the tricks which always worked before – trying to manipulate or talk her way out of it.

After that scene, when Thidias has gone and Cleopatra calms Antony's rage, she again seems very genuine. No tricks, no wiles, no games. She seems a very different Cleopatra from the one we met in Act 1.

No, the same person, just a different side.

We see a different side of her, okay, that's a better way of putting it. Then Antony orders a last supper, as it were, to say farewell to his servants [4.2]. She asks 'What means this?' and then to Enobarbus 'What does he mean?' That seems odd, because on the surface, at least, the meaning's obvious. It feels as if there may be a gap developing between them.

Isn't that immediately before Antony's men hear this weird noise, and they think his protector Bacchus/Hercules is leaving him [4.3]? There is a side of him that Cleopatra doesn't and never will grasp, and that's his soldiering side – the Enobarbus side, the side that gets on well with men and goes off to the football match with them in the afternoon, his male-bonding side – that Antony obviously has in spadeloads. That's a side of him that Cleopatra will never be able to engage with, or understand, or be a part of. That's one thing that will always take him away from her.

That's followed by a switchback series of short scenes [4.4–4.8]. Your star seems to be in the ascendant when Antony is victorious in the next battle and re-enters the city in triumph.

Yes, a brief moment of contentment.

Then there's the next battle in which he is defeated, and he believes that you've betrayed him [4.12]. He rages at you again, and you try to pacify him, this time without any success. You go to the monument [4.13] and send a message that you've killed yourself [4.14]. I wonder what you hope to achieve by doing that. It has a disastrous effect, of course.

Who knows why. There are these occasional, so to speak, authentic moments in the play, and sometimes you think 'Well, why the fuck are they doing that?' because there's no proper explanation for it. I guess it's Shakespeare just using a little bit of history and throwing it in without any real psychological unpicking, if you like. I think Cleopatra did do that in real life. But exactly what the historical circumstances were, I can't now remember. And then Antony went off and tried to kill himself, botched it, and was carried to the monument.

So he comes at death's door to the monument and you have to lift him up, just you and the girls [4.15]. How did that work out?

That's always a tricky moment. Again, it's pretty extensively talked about historically, so apparently it really did happen. That scene is always difficult to achieve on the stage because Shakespeare gives it just to Cleopatra with Charmian and Iras. Probably in real life there were a load of other people in the monument as well. Also it's a very difficult moment visually – it always looks silly because you can never be high enough. Imagine a real Egyptian monument, a pyramid or something, it would be amazing.

After Antony dies, she has this very simple, desolate speech: 'What, what, good cheer! … Ah, women, women!' Little disjointed phrases, almost as if she's going slightly mad.

No, that's a very beautiful speech. I don't see it as going mad. No. It's just very natural. He does give Cleopatra fabulously naturalistic things to say and that's one of them – an incredibly realistic, Pinteresque sort of speech.

I was quoting from a critic who wrote 'She flirts with insanity.'

Never listen to critics.

Later she has another extraordinary speech, in the scene with Dolabella [5.2]: 'I dreamt there was an Emperor Antony…' She becomes ecstatic about the memory of Antony in a way that catches Dolabella completely off guard. You then get out of him what Caesar's real intentions are for you. I wonder how much you're planning to seduce him, as it were, and how much it's a spontaneous celebration of Antony.

I think the stuff about Antony is absolutely genuine. It's so beautiful. And again, that's where love of the mythology comes in. 'His legs bestrid the ocean...' That's a glorification of Antony, building him up into this absolutely monumental character in her mind.

So the fact that Dolabella is lulled into telling you the truth about Caesar's intentions is, if you like, an accidental by-product.

I don't know. Maybe. Maybe not. I hate making pronouncements about that sort of thing. Not just on Shakespeare, but certainly within Shakespeare anything's possible. I think the most interesting act in *Antony and Cleopatra* is the fifth act, which is so weird. It's so weird, but less so if you see Cleopatra in terms of somebody who's intensely practical, out for the survival of Egypt above all, prepared to do anything for that. I'm not saying the love for Antony is not genuine – the two are not contradictory, you can love someone but at the same time be utterly practical. But that last act is quite extraordinary; the lengths to which Cleopatra will go, first to save both herself and her country, and then later when she realises that's not going to happen. I think all of that is pretty historically accurate as well.

Her treasurer Seleucus comes on and says to Caesar 'Oh no, she's got twice as much money as is on this list. She's hiding half of it from you.' That turns out, again, to be very useful, because Caesar then believes you must want to live. I suppose a subtitle for the last act might be 'Will Cleopatra manage to outwit Caesar and commit suicide?'

Of course we know the answer to that, unfortunately, before the act begins.

But before she gets there, it seems as if she may have been caught out by Seleucus in a rather grubby lie. Or she may be playing a double-bluff, with his help. Do you remember which it was?

I always thought it was a double-bluff, deliberate. The way it's written is very sort of hokey. I suspect it was a double-bluff that also had its basis in truth – that they did want to keep half the money, hoping she might survive.

As Cleopatra prepares to die, she calls Antony 'Husband' for the first time: 'Husband, I come! / Now to that name my courage prove my title!'

Yes. United in death, married in death. I think the circumstances now give me the courage to come to you in death, to marry you in death.

Did you have a real snake?

I did, yes. We had real little adders. One night one escaped. I don't know if they found it – it might still be living in the bowels of the Olivier.

How do you think Cleopatra's feelings towards Antony change from start to finish of the play? Do they change?

I think if anything she feels more in love with him. At the end of the play she is genuinely in love with him, and I'm not too sure that she is at the beginning. Possibly. And that's really only happened, if it's happened at all, because of the march of circumstances and where it's brought them. She certainly throws her lot in with Antony in spite of the so-called betrayal of her fleeing at Actium, which is ambivalent even in Shakespeare's play. She definitely didn't flee straight to Caesar's camp and say 'I'm giving myself up. Come on, I'll get Antony for you.' She doesn't betray him like that. She has thrown her lot in with Antony and she is consistent with that. I think she thought Antony would win.

Do you see changes in Cleopatra during the course of the play? A journey, if you like?

No, not really. No. I think they are both people of circumstance. They're not psychological people. They're people of their moment in history, of what's happening today, right now. 'How do I deal with it, what do I do?'

So you don't really think of it as one of the great love stories – or I should say Shakespeare's play as being about a great love story?

No, I don't. I think that there is a love within it, definitely, but I don't think the play is about love.

Tim Pigott-Smith
on
Leontes

The Winter's Tale (1610–11)
National Theatre
Opened at the Cottesloe Theatre, London
on 18 May 1988

Directed by Peter Hall
Designed by Alison Chitty
With Eileen Atkins as Paulina, Sally Dexter as Hermione,
Shirley Henderson as Perdita, Basil Henson as Camillo, Ken Stott as Autolycus,
and Peter Woodward as Polixenes

The *Winter's Tale* is one of Shakespeare's haunting four final plays, often referred to as 'romances' or 'tragicomedies'. It tells the story of King Leontes' mistaken conviction that his best friend has slept with his heavily pregnant wife, and that she is about to give birth to a bastard. Insane jealousy takes possession of Leontes with startling rapidity. His inner turmoil is expressed in tortured and, at times, well-nigh impenetrably difficult language [1.2]:

> Affection, thy intention stabs the centre.
> Thou dost make possible things not so held,
> Communicat'st with dreams – how can this be? –
> With what's unreal thou coactive art,
> And fellow'st nothing. Then 'tis very credent
> Thou mayst co-join with something; and thou dost,
> And that beyond commission, and I find it,
> And that to the infection of my brains
> And hardening of my brows.

This speech has been called the obscurest passage in Shakespeare. He wrote very few stage directions, but clues for actors can often be found buried in the text itself. In this case its jaggedness can be said to reflect the character's torment and confusion. The actor playing Leontes has the challenge not only of negotiating his dangerously mad behaviour – he also has to make sense of such a text, and lead the audience through it. It is not an easy part.

A sixteen-year gap separates the bleakness of the first half from a comedic second half. The play concludes with a truly astonishing *coup de théâtre*, whose impact can scarcely be reproduced on the page. It is Shakespeare's most daring and moving reconciliation scene. I've been in *The Winter's Tale* three times, and have regularly seen casts of grown-up actors awash at that moment.

I first met Tim Pigott-Smith in 1971, when we toured together in Ian McKellen's *Hamlet*. In Vienna the actor playing Claudius was taken ill, and the as-yet-unknown Tim was his understudy. He seized his opportunity with dazzling assurance. Since then we've worked together on several occasions, twice with him directing me in works by Samuel Beckett. He was my first interviewee for this book. We met between shows in August 2006 in Tim's tiny dressing room at the Duchess Theatre, where he was playing the Bishop in Philip King's farce, *See How They Run*. It's three floors up, and seriously cramped, not at all the typical star dressing room. Tim told me that they forgot about dressing rooms when the theatre was designed.

Julian Curry: Where did you play Leontes, and when?

Tim Pigott-Smith: It was for Peter Hall in 1988, at the National Theatre. We did three late Shakespeares. I played Leontes in *The Winter's Tale*, Iachimo in *Cymbeline*, and Trinculo in *The Tempest*. All three plays were rehearsed at the same time, which is a recipe for a nervous breakdown. There's so much to do, even over three months, that you have long gaps between rehearsing scenes, so the schedule was very strenuous, very taxing.

This was the end of Hall's regime, wasn't it, his farewell productions as Artistic Director of the National?

Yes. It was great, because he wasn't doing masses of bureaucracy, he was very present. But towards the end he did start bringing in an increasing number of assistant directors, just because of the logistics. We opened in the Cottesloe with *The Tempest*, two weeks later *The Winter's Tale,* and two weeks after that with *Cymbeline*. And then a fantastic tour. We went to the Moscow Art Theatre, and the Tokyo Globe, and we played Tbilisi. Originally we were supposed to play in Leningrad, but that fell through, because the Rustaveli company from Tbilisi were playing in the very theatre where we were supposed to be. Somebody said 'Well, why don't we go to the Rustaveli Theatre?' which we did. But they hadn't looked at the map. Leningrad is six hours from Moscow by road, whereas Tbilisi is six days away, with the result that our sets and costumes arrived on the day we left Tbilisi. So we had to perform without them.

The building was good and watertight, was it?

We first played in the studio, a smaller space, and then we moved into the main theatre, which did leak rather.

I read that hailstones came through the roof.

Nice idea but no, that's embroidery. It's a fish story, that got bigger and bigger. But we had to use whatever was to hand. I remember, for instance, the only thing we could get to represent the monster in *The Tempest* was a sort of gaberdine – a bit of upholstery from an old sofa. I'll never forget hearing Georgian children just pissing themselves laughing at this weird object. We learned a great deal. It's the only time I've ever done a play when you start off in costume, and then perform in jeans and T-shirts, and finally play again in costume. It was a surprise to discover how much all the wigs and swords and everything had been slowing us down.

The Winter's Tale *has been described as 'the most intractable, broken-backed and diffi-cult of the late plays'. Would you agree?*

I would have said that, compared with *Pericles*, it's an absolute doddle, a hymn to being joined in one piece! No, it *is* difficult. And there's a huge chasm, isn't there, in between Sicily and Bohemia. But it seems to me to be an absolutely intentional one.

For a director I suppose there's a choice between trying to make it one homogeneous play and accepting that it's basically two plays – the first half being a tragedy and the second half a comedy – with a sixteen-year gap in between.

Yes, and the two come together in another world at the end. One of the things that made our life slightly difficult was that Peter saw Autolycus as a serpent in the Garden of Eden. He didn't really want him to be funny. So the relief that the audience usually get from that wild zany comedy in Bohemia was somewhat missing. Ken Stott was deeply loyal to Peter's concept. I said to him one day 'You realise there's a big laugh there,' and he said 'Yes, I know, but Peter doesn't want me to get it.' So it was quite dark, and actually that doesn't help. It just makes the play seem rather long. I think Autolycus is probably better being funny, for the audience anyway. Ken could have done it standing on his head.

Forcing it a bit, that.

Well, I think so, to suppress laughs. Those first three acts are so intense. There are just three or four laughs in them, you know, really good laughs, justified laughs, but not a lot else. But I think Peter was looking for a join. He was examining the late plays. He was looking very much at madness, and the things that afflict people later in their lives, desire for revenge. He pushed Michael Bryant to be a very, very angry Prospero. So I think he was search-ing for more than just a theme in one play – he was looking for what joins the three plays together. The sort of madness that afflicts Posthumus in *Cymbeline* when he thinks that Imogen's being faithless. And that afflicts Imogen when she thinks that Posthumus is dead.

And Leontes.

And Leontes, of course. In a way Leontes is easy, because it fits that theme, doesn't it.

This man, Leontes, is King of Sicilia. John Gielgud referred to him as 'a highly imaginative poetical tyrant'. Ian McKellen called him 'a soldierly type, ruling Sicilia as a one-party state'. Do you think of him as a soldier, or a statesman, or a poet, or what?

I don't think he's a poet. And I don't think he's a soldier. I think he's a king, in the respect of being tyrannical. He hates being contradicted. He can't stand it when people start telling him that he's behaving wrongly. There's a bit of business that Gielgud did when he plucked a hair out of Antigonus's beard on the line 'I do see't and feel't / As you feel doing thus' [2.1]. Clearly he does something to Antigonus. But it seemed to me that pulling a hair out of somebody's false beard was a less than felicitous piece of business. I didn't want it be weak, I wanted it to be shocking and surprising. So I did something extreme: I took out my dagger and cut his hand. 'Did that hurt? Of course it did. Well, that's how I feel my jealousy!' That was the context of it.

You had a kind of infantilism at the very beginning of the play. Messing about with kids' toys, not being quite grown-up, as it were.

Yes, I saw him as being quite immature emotionally. I seem to recall that I played quite a lot with Mamillius. We did little sword fights and things, stuff like that. I found that the best way to prepare for it was to fool around with Mamillius. To come onstage not anticipating the outburst at all, but having fun. At the beginning of the play you've had Camillo and Archidamus talking about Leontes and Polixenes, and their wonderful lifelong friendship, and the 'unspeakable comfort of your young Prince Mamillius' [1.1]. And then who comes on but Leontes' very pregnant wife, between the two friends. And the first thing Polixenes says is 'Well, I've been here for nine months now, I think it's time to go home!' And everybody in the audience goes 'Hello!' In that sense, Shakespeare is doing your work for you. It's extraordinary writing.

How was it set? What was it like to play on?

It was designed by Alison Chitty. It was pretty easy to work, with the exception of one very complex scene change. The centre of the stage was a disc. If you looked at it beforehand you might have thought it would be a revolve, but it wasn't, it was two discs that came up vertically. One came up from the back, and the front one dropped down, and they swapped over. You got a bald, bare stage to begin with, very austere – it meant that you could move on and off quickly, very little furniture. And then the central rotunda became green grass for Bohemia, a completely different look. But the scene change back from Bohemia into Sicily was always a nightmare. Indeed on the first night we very nearly had a disaster. Something went wrong with the mechanism. A stagehand was underneath, and there was one moment when he had to put his hand into a piece of revolving machinery, grab hold of a bar and pull it out. If he hadn't got it right he might have lost his arm. It was hairy. The guys were underneath the stage hammering rhythmically in time with the Satyrs' dance [4.4]. But it did settle down. What was so interesting was that we saved twenty minutes on each of the plays in Georgia, because it didn't seem to be a cluttered or a fussy set at all. And yet without it we lost all that time. We managed to keep quite a lot of the time off when we got back. The design worked tremendously well for the trial scene [3.2] in the Olivier Theatre. Peter's staging was very clever. Hermione was dead centre of the rotunda, and Leontes was sitting as if he was part of the audience, at the bottom of the central steps. So she could play right out to the audience as if they were all her judges. We did the same thing in the Cottesloe, but it worked better in the Olivier. And that staging was mirrored for the final scene [5.3], when she came on as the statue on a plinth, on runners, right into the middle of the stage. This meant that we were able to walk upstage of her, around her. It's difficult with the normal staging, when you often can't get above or behind her, because everybody's lines then have to be delivered upstage. They may have had the same problem originally, assuming it was staged in the inner room of an Elizabethan theatre. But the cleverness of Peter's staging was that the plinth just glided on with a curtain round it, which Paulina then opened. It was very effective.

What period was it set in?

Carolean. There was a very strong sense of period. Peter is quite rigorous about that. I think nearly all those plays which involve kingship need some sense of panoply. It's harder to catch in modern costume, that business of kingship. Trevor Nunn achieved it brilliantly, I thought, in the Kevin Spacey *Richard II* [at the Old Vic, 2005; see pp. 199–211], with all that ceremonial stuff at the beginning involving the lords and earls, and the King being elaborately robed. But it's tricky. As we were doing three of the late plays on this occasion, they were all staged using the same set with the disc in the middle. For *The Tempest* it was filled with sand.

How was your appearance?

I must say that my costumes and the look were really fine. For the first half I had a smashing wig. Period hair with locks, which made me look young. And when we came back sixteen years later I'd taken that wig off, and had a long extension that fitted into the back of my own hair. It was grey, and with my thinning scalp you got a powerful impression of a different older man.

Which seasons does the play cover?

I think it should be played through the four seasons. In fact we didn't quite follow this through. It's not particularly to do with Leontes, but in my opinion it is really important in the play. It's frequently done with the first scene in winter. You see snow falling, or people in big bearskins. But it seems to me that when Camillo says 'This coming summer, the King of Sicilia means to pay Bohemia the visitation which he justly owes him' [1.1], it suggests that we're actually in spring, rather than in winter. And when they ask Mamillius to tell a story, he starts off 'A sad tale's best for winter. I have one of sprites and goblins' [2.1]. It's often played as though it was winter at the time. But he doesn't tell a sad tale, he tells one of sprites and goblins. So I think the first scene should be set in spring. And then you get to summer when the emotion is at its height. Those acts take place in Sicily, with the volcanic passion erupting in that central, highly dramatic scene [3.2]. Leontes is mad and Hermione is dragged on trial. I always think she should be wearing something absolutely minimal, like prison clothes, with blood appearing on the front halfway through the speech. She's just had a baby in prison. If it was hot and summery that would be quite plausible. Then you have to play the sheep-shearing in autumn, when it is very specifically set. And when Hermione comes back at the end of the play, that would be the scene of winter. She would be frozen like a statue for the final scene, and there would be the promise of life to come with the thawing and reawakening of the statue at the end.

Peter Hall described the play as a fairytale. But the critics refer to a naturalistic frame-work, and to the poetic intelligence, clarity and precision of the performances. They also refer to blood being drained out by intellect.

I think because of the way we rehearsed, when we opened, the plays were a bit bloodless. I don't think that's unfair. It took me a good six weeks to crack how to take an audience through Leontes' journey, which is not easy. It's not sym-pathetic. And Peter had a specific image, that the opening of the play was a sort of paradise. You get these two old codgers who come on and say 'Oh, it's absolute bliss. Nothing can possibly go wrong in this wonderful world here we have, between these two good old friends.' And what goes wrong? *PPPPPPGGGGGGHHHHHHHH!!!!!!!! [Making a massive explosion noise.]* Peter decided that the volcano was an important metaphor. I'm sure it's set in Sicily for that reason. The volcano would spout, as it were, on the half-line 'Too hot, too hot!' [1.2]. He's very suddenly deep into jealousy, and the scene just goes off on two wheels. It's an astonishing moment. Very tricky. The earlier stage direction *'Leontes draws apart'*, when Polixenes and Hermione are talking, is not a First Folio instruction. If you do it, it's almost impossible to keep what Leontes is thinking from the audience, which pre-empts the moment. But if you don't do it – if he just stands and listens to Polixenes and Hermione – then when he turns to the audience and says 'Too hot, too hot…!' it really is a huge shock. It took me a long time to learn how to do that so it didn't blow the audi-ences out of their seats, and make them think 'What's going on here? Why's he so upset? I don't understand this at all!' Sometimes an ambassador comes in with a clipboard, and Leontes signs a few papers, or he distances himself and becomes preoccupied in some other way. It's more difficult then for them to read, and I think you should play it like that. But it's a major problem of the part, to take the audience round that corner.

The verse in that opening scene is very fractured.

Fractured to hell.

Extraordinary jagged rhythms. And a total contrast to the last act. Did you find it helpful, that jaggedness?

Yes. But the problem is that you want to keep the jaggedness, but somehow explain what on earth he's talking about.

More so because Peter Hall, I believe, is very keen on end-stopped delivery.

Yes. That's an expression I don't terribly like, actually. I think, to be fair to Peter, he only uses it out of a desperate dogmatism. Because so few people do what he wants. I think what he would say is 'Why is the end of the line where it is? Examine that, and answer that for me in the way you deliver it, and I'll be quite happy. It's either there to be emphasised because it's at the end of the line, or it's at the end of the line in order to be emphasised before leaping on to something more important at the beginning of the next line.' He was less dogmatic with me because he knew that I respected the system. And in general I found it hugely helpful. But Peter's notion of how to do 'Too hot, too hot!' was based on the fact that it's a half-line pick-up. Hermione: 'Th'other for some while a friend.' Leontes: 'Too hot, too hot!' Doing that in Peter's way, it's not easy to get the audience onside. Because their initial reaction is 'Jesus, wow, that volcano's blown!' Some editors even think it cannot rationally be fully explained. They believe Shakespeare's writing somebody who suddenly starts talking poppycock. But as long as you've got the audience inside your head, you can take them on that journey too.

At the outset, Leontes seems very solicitous with Polixenes. He tries over and over again to persuade him to stay. Do you think it's a subterfuge to test Polixenes? Or do you think it's genuine friendship, which suddenly at that moment turns?

I explored the meaning of 'tremor cordis'. Leontes says 'I have tremor cordis on me: / My heart dances,' a moment later. I discovered a disease called myocarditis. It's a disease of the heart, but it afflicts the brain for about three months. And it can come on instantaneously, without warning, and go off the same way. When I read about it I thought 'My God, Shakespeare knew somebody who'd had this! He'd seen it.' You know what a blotting-paper sort of a man he was. He sucked in any experience. Maybe he'd seen it twenty years earlier, and this is how it came out. That's how I played the part. I didn't try to justify that moment of explosion at all. It was just something that happened to him. And it does go off exactly like that when you're playing him.

The other major jealous part is Othello. But he has much more motivation: he's got Iago to deceive him. And it's a much more gradual thing. Whereas Leontes is on his own, and plunges straight in at the deep end.

It seems to me that the real play about jealousy is, as you suggest, *Othello. The Winter's Tale* is always considered to be a play about jealousy. But in fact it's much more to do with madness. How does a country behave, how do a group of governors and people behave when the King has gone mad, but is convinced he's completely sane? The only person who has the courage to tell him is Paulina. She just whams in with the truth: 'YOU ARE MAD!' [2.3] and he can't take it on board at all. It's not until the death of Mamillius [3.2] that some sanity creeps in. I think the element of it being a fable, a winter's tale, an old folks' tale, if you like, is appropriate. It's in that sort of spirit. You don't have to justify something terrible. The wolf comes out of the undergrowth – WHOOSH!!! There he is – Bang! But it was useful to be able to justify to myself what was happening, with a medical explanation. The problem is that the irrationality of it has absolutely no significance for the person who's suffering.

You had wonderful reviews. But they do refer to extremes, to a madness of jealousy. They found you almost unacceptably mad, sometimes.

Yes, you see I thought he had gone off the scale. I thought he goes completely mad for three months. You watch people trying to deal with it, and nobody can. He just will not be gainsaid. In Act 2, Scene 1, Leontes says 'There may be in the cup / A spider steep'd...' – you're alright until you've seen the spider, but once you know it's in there you can't drink. Later in that scene I invented a piece of business that I was proud of. He's gabbling away to the lords about Hermione and suddenly in the middle of a speech he says 'Oh, I am out!' – which was the Elizabethan for 'I've dried... I've forgotten my lines!' I had a goblet of wine, and when I got to that moment I looked in the goblet as if the spider was actually there. I threw it on the floor, and stamped on an imaginary spider, and then said 'Oh, I am out!' – because he never finishes that sentence. So I played him really extremely mad. Well, he was having hallucinations. And when the King does that, the question is 'What do we do?' It's a bit like *The Madness of George III* – 'We've got to persuade him that he's mad, and every time we go near him, he just goes berserk, he cuts this guy's hand, he's irrational!' 'Tyrant' is a word that you could use, but I think he's just a sort of child-king. I don't think I'm very good at talking about this, because I can't rationalise it. There's something about the part that you can only make sense of in performance, and it took me different ways each time I did it. I think the person who's really mad is the one who hands you a teacup and says 'Hold my crown for a minute, will you?' That's real madness. And when I got it, I didn't have to work very hard at it, I didn't have to do any sort of mad acting. People just had to be really careful, because they thought 'Jesus, he's going to go in any direction!' And that becomes really quite potent.

There are other things that happen very suddenly. The dispatching of Cleomenes and Dion is announced out of the blue – seemingly there's no premeditation. Likewise, after the death of Mamillius, when the Oracle says that you've made a terrible mistake, you're immediately totally contrite.

Exactly.

From one extreme to another. The whole thing's turned on its head.

I think that's partly why I saw him as childish, just to help me play it. What he learns in the next sixteen years from Paulina is some kind of emotional maturity, and growth into adulthood. So at the end of the play there's a possibility that he will be able to repair with Hermione the appalling damage he's done.

It's remarkable that even when Leontes is talking about dashing the baby's brains out, I'm not sure that we ever quite lose sympathy with him, do we? In Act 2, Scene 3, with the baby there onstage, he says 'The bastard brains with these my proper hands / Shall I dash out. Go, take it to the fire…' It's an escalation of the violence and madness of the early scenes.

I think that's where I went wrong to begin with. I played it so truthfully, without giving any thought to the audience, that I did lose sympathy. Their reaction was 'This man's just mad, he's crazy, it's horrible. It's infanticide, he's gone barmy.' So it's a question of letting them know 'I'm not really mad, this is just something that's happening to me, and you've got to stay with me for a bit.'

After that, did you find it a problem getting the audience back in Act 5?

Act 5, Scene 1, which is his first scene after the long gap, is a great scene in terms of rhythms and the subconscious. You find him with his two ministers, a changed and calmer man. Paulina is talking about how he must carry on preparing himself. I played quite a lot of that scene with something like a prayer book. It set the notion that Paulina had been retraining him in a spiritual way during those sixteen years. But you only have to look at the structure of that scene on the page and listen to it and simply say the words. We played it one day in rehearsal quite early on, when we were newly off the books and not doing very much, and Peter came up to us in tears and said 'That was completely wonderful. You don't need to do anything more.' That's the impact of the verse. It's the most powerful scene I've ever played in. I'm very rarely completely submerged by the power of a play or a scene. Maybe a moment will suddenly swell up and take you, and then you become the performer again and think about technique or whatever – a weakness in my acting no doubt. But in that particular scene, on a nightly basis, something extraordinary seemed to be happening within the play. My God, there's such a wonderful line: 'Stars, stars' – he's talking about Hermione's eyes – 'And all eyes else dead coals.' Where did the old boy get it from?!

Talk to me about the last scene [5.3].

I think it only really works when you catch a slightly religious sense, a feeling that you're in a very hallowed space. Paulina has a line about it. 'If you think this is black magic that I'm working, then please leave.' It should be the opposite of that: holy magic. It was very beautifully lit, very atmospheric. I'll never forget one night when we were performing in the Cottesloe, and there was a blackout over the whole of Waterloo. One of the actors, who was about to come on and describe the statue by Giulio Romano, suddenly found his dressing-room corridor in complete darkness. He had to feel his way down three floors and along to the studio, and missed his entrance. But it meant that we played the last scene with the statue entirely in candlelight. And of course it was absolutely gobsmacking. Because the point about candlelight is that it flickers. In that context, your vision is much less clear than even in dim electric light. It was a phenomenal experience to play that last scene just with two huge candelabra. They were part of the set-up anyway, but much more effective on that one night when they were all the light we had. In any case it was always lit with that feeling, dark and mysterious and sacred. I did the play later on radio, playing Polixenes. It was a pretty good production, but we failed to catch that atmosphere. Therefore it came across as being a little bit mundane. Peter was incredibly fastidious about the verse in that scene, which is quite intricate, lots of little pick-ups. He created a very holy, fragile atmosphere.

There's a photograph of you holding a candle, but that was always part of the action, was it? [see p. 185]

Yes. It gave me the idea that maybe Shakespeare got the inspiration for the play one day when he was watching some performance at the new indoor theatre, which had just opened in Blackfriars. He saw an actor standing, say waiting to come on in the candlelight, and suddenly thought 'I haven't seen him move for several minutes – he's like a statue. That's not a bad idea, I could make something of that. I could bring a statue to life!'

How complete a coming together was there at the end?

We played the ending quite unresolved. One or two people got upset by that, they wanted it to be more positive. But we thought that quite a lot of china would need to be thrown around the kitchen before they really come to terms. 'For goodness' sake, how many *more* times are you going to bring up Mamillius? Will I never be allowed to forget!' It's a huge thing.

There tends to be some form of redemptive journey in many of Shakespeare's plays. But I suppose you're suggesting that in your case it's more complete for Leontes – maybe Hermione wouldn't find a resolution quite as easily. She'd be the china-thrower?

Yes, it's for her to forgive. It's interesting that in the last scene Hermione doesn't speak to Leontes. Her speech is reserved for the daughter. Leontes says 'Oh, she's warm!' so they appear to be reconciled physically. But she doesn't say 'I've been waiting sixteen years for this moment, how good it is that we can be together again.' Nothing is said, it's left unresolved. And even in Leontes' last speech you get the feeling that it isn't knotted up all neat and tidy. Have a look and see, but I don't think the play ends on a rhyming couplet. There's something in there that made us feel it should be hovering. But you have to find a balance in the playing. If we got it wrong and it was too cold, which I think it was when we opened, they really thought 'Well, why on earth have we been sitting here for three hours!'

It needs some kind of resolution.

It does. An audience needs a resolution, whether you do or not. You've got to find a healing, a positive, a step forward. This is a play at the end of which Paulina suddenly gets hitched up with Camillo, somebody she's hardly spoken to. Her husband's been eaten by a bear, and she gets fobbed off with an old widower. We're not in the real world, are we, and you do need to offer an audience something. 'They're going to be alright' is what the audience need to feel. It's a bit like *Measure for Measure* in that respect, a problem play. What are you going to do? Are they going to walk off separately, or are they going to be married? An audience likes to feel they're going to go forward together.

Looking back, do you remember a particular moment when you got it, as it were – when you found your performance?

Rehearsal was very fractured, as I said. I had one terrible day working on Act 1, which I knew backwards, but I had to take a prompt on every line. Next morning I got in the car and thought 'I could just drive off in the other direction, get out of all this, and save myself the trouble.' It was very, very, very taxing. But there was a glimmer some time later when we ran the first three acts. I realised then 'I've got something together, a journey that I can hang on to. I've found a character that I can develop, an internal story that I can share with the audience.' That must have been in about the third month of rehearsal, quite late on. It was very difficult. Sometimes we didn't rehearse a scene for two weeks.

The subconscious is helpful though, isn't it.

Drip-feed time is very useful, yes. But the trouble is you have two other drip-feeds going on at the same time. Funnily enough I think I really found it in Russia, on tour. It was somehow easier that you had another perspective on the audience. You knew that they would read you in a slightly different way, which was a release. And when we came back into the Olivier, I found that very liberating too.

You started in the Cottesloe before the tour, and ended up in the Olivier when you returned.

Interestingly with *Cymbeline*, which Peter did as a huge production, it was easier to be epic in the Cottesloe than it was in the Olivier. Something about the size of the theatre diminished the size of the play. And I thought almost the reverse happened with *The Winter's Tale*. Peter staged the first scene very intimately. We didn't have a lot of courtiers and suchlike. When there's nothing else, it's wonderful. You could play it big, because you'd got this big space.

Was there anything in particular about your performance that you feel specially proud of... or specially unproud of?

I think I was on to something quite unusual in interpreting the physical affliction 'tremor cordis' as being related to a mental breakdown.

Myocarditis.

Yes. It came on, and it went off, bang, like that. We had a poor man in the company at the time who suddenly became really unwell, and it turned out he'd forgotten to take his medication, all he needed was a pill. He took one of his tablets and he was fine. It was really quite bizarre, and it completely changed my notion of mental health being solely a mental problem. I think probably a large portion of it is physical. People with manic depression now, who have huge highs and huge lows, take medication – which reduces the height of the highs and the lowness of the lows. It's fascinating, and in that respect Shakespeare was hugely ahead of his time. I often think playwrights were early psychoanalysts. But again, I'm convinced he'd seen it. Poached it from somewhere, and put it together with *Pandosto* and the candlelit statue. He was so voracious in the way he just nicked ideas and pulled things in! I reckon actors would also make wonderful counsellors, because that's our job, working with the mind. And we're relatively sympathetic people. No, I was proud of the interpretation. Stanley Wells reviewed it, and said it was the most original Leontes he'd seen since Gielgud. Even to be mentioned in the same breath as the mighty man, I felt I'd achieved something. But I was a little bit callow in my notion of how to put it across. I only learnt how to do it, really, through failing.

And touring, doing it in other countries for people who spoke different languages.

Having the freedom of playing it in front of people who didn't really understand what was going on!

What do you think is Leontes' journey through the play?

From childish irrationality towards emotional maturity at the end. I don't think it's particularly plotted by Shakespeare. It's something that each actor has to find his own ladder to explain, and that was mine. Perhaps it has something to do with my own feeling about myself, involving the fact that it took me a long time to overcome a sort of callow emotionality.

You'd like to direct this play one day, would you?

Oh, I'd love to. I'd love to have a go at it. I usually grab any opportunity to see it, because it's such an extraordinary play. I saw a wonderful production at my old school, funnily enough. On the first night the bear's costume didn't turn up, so the boy playing it came on wearing a fur coat backwards. Didn't matter at all! I have a lot of ideas up my sleeve as to how it might go. My Bohemia would be raucous and hysterical. I've seen many fine productions, one of which had millions of sheep, which was terribly funny. And then that ludicrous one that you were in [RSC tour, 1984], when the satyrs had enormous pricks which they banged against each other. It was fabulous, hysterically silly. I seem to remember you turned up at the sheep-shearing as Polixenes in a pair of little black Beckettian glasses. It was very droll. Bohemia's full of narcotics, it's set up in the first scene when Archidamus says: 'We will give you sleepy drinks...' I suppose that was part of the pleasure of the famous white production, when Bohemia was a sort hippy land and you got a sense that everybody was on dope. It was a Trevor Nunn production – oh, it was wonderful! The only thing that was bizarre about it was that Judi Dench doubled Hermione and Perdita. Which is fine except for the last scene where you have both characters onstage at the same time.

How did he manage that?

He had a double. But that weakened it, because you knew one or other of them was not Judi. As I said before, Hermione's speech is reserved for Perdita at the end. She doesn't say anything to Leontes, which is very important.

Kevin Spacey
on
Richard II

Richard II (1595–6)
Opened at the Old Vic Theatre, London
on 4 October 2005

Directed by Trevor Nunn
Designed by Hildegard Bechtler
With Oliver Cotton as the Earl of Northumberland, Peter Eyre as the Duke of York,
Julian Glover as John of Gaunt, Ben Miles as Henry Bolingbroke,
and Genevieve O'Reilly as Queen Isabella

Richard II is the first in Shakespeare's great cycle of English history plays revolving around the Wars of the Roses. The play has the symmetry of a see-saw, with Richard falling as his cousin Henry Bolingbroke rises. Richard starts as King of England, halfway through he is deposed, and at the end he is assassinated. Conversely, Bolingbroke is banished at the start. He returns to lead a rebellion, deposes Richard, and by the end he has been crowned King Henry IV.

The fundamental differences between the two men provide much of the play's tension. Richard has a medieval belief in the divine right of kings. He considers that he is chosen and guided by God. He is sensitive and poetic, but arrogant and incompetent as a ruler. Bolingbroke represents a more modern view of the throne. He is a pragmatic man of action who is popular with the people and acquires de facto power. Richard expresses himself with dazzling eloquence, using flowery, metaphorical language. Bolingbroke employs more plain, direct speech.

This production, directed by Trevor Nunn, opened at the Old Vic Theatre in 2005. It was revived the following summer for a festival in Germany. Several parts were recast, and I took over the Duke of York. I was thus able to enjoy Kevin Spacey's performance at close quarters. It's not always a happy experience to take over from another actor, but on this occasion it was fine. The production was so clear and strong that I felt as if I was riding in a Rolls Royce. The show was a tremendous success. Every performance was packed and the entire week was a joy, except for the Saturday matinee. It was the last match of the football season. Spurs needed to win at West Ham to clinch fourth place in the premiership, and qualification for the European Championship. However, news reached us before the curtain went up that no fewer that fifteen members of Spurs' squad had, most mysteriously, gone down with food poisoning. We lost the match 2–1 and the dastardly red shirts of Arsenal usurped fourth spot from the valiant white shirts of Tottenham.

They say 'If you want something done, ask a busy person.' I wasn't sure whether Kevin Spacey would fancy fitting me into his tightly packed schedule of administrating, acting and directing at the Old Vic Theatre, on top of his career as an international film star. But as it turned out he was entirely amenable. We met in his dressing room at the theatre in 2008 and talked for an hour before he had to go down onstage for the pre-show warm-up, prior to his performance that evening in David Mamet's *Speed-the-Plow*.

Julian Curry: I believe your first Shakespeare role was a messenger.

Kevin Spacey: In *Henry IV, Part 1*. I played the guy who comes on and says – I think it's something like four lines – 'These letters come from your father… He cannot come, my lord; he is grievous sick…' [4.1].

Good heavens! [Kevin did that with remarkable, highly authentic-sounding, olde Eng-lishe pronunciation: 'lord' became 'larrd' and 'grievous sick' was more like 'greyvus sack'.] You later played Buckingham opposite Al Pacino in Looking for Richard, *his film about* Richard III. *But this was your first Shakespearean lead on stage on either side of the Atlantic, is that right?*

If you don't count monologues and performances with Shakespeare in shop-ping malls as a young lad.

Why choose Richard II*?*

Well, Trevor Nunn and I chose it together almost by accident. We began talk-ing right away when I knew I was going to come and run the company at the Old Vic. I wanted to tackle Shakespeare but I didn't know what or when. I've always been encouraged to play Iago or Richard III. But I was a bit reluctant to do what might be the obvious, or perhaps perceived as the thing that would come easy. And I remember we were sitting at dinner one night, I think it was just as he was in rehearsal for *Hamlet* with Ben Whishaw. *Richard II* was always in the mix, but sort of down the list, and he said 'You know, I've never directed it.' And I replied 'Well, that's the one we should do! For God's sake, let's have an experience where we both discover a play for the first time, rather than I'm your fourth Henry V or your second Richard III. Let's do something you've never done.' So in a way it just fell to us that in all his seventeen years at the RSC and his time at the National he'd never directed it.

I don't imagine the accent was a problem, because I know you're a famous mimic. You can take off Judi Dench and Katharine Hepburn, among others.

I was nervous about it though. The truth is that with imitation in a form like high comedy, or sitting on a chat show and doing Clint Eastwood, it's very easy to make it work and get a laugh. But to sustain the King's English through a three-hour production – standing onstage with twenty-six actors who've been trained in the craft and who have much more experience at it than I do – was daunting. It was incredibly important to me to achieve it, and it was a deal-breaker for Trevor. 'You have to be an English king,' he said. 'You must speak the King's English.' Normally, when I go into rehearsal I don't learn the lines beforehand. I like to discover the play with the company, because I think there's always a danger of not only learning the lines but getting a fixed idea of how to say them, if you're on your own. But in this case I was off doing a film before we started rehearsal. I was away for six weeks, and in that time I learned the first three acts, then I learned the rest of it while we were in rehearsal. I felt that since the language would be so new for me, I didn't want to be thinking about what word came next, I wanted to be working on what the word meant, and what was behind meaning and double meaning. So I came more prepared in the sense that I knew more of the play on the first day of rehearsal than I normally would have, because of the fact that I had this other thing to achieve, which was the sound.

Did you have an accent coach?

I did. Yes. A very good one.

You won the 2005 Critics' Circle Award for the Best Shakespeare Performance. And you received it with: 'This is from the critics, right?', which got a nice laugh, as you had been quite savaged for some of the earlier shows at the Vic. Can you describe the production and the set?

Trevor wanted to modernise the production. And he felt that although it's perceived as a history play, it really is a tragedy. He wanted to set it in the Houses of Parliament, in the sense of them being the centre of power, to update it in fleshy ways and scenic ways, and to introduce the media as an important element in the piece. Therefore you had cameras and television screens and you had boom microphones. And John of Gaunt's speech, for example, instead of being a soliloquy in a room with twelve people, was done on television. And sections of it were repeated again and again throughout the play. So in that way, Trevor was carving out how politicians and those in power use the media to influence the public. And we can see how easy it is to manipulate, to put across your point of view. You can have half the country for something or half the country against, depending on how you use the media.

We were wearing Armani suits. Richard II was known for being rather fashionable. He liked to party and enjoyed being surrounded by young and lovely things. Whether he was homosexual or not is unsure. Certainly in history it's often referred to in that way, and there were implications of it in this production. There was this decadent, privileged world that Trevor wanted to illustrate, the only thing that Richard himself had experienced. He'd never known anything but being King. Probably was raised by nannies and mentors and teachers, and didn't have a great relationship with his own father and mother.

I think what was exciting about the production, and one of the reasons it was received well, was because it became very immediate, particularly for a younger audience. Even if they didn't understand every word, they got into the play in a more direct way. Nonetheless, it began with pomp and circumstance. I thought Trevor did a very clever thing. Because it was my first major Shakespearean role, and it was at the Old Vic, he actually showed Richard being robed and crowned and becoming King in a four-minute sequence of pomp and circumstance. I felt very elegant and majestic, huge. I can't remember the music that was used, but it was quite extraordinary.

It was Handel's Zadok the Priest. *In stereo – very loud!*

That's right. We did a very formal procession, and I went passing through all the lords (dressed, incidentally, in the same ermine that they wear to this day). And by the time I sat on the throne, which was brought in behind me, I think the audience assumed it was going to be a traditional production. Then suddenly, everyone was wearing suits and ties. And they went 'Aha!' But they had witnessed the King being crowned. Whether it's a daily exercise, or only happens when he's going before the lords, they had witnessed it. It's not in the play of course, it was an invention of Trevor's. But I thought it was a very clever way to establish that I was the King before a word had been spoken.

There were some critics who were worried by the modernity – mobile phones and Queen Isabel being snapped by a fashion photographer and so on. They thought that in a play about the divine right of kings, and the monarch as God's anointed representative on earth, it didn't sit properly. Did you feel it worked?

I felt it worked fine. I think the great thing about Shakespeare, or I would say any playwright who continues to survive, is that the plays are elastic. How many countless productions have we seen of Shakespeare's plays that don't work as a whole? There may have been a few who had niggling problems about this, that or the other. But I think as a whole the production did work. It was primarily embraced. When they're performed well these plays are strong enough to survive any concept, even a bad one. Because they don't go away, they keep coming.

One critic wrote 'The play works inversely as a political icon searching for an escape through self-expression.' What do you think that means?

Well, maybe that has to do with the way we interpreted it. I felt that there was something in the writing, in the way Richard spoke at a certain point of the play, that was different. It shifted. For me, the turning point is the moment in the abdication scene when he says 'There lies the substance' [4.1]. If you work backwards from there it is a play about a man who only deals with things from the outside. He's never been asked to go on an internal journey. From that moment in the play, when he realises that it's inside himself that he has to go, it becomes an internal play for Richard II. If someone is a political icon, meaning that he is King, it's all he has ever known. That's the way people view him, the way they treat him, how does he escape from it? Ultimately, of course, his escape turns out to be death. The journey he goes on from that point in the play until he gets murdered is one of self-reflection and self-inspection, in a manner he's never ever been called upon to do before. And I suspect he would then be a better king than earlier when he was King, because now he's a better man.

If he could go back and do it all over again.

Yeah. If he could go back and do it all again. Because I think the play is a journey of a king becoming a man.

Tell me about the first night. You had a technical problem, didn't you? The electrics failed, I think.

Oh yeah. There was a South Bank-wide power surge, when the performance had already started, which knocked the computers down. And all the lighting cues are done via computer. What happened was it got stuck in the lighting pattern of one particular scene, which didn't change until we were able to reboot the whole thing at intermission, and then we had it back. I know it drove Trevor nuts because there were five or six scenes that were in the same lighting. He was upset because of course he had evoked a variety of different moods and feelings through the look of it. Unfortunately those variations weren't seen, at least on press night by the critics. But it was just a hiccup on that particular evening.

So you did it with unchanged lighting.

Yeah. For those five or six scenes before the intermission, we just went out and did it. The scene changes happened but the lighting changes didn't.

I read that it gave an impression of instant Brechtianism. So it can't have been all bad! Moving on to the man himself. Richard has fantastic skill with words, a scintillating poet's skill with words. But reading these wonderful arias (and that's what they can easily resemble), you sometimes think 'Where is his motivation, what is he driving towards?' I don't know what your acting process is, but in Method terms, was it easy to find the character's 'want'?

No, not always. In rehearsal and in the prep that I did beforehand, trying to investigate what motivated him, how he felt and what he desired, it wasn't always easy. I remember having several very good, I would say productive but animated arguments with Trevor about the poetry, and the floweriness of it, and how much he was in love with his own voice. I just objected to that at a certain point in the play. Of course that's its reputation, and people still talk about Gielgud's performance. I was the twelfth actor in the history of the Old Vic to play Richard II. I'm glad I wasn't the thirteenth! – nonetheless, I was the twelfth. And it has this reputation that I found I wasn't so interested in. I felt that when he realises his world is beginning to crumble, and people are out to usurp his power, have him lose his crown, and in fact perhaps kill him, it's no longer about some strange affection for your own voice. He was fighting for his life. I remember several good tussles with Trevor encouraging me to love the language more. And I said 'I'm sorry, but I just don't think at this point in his life that's his concern.' His concern is to try to save his position. It's a moment of desperation. He's facing what is, perhaps, the end of what he's always known. For Richard it's an abyss, it's the edge of a cliff on which there is nowhere to go but down, and he doesn't even know what's down. Ultimately, I believe he does succeed in finding a redemption for himself as a human being. But up to that point, until he says those words 'There lies the substance', I think he's fighting for his life. Therefore I did not want to fall into the trap of him being in love with his own voice, or falling in love with poetry or expression. So it became, for me, far more visceral and real. And I was able to get into the heart of the matter, which made it much more immediate for me to play. But also I tried to understand that this is a man who's ill-equipped to fight for his own life. He doesn't know how. He's never had to. Everything he's ever had in his entire life has been given to him.

He's intensely aware of his own drama. He often seems to perform his own life. How much do you think he's an actor playing a part?

Oh, I think he is. I don't think he starts to know who he really is until he loses everything, so he is playing the role of King as he sees it, and as he has been raised to see it. I do think it's role-playing. And then when the rug starts to get pulled out from under his feet, he suddenly realises that in fact, as a man, he has no foundation whatsoever. I think that's when he begins to question what is it that he really believes, what is it he really wants, or who is it that he really is. But up to those moments in crisis, when he's challenged, I think a great deal of it is role-playing.

Did you have any model in mind for your performance? Any particular royal model? A royal who might be expected to abdicate, perhaps, in the near future?

Well, you know, it was very interesting. I remember hearing people having discussions about some kind of parallel between Blair and Brown, and the King and Bolingbroke. But I'm not quite sure I saw it. Maybe it was just a function of the fact that we were wearing Armani suits and standing in front of television cameras. It was at a time when the power struggle between Blair and

Brown was at quite a height. Blair was under an enormous amount of pressure over the decision to go into Iraq. There had apparently been promises that he was going to withdraw and Brown would become Prime Minister. But of course that didn't happen until years after this deal took place, if one's to believe the deal existed. So I heard those kind of parallels. But I'm not quite sure I ever really heard the one involving Prince Charles. I don't know whether Prince Charles gives the impression that he is driven by self-interest or personal arrogance, he doesn't quite come off that way to me. So I never really did, no. I just tried, with Trevor, to create a man that we thought could both reflect the time in which this play took place, but also a more modern version.

So those perceptions were other people's?

I think so, yeah.

About his sexuality, Laurence Olivier described Michael Redgrave's Richard II as an 'out-and-out pussy queer'. On the other hand, Edmund Kean was criticised by Hazlitt for making Richard 'a courageous figure, a character of passion, that is, of feeling combined with energy'. Do you have a reaction to that?

You know, I think that's one of the great things about the living theatre and about these kind of parts. Our job as interpreters is not necessarily to listen to the way anyone else has ever done it. I didn't pay any attention to what people had said about other performances.

I didn't necessarily imagine you had. But I was offering those two as polar opposites.

So what if he was gay? I'm not sure it would have changed his fate. For me, it wasn't hugely important to highlight that as a characteristic. I think Trevor wanted to introduce the idea – which we did in subtle, and perhaps for some people, not so subtle ways. He obviously had this marriage that didn't mean a lot to him. He barely spent any time with his wife. And he liked to be in the company of his young cousin more than anyone else.

He's tremendously egotistical, completely self-obsessed. As things go wrong he has self-pity in spades. He doesn't 'rage against the dying of the light' by any manner of means. How do we engage with him?

Well, I think you have to tip the scales away from self-pity and towards something else that's just a little bit more driven. Rather than 'Oh, woe is me!', it was 'Why are they doing this?' I tried to lock into 'Why is this happening to me?' He's been so insulated that he doesn't see it coming. He believes in his unique status and the divine right of kings to the extent that he can't imagine people would turn against him. He can't conceive of people who were on his side or in his family suddenly becoming traitors, enemies.

So it's the shock.

It's the shock, yeah.

Do you think you were implicated in Gloucester's death?

Well, that's the five-hundred-year-old question, isn't it! I certainly think we played it that way. There were all kinds of little looks and things that Trevor built in between characters who knew the true story, people who were behind the scenes, as it were, and the ones that would have done the dirty work. So you definitely got the implication in our production that he was culpable. He knew, and perhaps had sanctioned it or ordered it. But also, you wonder if he was even that clever. Maybe it was something that he was convinced he should agree to, but not necessarily something that would have been his idea. I just don't think he was that politically savvy. If he'd been more so, he probably would have survived.

In Act 1, the Bolingbroke/Mowbray duel is first on and then it's off. Why does he change his mind?

In our production this was severely reduced. The full uncut text of that first scene is very long. You've got both sides coming up and arguing. You've got this happening and that happening. Trevor felt that we spend so much time talking about something that will never be raised again in the course of the play, and no one will ever know the truth about, that he cut a good portion of it. He also removed an entire Duchess part from the original text. And he brought in some sections of *Henry IV, Part 1*, in order to make the Bolingbroke story a little bit clearer. Those were things we talked about very early on.

So the text was quite heavily edited.

It was, yeah, for our production. Which I thought was to its benefit.

And the Duchess of Gloucester went?

She went completely. And a number of other lines. Trevor's clever at excising things that are not helpful to his concept of the play.

I'm still not quite clear why Richard first allowed the duel and then aborted it.

Well, I think he wants to get rid of Bolingbroke. He's been warned that the man's a threat, so he banishes him. Off they go!

He banishes Bolingbroke because of his growing power?

I think so.

In Act 1, Scene 4, you suddenly showed a very different side of Richard. I quote again: 'In a private club, smoking among friends, those dark Spacey eyes twinkle with devilry, and his voice is mordant with pent-up malice.' Can you describe the nightclub scene?

We liked to call it Annabel's. Yeah, it's not a long scene, it's one of those little peeks into his private world. You've seen all the pomp and circumstance of the robing and the crowning, and the way in which he handles the Bolingbroke/Mowbray situation, all very regal and proper, following the rules of this and the rules of that. And suddenly you get behind the doors. They're sitting around talking about what really is going on, and having a drink and a bit of a laugh at Bolingbroke's expense. I think that choice of Trevor's, to place it in a nightclub scene, was very clever, because it illustrated clearly the arrogance, the sense of being above it all. I don't think Richard II would ever have been called the 'King of the People'. For me, that scene contains the seeds of what will come. He gets his comeuppance for that attitude of 'we're better than anyone else'.

What were you thinking as you listened to Gaunt berate you in his famous speech [2.1]? You stop him eventually, when he calls you a 'landlord', but you could have stopped him much earlier, couldn't you? Was there any particular reason why you didn't?

Well, I think at first it's a bit like watching a train wreck, you know. You can't believe what you're seeing, and you can't stop it from happening. I don't think anyone had ever spoken to him like that before. So I don't think he was equipped to know how or when to stop it. I'm not even sure he completely understood what was happening until it was halfway done. And the way I tried to play that scene was – 'Why isn't anyone stopping him?' I remember looking around at various of my attendants and lords with a sense of 'Is it *my* job to stop him?' I tried to play it that way, slowly realising 'Oh, this is *my*... Oh, *I* have to stop him!' Because I don't think up to that point Richard had ever been treated that way. And certainly not by a member of the household.

Had you already planned to seize Gaunt's estate, or was it on a whim?

I think it's, unfortunately, an unbearably misguided whim. They try to talk him out of it. But he's so furious that he just snatches it. Because he can. For no other reason.

Then there's quite a long gap for Richard until you come back from Ireland. You have two monumental scenes in Act 3, Scenes 2 and 3. Early on, when you're blessing the ground that you've just set foot on again, you say 'Mock not my senseless conjuration, lords' [3.2]. The line leapt out at me as I read it, and I wondered what was going on at that moment.

The way we played it, some of the soldiers giggled at the previous lines, when I'm saying lovingly 'Dear earth, I do salute thee with my hand…', and I told them 'Don't make fun of how much I love this land. I may be talking in rhymes and poetry, but don't make fun of this, because what I'm saying is exceedingly important. Take it seriously. Don't mock what I am doing here.'

It just struck me as early in his downward graph, as it were, for that to be happening.

Yeah, for him to recognise that he could be mocked. I always rather liked that.

In these scenes there seems to be a kind of a switchback. He comes on first of all with 'Not all the water in the rough rude sea / Can wash the balm from an anointed king.' Then he receives a triple whammy of bad news, and plunges into an orgy of self-pity. And by the end of that scene he speaks of 'that sweet way I was in to despair', which seems to me very telling. You know Romeo's line: 'Come, death, and welcome, Juliet wills it so.' It's almost as if there's something pulling Richard towards that attitude, towards his fate. Is this striking any kind of chord with you?

The self-pity thing, yes, I've heard that, read that. I was more interested in the idea that he saw what was coming, and he walked towards it and made it happen even faster. At a certain point in that scene he embraced his destiny. He walked away proudly as they arrested him. If he was going to go, he was going on his terms. He was not going to fight it, avoid it. That's what the end of that scene meant to me. 'Alright, this is my fate, come on. Bring it on.'

So it was with head held high?

Absolutely head held high, rather than 'Oh, poor me.' And I also think the line you just quoted is him saying 'I was on my way to despair, but something else happened.'

The switchback continues in Act 3, Scene 3. Again he enters and says to Northumberland 'We are amaz'd… how dare thy joints forget / To pay their awful duty to our presence?' A wonderfully imperious line. But then within the space of another seventy lines he's crumpling again: 'What must the King do now? Must he submit?' It's curious.

Well, I think he doesn't understand. He's still the King. He's there to give up the crown. They make him do it publicly, which is horrible. But at that moment when he walks into the room he's still the King. The only way you know you're King is how people respond to you. Trevor used to say that all the time. I would ask 'Well, how do I act like a king?' And he'd answer 'It's not how you act like a king, it's how people react to you when you come into a room.' So when suddenly they aren't reacting any more, it's confusing. Until you take that crown off, until you go through the abdication, you are still the King, and you expect to be treated as a king.

Northumberland says later on in the same scene: 'Sorrow and grief of heart / Makes him speak fondly, like a frantic man.' Meaning he's gone mad. Do you think that's the case?

No. No, I never thought he was mad. I don't think he goes mad. I think he goes human. It's in that scene that he finally starts to discover who he is as a man. Because he hasn't known that. He has only known who he is as a king. I don't think it's madness. I think it's disbelief, I think it's shock at having gotten to this place, and terror at what's next. Until suddenly he finds this little window, realising that his entire life has been out there. Everything's always been on the outside. And suddenly he realises that no, actually it's inside, a place he's probably never gone to. So I actually think he leaves that scene in hope and not in despair. At least the way we played it.

In Act 4, Scene 1, the abdication scene, you seem to move between genuinely distracted grief and playing games with Bolingbroke: 'Yes... no. No... yes.' Is that accurate?

I think so. In that scene Shakespeare brilliantly shows that, even in the face of what is happening, Richard has not lost his sense of humour.

He's just having fun.

Yeah, I think so. He knows where it's going. But he won't play the suffering fool for Bolingbroke. And he won't be condescended to by Bolingbroke. So yeah, he plays with him.

There are so many unexpected twists.

Unexpected twists, yeah. Just when you think you know where he's gonna go, he suddenly goes somewhere else.

I remember very well, later on in the scene, the line you've already quoted a couple of times: 'There lies the substance.' You gave terrific weight to it.

Well, it came out of having smashed the mirror and then looking again at himself. Seeing himself, perhaps, for the first time. That was, I think, what the moment meant for him. It wasn't enough that he could see his reflection in a mirror. The self he had to see was inside. That's what he realises in the course of that scene.

In Act 5, Scene 1, you bid farewell to the Queen. And you turn uncannily accurate as a prophet, when you foresee what's going to happen to Northumberland in the Henry IV *plays: 'Northumberland, thou ladder wherewithal / The mounting Bolingbroke ascends my throne...' Then in the final scene [5.5] leading up to your assassination, alone in a prison cell, you seem at your most content. You're alone with your fantasy life. You seem happier and more relaxed than ever before.*

Yes. I think that whole long, beautifully written soliloquy is about a man who's finally at peace with himself in his little cell. He's dressed in these shabby clothes, given this crappy food, and yet is more content than he has ever been. He's finally gone on a journey that's been, in a way, a selfless journey. He's no longer surrounded by pomp and circumstance, or royalty and riches, or fabulously beautiful people and an adoring public. And yet at this moment, when he seems to the audience to be at his lowest, in comes this little person, a representative of the public. It's like an old actor sitting in a bar, who may have had fame and fortune, but whose career is over. And suddenly some little guy, a complete stranger, comes up to him and goes 'Oh, I thought you were wonderful, I saw you in that thing. I'll never forget you.' He finds another human being who believed in him. And that, for him, is enough. This one person who comes and says 'You'll always be my King. I believe in you, sir. Humbly believe in you.' And they embrace. It's such a gentle moment of finding solace in what could be described as the worst of times. But in many ways, internally for him, I think it is the best of times.

Patrick Stewart
on
Prospero

The Tempest (1611)
Royal Shakespeare Company
Opened at the Royal Shakespeare Theatre, Stratford-upon-Avon
on 8 October 2006

Directed by Rupert Goold
Designed by Giles Cadle
With Julian Bleach as Ariel, Ken Bones as Antonio, Mariah Gale as Miranda,
John Light as Caliban, and Finbar Lynch as Alonso

The Tempest is the last of Shakespeare's four late romances. It is one of his best-loved, and strangest plays. It tells of the sorcerer Prospero, an exiled duke, who exacts revenge upon his usurpers by calling up a tempest that shipwrecks them on his island. Elements of the story have the weirdness and wonder of a fairytale. It has inspired numerous diverse analyses. Some have considered it an allegory of divine learning, with the forces of evil conquered by Prospero, using his celestial authority to restore the power of good. Usurpation is a recurring theme. Recent focus has been directed at The Tempest's depiction of an island colonised by white Europeans, who enslave and exploit its native inhabitants. Contrasting themes of revenge and forgiveness are discussed by Patrick Stewart in the interview that follows. It can be seen as Shakespeare's swansong: at the play's end Prospero abandons his book and staff, the tools of his magic – Shakespeare was to leave the theatre and retire shortly afterwards. The Tempest is rich in theatrical illusion and allusion. Prospero abruptly halts the masque in Act 4, Scene 1, saying 'Our revels now are ended; these our actors… Are melted into air,' and immediately segues into an astonishing meditation on theatre, illusion, decay and the transitoriness of life itself, culminating with:

> We are such stuff
> As dreams are made on; and our little life
> Is rounded with a sleep.

The Tempest has never been my favourite Shakespeare play. I've admired different productions this way and that, but it has seldom previously grabbed my entrails. However, this was a staging with a difference. An opening radio gale warning led to a stunningly choreographed storm scene and shipwreck. The desert island setting was brazenly perverse, revealing a frozen polar wasteland. An unnerving soundtrack was suggestive of reinforced concrete. The 'airy spirit' Ariel was rivetingly creepy, labelled 'Beckettian' by several critics. A gale of fresh air blew through the play. At the eye of this tempest was Patrick Stewart's highly energised, fast and furious Prospero.

I used to play football with Patrick when we were at the RSC together. He was our right back, and God help the opposing left-winger. He went into tackles like a combine harvester. So it was no surprise to see the power and rage he brought to Prospero. Off stage and pitch, however, he's jovial and delightful, and spoke eloquently about this highly original production. We talked in June 2008 in the kitchen of his Oxfordshire home during his run at Stratford, doubling Claudius and the Ghost in Hamlet.

Julian Curry: Where and when did you play Prospero?

Patrick Stewart: I have a long and colourful history with *The Tempest*. I've been in it six times. I played Caliban on the radio with Paul Scofield as Prospero. I played Stephano at Stratford, and I've played Prospero four times. The first was as a schoolboy. I used to go on residential drama courses organised by the very enlightened West Riding County Council, where they had professional teachers. When I was fifteen, we did a somewhat cut-down version of *The Tempest*, but still a two-hour show, and I played Prospero. Somewhere in the files there's a photograph of me in a long velvet gown and a bad beard, and a staff.

And lines painted all over your face?

Exactly. And my recollection is that I was wonderful. Fearless, of course, carefree. Simply learnt it and bellowed it out. My next experience of it must have been Stephano at Stratford, which is a great role, a really great role. Each time I played Prospero I've thought 'God, I wouldn't half mind playing Stephano tonight!' That was Ian Richardson's Prospero. Then I went to Oberlin College in Ohio and spent two months teaching as an artist-in-residence. One of the things I did was play Prospero in a full-scale production. It was a very, very bad production, with a mixture of some Equity actors and a lot of students. But it was there that I really began to form a sense of how I would like to play the role, and who I thought this person was. I was then approached, to my astonishment, by George C. Wolfe when he was running the Public Theatre in New York, to play it in the Delacorte in the Park. This was to be his first ever production of a Shakespeare play. He'd never done any Shakespeare before, and knew nothing about Shakespeare at all.

But luckily you did.

Yes. He assembled a really wonderful cast. And it was an outstanding production. Very bold, very colourful, multiracial, with a sort of Cuban feel to it. There was a fiesta air about it. The masque, I remember, had goddesses on stilts, huge stilts, in outlandish kind of carnival dress, and we were in a vast sandpit. The Delacorte, the open-air theatre in Central Park, is a big circle, an empty space. They filled it with sand, which stuck to your feet when it rained, and it would build up like snow, so you had pads of sand under your bare feet. But that was the first time I got an opportunity to really explore my feelings about this character. I'm not sure when I did Caliban on the radio, but I remember sitting back and listening to Scofield and thinking he sounded wonderful, rather mellow, but resonant. I'd never played Prospero in England, at least as a grown-up. So when I came back to the RSC three years ago to be in *Antony and Cleopatra*, I started a little campaign to do *The Tempest* as well. And they agreed. They said there's this young chap Rupert Goold who's been running the theatre in Northampton. Would I like to meet him, and see if we get on, because he's interested in directing it. And it was one of the grandest and the most fortuitous meetings ever. We worked together back-to-back, because *Macbeth* was the next thing I did after *The Tempest*.

So this one is a distillate of your fifty or so years of tempestuous experience.

It is. And I think it has brought closure, at last, to my relationship with the play.

Somebody described the text as 'a rump of very chewy Shakespeare'. It's an odd text, isn't it. You probably know it so well now that it doesn't seem odd to you, but I think a lot of people find it quite difficult.

Well, it's as late a play as could be. And they're all tricky. They don't have the fluency and the ease of language of the middle period, even a play like *Hamlet*. Certainly not like *Macbeth*. But I think, for me, the fact that I have known it for more than all my career has made me very comfortable with it. What I do know is that from a technical point of view you need a huge amount of breath to play Prospero. I found that it was not a text that you could break up or modernise or make too spontaneous, that it needs to flow, largely to make the sense of it work. You need two or three uninterrupted lines very often, to get the whole significance of an expression out. The thoughts are often somewhat convoluted, a bit like *The Winter's Tale*, and there are clauses and subclauses. Well, if you break those things up too much, I found, it becomes harder to understand. But taken as one progressive thought, I think people grasp what's going on. That was my sense of it. That certainly applied to the long Act 1, Scene 2, telling the story of their arrival on the island to Miranda. I'd like to think that was probably the quickest that scene has ever been played, for two reasons. I felt that it had to be as fluid as possible but, also, I determined that the one dominant characteristic of Prospero was that he was very, very angry. This fury – and I think it is a fury – has been stored up in these years and years of relative solitude. At first Miranda was an infant, two years old, who apparently didn't yet have language, just smiled. Then there were the encounters with Ariel, and with Caliban, which filled out his life a bit. But when you think about it, for a man who had been running a state (albeit not well, I think – carelessly), other than his experimenting with magic and the spirit world of the island, his isolation must have been very bleak and grim. I imagined an increasing pressure-cooker build-up of anger, frustration, fury in this man. And on learning that his enemies are within reach, so that he can now have some power over them, it simply erupts. And because there is also a pressure of time in this play, things such as the telling of the story to Miranda, have to be achieved quickly.

The whole play takes place within twenty-four hours, observing the old unities.

Yes, it does. You never have to worry about which day we are in. Prospero has obviously devised a programme with Ariel. He refers to him – 'At this time such-and-such should happen', you know. And Ariel at one point says 'You said by now I would be free.' So they'd worked out a schedule when all these things will happen. Almost as though Prospero was fearful that his control might evaporate, rather like the Ghost in *Hamlet* when he scents the morning air. And so I found that what fuelled that long Act 1, Scene 2, which can be tedious, was the urgency of the situation coupled with the man's barely controlled fury, and his appetite at the possibility now of having revenge. All he considers is revenge, there are no alternatives. His actions are going to destroy these people, and he will make them suffer.

There are many different interpretations of this play. There's the revenge play you're talking about; there's the colonial/slavery interpretation; there's Shakespeare's farewell to his public. There's also (which I suppose is related to revenge) getting your daughter so well married that you create an Italian dynasty, bringing together Milan and Naples. But you would reckon that out of all of those, revenge is perhaps the principal one?

Well, you raise the daughter issue, and I think it's terrifically important. Prospero has come to realise that, although he can possibly survive indefinitely on this island, his daughter needs to be set free from it. I had a wonderful Miranda, who is also our Ophelia in *Hamlet*, Mariah Gale. He has begun to sense that he might be in danger of harming her in some way by his anger, by his frustration, by the resentment that has built up in him. Caliban has been a problem for her too. But she doesn't know about Ariel, she's completely ignorant of the existence of Ariel.

Oh, really?

Yes, I think so. If you look at it, she has no sense or knowledge of him at all.

So Ariel is just yours?

Ariel and Prospero, it seems to me, have an entirely isolated relationship. And in Rupert Goold's production we went out of our way to emphasise that it really was a one-on-one relationship. The putting of Miranda to sleep immediately before Ariel arrives, I think, makes it perfectly clear. Ariel is coming, therefore I put her to sleep, and I wake her up the moment he's gone.

Some people say, don't they, that Caliban and Ariel are the dark side and the light side of Prospero. Do you go along with that?

Well, our Ariel, as you probably recall, was pretty dark.

I do, yes. 'Beckettian,' they said.

Oh yes! People liken him to Nosferatu. I don't know whether you know Julian Bleach as an actor, he's a pretty intense and scary individual. Well, Rupert will occasionally say things quite lightly and off-hand in rehearsal, things which end up being very resonant in the production. I remember one day rehearsing with Julian, and Rupert said to me 'I wonder if Prospero's frightened of Ariel.' Well, I'd never considered that as a possibility! Ariel was Prospero's creature, I'd assumed, I was completely in control of him. But if for a moment you say 'Oh no, there are powers that Ariel has that Prospero is not in control of,' the violence of some of his threats towards Ariel makes sense. Whereas if Ariel is completely his thing, he doesn't need them.

Much more interesting dynamic.

Well, it gave a terrific dynamic. It meant that there was, at times, a head-to-head battle between the two of them.

The word 'malignancy' was used.

Yes. Yes. 'Malignant thing,' Prospero calls him [1.2]. The relationship with Ariel in this last production was, I think, the strongest and most interesting thing to come out of it.

This was a very original production, with all sorts of innovative ideas running though it. But what strikes one right between the eyes, of course, is the setting. You're supposed to have been shipwrecked somewhere off the coast of Italy, but as the play opens we see this bleak Arctic landscape. And Gonzalo gets a laugh when he says 'How lush and lusty the grass looks! How green!' [2.1], and he picks up a handful of snow and tosses it. How on earth do you justify that?

Yes. You know, really, these are questions for Rupert. You should ask him.

You must have had some conversations about it.

Well, you know, very little. I bought into the whole concept. I sensed that Rupert was kind of exploding the play in a really unusual and original way (just as he did later with *Macbeth*), and I decided to make an absolute total commitment to it and simply go along with him.

Can you enlarge on that, when you say you 'bought into the whole concept'? You presumably had a preliminary conversation with him, which persuaded you that you wanted to work with him. Can you remember the essence of what he was saying, that made you keen to do so?

Well, he certainly didn't talk about the Arctic when we first met. He talked about it being a violent play, and about the morality of the play being a strong issue, that wickedness was always just under the surface, and danger too. And that there was a political aspect. Not political in a colonial sense, but in the power struggles that exist between individuals – a kind of personal-political aspect. And that ultimately, also, salvation had to be the dominant theme of the last half of the play. I was thrilled to hear that, because I had sensed (I think probably from the time before when I'd done it) that the turning point in the play for Prospero is when Ariel says 'if you now beheld them, your affections / Would become tender.' Prospero answers 'Dost thou think so, spirit?' And Ariel replies 'Mine would, sir, were I human.' And in our production, after a very, very long pause, Prospero said 'And mine shall' [5.1]. And, in that moment, he resolves to put aside his murderous revenge and, instead, choose forgiveness. Hard though it is for him. In fact, when he finally comes face to face with his brother and Alonso, the rage against them still erupts and bubbles up. It's hard for him to be a forgiving person.

Jumping forward for a moment to the very end of the play, the forgiveness still seems to be incomplete. It doesn't seem to be a very satisfactory forgiveness.

He gets it theoretically, the argument that Ariel presents to him. Ariel is saying 'If I were human, I would pity them,' and what Prospero hears is 'You therefore, who cannot pity them, cannot be human.' And I think that is a huge realisation for Prospero: that in my rage, in my fury, I have become inhuman. I have become less human than this spirit. He says:

> Hast thou, which art but air, a touch, a feeling
> Of their afflictions, and shall not myself,
> One of their kind, that relish all as sharply
> Passion as they, be kindlier mov'd than thou art?

So he learns from Ariel?

Oh yes. Oh, completely. Ariel redeems him. He doesn't have to choose that path, he could have said 'Fuck off, I'm gonna kill them all.' The realisation that Ariel brings to him of his lack of humanity, I think, is huge. But still it is a struggle for him. It is not like the end of *The Winter's Tale*, a tranquil, peaceful redemption, but it shows very clearly that to redeem yourself can be a struggle. It's a constant battle. It's interesting, I was having a conversation with a Christian the other day, a woman of faith, someone I'd been dating. And I began to discern that she prayed every morning. Well, I don't know people who pray every morning! And she goes to church every Sunday. So we got into these conversations about religion, which apply to this in a way. I said

'But surely, you must have doubts.' Because she's a smart woman, a Harvard-educated woman. And she replied 'Of course. That's part of being a Christian. The doubts are everything, and you struggle with these doubts constantly. This is the battle you have.' Well, that's not good enough for me, but certainly how it seemed in Act 5 of *The Tempest* for Prospero. It is a constant struggle to hold onto his humanity in the face of these people's wickedness, and to actually forgive them.

Prospero's a very complex character. There have been diverse readings from 'noble and full of lofty sentiments' to 'irascible and distinctly unpleasant'. I was going to ask you where you were, but I think I'm getting a good idea about that! One of the critics called you 'a bitterly abusive supremacist'. Does that ring a bell?

Yes, it does. I don't know who wrote it, but it was certainly so. Certainly abusive and physically violent towards Caliban. I tortured him. I spat into his food, yes.

Quite vindictive.

Yes, yes. Although it's interesting, that action comes immediately before Miranda sees Ferdinand for the first time. I had always felt that was one of the reasons why Prospero winds Caliban up so much. He provokes him and provokes him and provokes him, abuses him with language. And indeed, I grabbed him and tortured him, twisted his arms. This is very cruel and not pleasant. But given that Caliban was the only male creature she'd ever known, apart from her father, and knowing that she was about to encounter Ferdinand, which Prospero wants to go as well as possible, he creates the most contrasting scenario. So that in one instant she is exposed to the savagery and brutality, sexuality and lust of Caliban, and then here is this gentle, grieving, delicate young man who only speaks to her in the mildest, gentlest terms. Those two scenes come right on top of one another [1.2]. So there was an objective behind the cruelty to Caliban which was partly to do with Miranda. But in the same way, almost as though there is a kind of dichotomy in him, Prospero chooses to treat Ferdinand harshly as well.

Making him prove himself.

Yes, it's a test. He wants to be certain that this man is worthy of his daughter. He doesn't know him yet. He only hopes for the best. He wants this to be for the rest of their lives. But nevertheless, behind that, it seemed to me that anger was the most accessible emotion for Prospero so much of the time. And in a sense this is why he too has to leave the island. It's killing him, this rage which doesn't abate. It's going to destroy him and it could destroy his daughter too, if some relief for it isn't found.

Let me ask about your costume. 'Shaman' is a word that recurs. You're described as 'a shabby Lapland shaman clad in a bearskin cloak and reindeer-skull headdress, raising the spirits from a burning brazier'. And as 'a vast furry figure, part totem pole, part elephant God, part yak'.

Oh, I don't think I read that! Well, I excitedly committed to Rupert's idea of an icy waste, which I think he would say was also meant to represent the icy waste of Prospero's own nature and soul. I can remember this now quite clearly: he wanted the environment to be as harsh and uncompromising and as uncomfortable as possible. He wanted to see everyone suffering, particularly the lords when they arrived. Very often it's a desert island, and perfectly pleasant. Although if you read the whole play, the actual topography is confusing. Gonzalo speaks about the grass being green, about trees, and then at other times it's moorland and wasteland.

Ariel refers to a 'desolate isle' [3.3].

A desolate isle, yes. Shakespeare didn't seem to be too worried about being consistent on that score. So once this Arctic world had been created for us, one of the most important things is to decide on the cloak: 'Lend thy hand / And pluck my magic garment from me' [1.2]. I think I've actually worn a cloak with moons and stars on it in my time. I didn't know what to do about it. But I have quite a growing collection of Inuit art – you passed a couple as you came in. I've seen a lot and read quite a bit, and seen films on the Inuit. So I was up to speed with this stuff, and knew something about their myths and legends, beliefs and so forth. It was my idea, instead of having a 'magician's' cloak, to assume an animal skin. You know, you make do with what you've got. And if some monstrous bear had shown up and he'd managed to kill it and skin it, well, that would be his cloak. In fact it was something of a mythological creature, because the skull at the end of it wasn't really anything at all. It had a kind of a bear-snout look, but it was very extended beyond that, so it wasn't naturalistic, and there were huge claws on the end of it. But what pleased me was the idea that Prospero himself became animal-like, had kind of taken on the spirit of the creature that he was wearing. Actually I watched a movie on Inuit, and underneath the fur parka that they wear with a hood, they have nothing else. They take that off and they're naked. So that's how I was, and then later I put on my old jacket, having finally taken off the cloak.

You were stripped to the waist, but you were not completely naked.

Not completely naked, no. I had my pants on. Although it did prompt Charles Spencer (who had mentioned my body, which was exposed quite a lot in *Antony and Cleopatra*) to say something in his review of *The Tempest* like 'And thank you very much, Mr Stewart, I think we've now seen enough of your body.'

Where and when and how did you acquire magic powers?

Well, he was studying it back in Milan. The books that Gonzalo gave him on their little boat before they were cast adrift were his magic books. He had been studying these – he says the library was the only place he wanted to be. And the fact is that the state, I'm sure, was beginning to founder, because Prospero was a failing prince. I think this is an important theme in the play, but we didn't examine it in our production.

A bit like the Duke in Measure for Measure *in that sense.*

A bit like the Duke in *Measure for Measure*, and you might even say Old Hamlet in *Hamlet* too. He was not doing his job, which was, first and foremost, to govern. That's what a Renaissance prince does: he rules. Well, Prospero clearly wasn't ruling, so the coup was easy enough to pull off, because he was spending all his time with his magic books. He was studying necromancy and the dark arts, and had become obsessed with them. So he has these books when he arrives on the island. And I think then coupled with what Ariel can bring him, and the other spirit world, he developed his magic powers. Because Ariel, and only Ariel, gives him access to the spirit world. Ariel is his conduit. It's consistent all the way through. He needs Ariel as a conduit to the spirit world. He, by himself, cannot conjure it up.

He drowns his book and breaks his staff quite a long time before the end of the play [5.1]. You tell Ariel to set Caliban free after you've renounced your own magic powers. So you still use him as a conduit at that stage.

Yes. I give him one more task, which I think is:

> Set Caliban and his companions free:
> Untie the spell.

Finally I say:

> That is thy charge. Then to the elements
> Be free, and fare thou well.

And in that farewell, having already renounced my magic – and I don't know whether you remember – I threw my staff into the hut, which exploded. Do you remember those huge bursts of flame? Unless you happened to be there on a night when the flames didn't occur – which was once or twice!

I certainly do remember them. Yes.

There was a huge explosion. It was terrific. And so he chooses not only to become human, but to free himself from the spirit world that has been so important to him, and to become, in every way, a man. No longer a shaman, or a godlike creature, but a frail and vulnerable human being. And to that end

– and this really began way back in Oberlin – I tried to acquire a different tone, almost a different voice, during the last speech:

> Now my charms are all o'erthrown,
> And what strength I have's mine own;
> Which is most faint...

Someone much frailer, much more vulnerable than before. We used a trick in the Delacorte, which I've never been able to do since. In the Park we were miked, because it's such a huge open space, and you've got planes going over and all kinds of things, so we were radio-miked for the whole performance. But in the final speech when I got to the line:

> Gentle breath of yours my sails
> Must fill, or else my project fails,
> Which was to please.

At that moment I pointed to the sound booth and did a throat-cutting gesture with my finger, and they turned off my mike and cut the sound. The next thing I said was:

> Now I want
> Spirits to enforce, art to enchant...

And what the audience heard was totally different. Because there was no longer amplified sound, it was just a rather faraway human voice.

So you renounce Ariel, you renounce the island, you renounce magic, you renounce your daughter, up to a point. It's almost Franciscan. Why do you make these choices?

He chooses, yes, to give away daughter, magic and spirits. And you might say, also, his governorship of the island. He abandons them all. In return, he is going to be Duke of Milan again. Where, as he says 'Every third thought shall be my grave.' So the suggestion is that he is preparing himself for death, he's preparing himself for the end. In a sense it's a kind of purification of letting things go, giving up not only the spiritual but the worldly as well. What does he say finally:

> And my ending is despair,
> Unless I be reliev'd by prayer,
> Which pierces so that it assaults
> Mercy itself and frees all faults.
> As you from crimes would pardon'd be

(Because I have committed crimes)

> Let your indulgence set me free.

So freedom, in every possible sense, is what he is embracing at the end. But you cannot be free, as indeed the Franciscans know, if you have tried to hold onto things. What is it that Claudius says, in *Hamlet*? 'May one be pardon'd and retain th'offence?' No, you can't be pardoned, you've got to give things up.

Tell me how you resolve your relationship with Caliban. 'This thing of darkness I / Acknowledge mine' [5.1]. Is Prospero about to adopt him and take him back to Milan?

I think he means that he takes responsibility for him.

Why?

Because he is another creature. I don't know how old Caliban actually was when Prospero got there, but he was pretty young. Caliban's experience of the world has been through Prospero.

He taught him how to speak.

'You gave me language' [1.2].

And taught him about the sun and the moon.

That's right, yes. But also tied him up and put him in a cave and abused him.

Even so, the word 'mine' is surprising, isn't it.

Well, I think in a Christian sense he is saying 'I take whatever this creature is, to be me also.'

So in that sense he is linked to the dark side of Prospero.

Yes. Yes. I think Prospero's acknowledging that there is some form of bond. Caliban does eventually say 'I'll be wise hereafter / And seek for grace' [5.1]. Which is a good lesson.

So he learns from him as well?

Well, he says that after Prospero's line: 'This thing of darkness I / Acknowledge mine' – 'I take responsibility for him.'

Curious fellow, Prospero, isn't he. Does he have a sense of humour? Did you have any fun? Were there any jokes, a sense of irony?

Yes. We actually found quite a bit of humour in that first scene with Miranda, largely brought about by misunderstandings. But he's not a man who makes jokes, as Macbeth does. Macbeth has an ironic side to him. We found a lot of jokes in our production. But I think it was largely in Prospero's relationship with Miranda that we found humour. I remember we used to get one very good laugh in that scene. But I was doing Antony in that same season, and playing Mark Antony was fun. It literally was fun. The character is so diverse, so colourful, so extreme in all of his emotions and experiences. He's up one minute, he's down the next – he's having a party, he wants to kill himself. He's all over the place, is Antony. I think that's what gives him a lot of his charm. So playing him was always entertaining. It was never fun being Prospero, I used to feel playing Prospero was hard work. You put your head down and charged, playing Prospero. And those speeches are tough, they're gruelling. It was like digging ditches at times, I used to feel, getting through some of those speeches.

But you did it again and again and again. Was that for the last time?

Oh yes. I felt able to explore the darkness in him thoroughly, the anger in him, and investigate the attempt at finally redeeming himself. I thought it was quite successful. And therefore, there's really no need. Maybe I ought to play Stephano again next time.

Penelope Wilton
on
Isabella

Measure for Measure (1604)
Opened at the Greenwich Theatre, London
on 12 July 1975
(Originally performed by the National Theatre Company in 1973)

Directed by Jonathan Miller
Designed by Bernard Culshaw
With Julian Curry as Angelo, David Firth as Lucio, Lucinda Gane as Mariana,
David Horovitch as Claudio, and Joseph O'Conor as the Duke

$\mathbf{M}$*easure for Measure* is one of Shakespeare's so-called 'problem plays'. It was written in the early 1600s, between *Hamlet* and *King Lear*, when he was at the height of his powers. In the 1623 First Folio it was labelled a comedy. However, it ends with two weddings which are enforced rather than romantic, and a marriage proposal that receives no response – hardly the stuff of conventional comedy. 'Enigmatic masterpiece' might be nearer the mark.

Isabella tells Angelo 'O, it is excellent / To have a giant's strength, but it is tyrannous / To use it like a giant' [2.2]. The use and abuse of power is a central theme. Other issues raised are the extent to which mercy should temper justice, and the validity of different relationships between men and women. To what degree is the Duke a benevolent deus ex machina, and to what degree a ruler by the seat of his pants, who moves from one hastily improvised solution to the next? Is Angelo really nothing but a villainous hypocrite, or is he basically a virtuous man whose newly aroused sexuality propels him out of control? And in Isabella, what separates saintly compassion from rigid and frigid morality? *Measure for Measure* asks many more questions than it provides answers to, and resists neat categorisation.

I must declare a strong personal interest, having played Angelo in this production. Jonathan Miller updated it to 1930s Vienna. It was originally put on in 1973 during the National Theatre's tenancy at the Old Vic, shortly before the company moved to the South Bank. The show was revived two years later at Greenwich, with some of the original cast and some newcomers, including Penelope Wilton.

It was small-scale, intimate, 'chamber Shakespeare'. There was very little that was either fast or loud. People, for the most part, simply spoke to each other. Jonathan Miller directed with the delicacy and precision of a watchmaker. Some of his suggestions bypassed theatricality. For example, when Claudio was told that death is certain [3.1], he turned away and yawned. As a physiological response to terror, it was piercingly accurate. In the final scene [5.1], after Angelo's unmasking, I stood in front of the Duke. Jonathan suggested I should remove a barely perceptible piece of fluff from the Duke's robe, as I confessed. I thought it was a daft idea. But in performance people found it inspired. Don't ask why, I've no idea!

Not long before this interview I'd played Penelope's simple-minded brother in an RSC revival of Middleton's *Women Beware Women* at the Swan Theatre. Besides being wittily and sexily evil, she brought a rigorous intelligence to her performance, and it was this quality that contributed to making her Isabella so remarkable. In my opinion, Angelo finds her attractive not only sexually but also cerebrally. We met and talked one fine morning in 2006, in her light and airy flat in west London.

Julian Curry: I've put together a collage of your reviews. They were terrific, by the way. It's in two halves, here's Part One. The critics were fascinated by how unattractive and dowdy you were. They described you as 'tight-lipped and determined, gauche and sex-frightened'. They referred to 'primness', 'religious mania', 'glacial self-righteousness' and 'puritan zeal'. They said you were a 'flat-chested, flat-footed nun in black rubber-soled shoes, and an ugly grey convent skirt... clutching with purple hands a nasty handbag, into which she claws for a handkerchief to scarify her raw nose'. And my favourite: 'A voice suggestive of both rigid morality and a severe head cold.' The best they could call you was 'a dowdily beguiling Isabella'... and 'appealing but utterly unglamorous'. One sexist critic wrote 'There is no doubt that this handbag-swinging, square-jawed, sanctimonious nun would be better off for a little of what she doesn't fancy.'

But with Part Two I can right the balance, give measure for measure. You found an extraordinary range and complexity in the part. 'She calmly listens to Angelo, not understanding to begin with, following his circuitous arguments as if at a seminar. But when she does understand, Ms Wilton is Boadicea, all knife blades and armour. Claudio's pleading turns her into a trembling tearful hysteric, banging at him with her handbag... she shudders and almost pukes with revulsion when the scheme of exchange is mooted by the disguised Duke... She goes through the Mariana intrigue in a mood of icy disapproval... At the last, Isabella and Claudio do not leap joyously into each other's arms, but simply stare at each other across a chasm of guilt and shame.' Does that ring any bells with you?

Penelope Wilton: Well, I can only say I'm very pleased, I really like those reviews. I haven't changed my view at all. Jonathan Miller had an unromantic perception of the play, and gave it a twentieth-century setting, in Freud's Vienna. We were taken down that route. It seemed to me the religious zeal, and the strength of Isabella's character are informed by the fact that she's just about to take holy vows and go into a convent. When Lucio comes to ask her to plead for her brother [1.4], the nun says to Isabella 'You must speak to him because you haven't taken your orders yet. I'm not allowed to speak unless I go through the Mother Superior.' So she was going into a silent order, a very severe order in other words. Shakespeare has written this girl – call her a religious maniac or what you will – and I think Jonathan's reading of it suited the text extremely well.

For a glamorous actress like yourself, it must have taken a deep commitment to make yourself so plain for the part.

I've never seen myself as a glamorous actress. I've only ever seen myself as an actress who does the parts that I do. If it suits the part, then I will be glamorous. But given that the rest of this production was altogether unglamorous, it didn't feel so very strange. It must be said that this wasn't the original version. You yourself, Julian, had done it with Jonathan, hadn't you, at the National Theatre, with Gillian Barge playing Isabella. So this was a remounting of a production. I think Jonathan probably refined it. People seemed to know what they were doing. I was fitting into a production that was quite clear as to where it was going. And I agreed with it.

You didn't feel straitjacketed?

I didn't feel in the least bit straitjacketed. Jonathan has a reputation for being a bit of a wild card, but actually he was very truthful to the text. He wouldn't do things gratuitously. I felt that the production, and my performance, fitted the text. But it's very, very serious. Isabella doesn't have many laughs, she's not blessed with a sense of humour. She takes herself, and the world, very seriously. It was quite a dangerous production.

Tell me more about the setting. You mentioned Freud's Vienna.

The set was a box with a row of doors at the back and at the sides, out of which people appeared. It suggested a prison, the courtroom, Angelo's office, a friar's cell, even Mariana's grange. It was multipurpose, minimalist. The whole thing was minimalist – all we could rely on was the words. I thought it was one of Jonathan's best productions. The lighting was very plain. Every single part was fulfilled and realised. And everyone was in the same play.

Was there music?

Yes. It was kind of pastiche Schoenberg, written by Carl Davis. It gave the feeling of that time and place. Mariana's song was sung on a record by Jean Boht, who was married to Carl Davis. It was beautiful.

Was there an arc for Isabella? Do you have an idea of what she might have learnt, how she might have developed, through the play?

The thing about Isabella is that throughout the entire play she's reacting to circumstances beyond her control. At the very beginning she has set herself on a journey, which is to go into a convent of a silent order. And then this information is received. She finds out that her brother is going to have his head cut off, for having sex before marriage with his girlfriend. In fact he was just about to marry her anyhow, but they had to wait for certain marriage money to be arranged, for him to receive her dowry. From then on Isabella reacts to the situations around her. She is asked to plead for her brother's life. At first she isn't keen (and I think that is where she is somewhat religiously fanatical). But she is cajoled. She doesn't approve of sex before marriage, but her love of her brother overcomes her own moral standpoint. From then on she reacts to situations that are thrust on her, rather than ever instigating anything on her own behalf. So she is always on the back foot, and the story is changed by people around her. But by the end of the play she has learned something. Her journey is one of realising. The outside world has shown her that you cannot afford to live in such a narrow scope. You have to be aware of humanity. But at the very end of the play, when the Duke offers her his hand in marriage [5.1], would she then leave holy orders and marry him? We decided, and I certainly felt it was right, that her long silence amounted to 'No'. Silence is unexpected from this articulate young woman, who could plead for her brother so coherently [2.2], this intelligent, well-read girl.

But it is an odd sort of play. That and *All's Well That Ends Well* are really back-to-back problem plays, because of the disarray of the morals. They don't follow just one path, they go all over. It's a very interesting end to the play. There is a long scene where everyone gets their comeuppance. Angelo is exposed as being hypocritical, and Lucio is ticked off for saying things about the Duke to the Duke's face when he was dressed as a friar. And at the end Isabella does not say a word. It's like she's opted out. So when you read those notices, saying that when she sees Claudio she doesn't embrace him – well, there are no words for her to say, she's given no words. Shakespeare gives her words when he wants to give her words. And when the Duke says 'Dear Isabel, / I have a motion much imports your good' and so on, again there are no words. I seem to remember that in our production, as he came towards me I backed away from him; because I think she goes back into the convent.

The games played on her beggar belief. First of all Angelo plays with her feelings and says 'If you don't have sex with me I'll cut your brother's head off.' Then the Duke finds out and says 'Look, Angelo was engaged to a young woman, Mariana, but he jilted her. She still loves him, she'll be happy to take your place in his bed, so you won't have to do anything that will hurt your moral feelings. But if you *say* you'll sleep with him, your brother will be saved.' Then the Duke finds out that, yes, Angelo has had his way with Mariana, but the brother is going to be executed anyhow, and his head must be delivered to

Angelo on a plate. When the Duke hears this he has another plan, to substitute the head of someone else that died in the prison. But he doesn't tell Isabella. He tells her that even though she's done everything he asked, and gone along with his plans, her brother has still died. There's no relief. It's so that she will still be angry, ready for a very showy trial, come the confrontation at the end. Well, it's beyond belief.

Still be angry, to publicly accuse Angelo?

Yes. She's manipulated into publicly accusing Angelo, which she could easily have done anyway with full knowledge of what had happened. But it's as if the Duke didn't trust her to have that passion behind her. Or thought perhaps she'd be tricky. But as she's gone along with the rest of it, why shouldn't she accuse Angelo even with the knowledge that her brother had been saved? There's no let-up. She's never let off the hook, throughout the whole play. Her emotions are played with. She is, in many ways, naive. She's not of the world, she hasn't lived. Shakespeare shows a very bustling, warm, sexy other life going on, with Mistress Overdone, and Pompey. There are great jokes and amusing mispronunciations, and people saying the opposite of what they mean, calling someone a villain when really they're not. There's Elbow the policeman who gets everything mixed up, and Barnardine. They're wonderfully rich, funny characters. She is separate from all of that, she's never a part of it. Angelo's a bit a part of it, and so is the Duke, even her brother Claudio is a bit a part of it. But she's by herself, she's an outsider to the world.

Going back to the beginning, when Lucio first comes to her and says that her brother's going to be beheaded for getting Juliet with child, she seems to be more casual than later on, more easy-going. She just says 'O, let him marry her!'

Well, she's no fool. She wouldn't approve of it, she wouldn't say 'Oh, go on,' you know, 'let's all have sex before marriage!' She doesn't agree with it, but goodness me, he was going to marry her.

It's a curious little scene, though, isn't it. At the end she actually says 'I'll see what I can do' – which is as modern and colloquial as you can get. Quite casual.

She doesn't think she's going to have too difficult a time when she starts off. It's a rude awakening when she realises. At first she walks away from Angelo [2.2], and she has to be persuaded back. She's stunned, I think.

Again in that first scene, it's interesting that Lucio suggests that she should use her femininity to get round Angelo:

> Go to Lord Angelo,
> And let him learn to know, when maidens sue,
> Men give like gods; but when they weep and kneel

> *All their petitions are as freely theirs*
> *As they themselves would owe them.*

And she's happy about that. She doesn't say 'I don't play that game.'

No, no. But I think it's with language. She's not going to use her feminine guile as far as flirting. She's an intelligent girl and uses language. She pleads to Angelo's better character. And certainly the way I played it, it's an intellectual approach rather than anything physical that she uses. She intellectually makes her appeal to him. And then her own momentum grows as, thinking on her feet, she realises the seriousness of the situation. Angelo keeps saying 'I'm sorry, no. He's going to die. I'm sorry, that's it.' And then she starts to use language in a wonderfully persuasive way.

So the idea of weeping and kneeling wasn't literally what you took from Lucio?

When she's not getting there with Angelo she does what *feels* like kneeling, but it takes her a lot to do so. She loves her brother, and life is important. The woman, Juliet, is going to have a child, and she's not a prude in that way.

No?

Well, she's a prude about herself. During her second scene with Angelo [2.4], before she goes to Claudio, she says 'Better that my honour be saved and Claudio dies, than the other way round. Because I'd be in damnation for ever, whereas he'd only be dead.' One of her arguments is that.

It's a form of vanity, isn't it. When she says 'My chastity is more important than the charity of saving my brother.' The glory is hers rather than God's.

You as an onlooker would say that, yes. I, playing it, didn't take that at all. Isabella doesn't think like that. She sees it as being asked to give up something that is impossible to give up, because it would be a sin.

What do you think it is about her that gets to Angelo? She doesn't appear glamorous, we talked about that already. However, she uses words which are provocative. She says 'Th'impression of keen whips I'd wear as rubies', which is very sexy. But I don't think she knows what she's talking about – or does she?

Well, I didn't. The Isabella I played didn't. You, having played Angelo, would be better able to say what Isabella's appeal was than I would. But I think it's a bit like the appeal of the Brontë sisters. Their imagination is extraordinary, and yet it comes from a very virginal base. It's not tempered by anything. It's sort of out there. And they're very vivid. They had a very vivid inner life, I think. Isabella is going to be a nun, and chose to be a nun. She came from a good family, I would suggest. She's not put in a convent because they're poor, or she's got anything to hide. She's chosen to take the veil, and join a silent order. She likewise must have a very vivid inner life – that's what I felt. I think there must be something very attractive about disturbing this virginal, pedestal-like creature. A virgin. A Mary sort of figure. Like having your way with something that is untouchable. I suppose that would be what it is. I hope I wasn't *so* unattractive? I didn't have a moustache, or eyebrows growing across one another? Or was boss-eyed, or had terrible body odour…?

Well, I didn't like to mention it… No, I think it was because you had a passion and a rigour and a very acute intelligence. And also, I don't believe Angelo's been near many women at all. I think it's all of those things. And she's uncompromising. In a way, they are birds of a feather. I'd say he recognises that, he gets turned on by that. She's got the same kind of rigour as he has.

Whereas Mariana is a bit too… I don't know…

Soppy?

A bit soppy. Isabella and Mariana are not going to be best friends, after the play ends.

In the first scene between them, Isabella says to Angelo 'Go to your bosom, / Knock there, and ask your heart what it doth know / That's like my brother's fault' [2.2]. I wonder if she's got any idea how accurate that is. Because it's uncanny. Do you think she knows, if only subconsciously, that she's hit the bull's-eye?

Well, it's only because we are all mortal sinners. If you're brought up in the Catholic Church, you are born with mortal sin. I know a little about this because I was brought up a Catholic – not that I still am. And the very thought of anything is as bad as doing it, that is how mortally sinful we are. She must have felt the same, because you have to give up things: you don't suddenly decide to go into a silent order – you struggle. And then when you take up the veil, you wear a wedding ring and you're married to God. That's what you do if you're a nun. I researched the nunning quite a lot. I thought it was really important, especially in our production, to know what all that involved. So to answer your question, I think she is asking him to look into his soul, to make sure that he hasn't had wicked thoughts, if not sexual thoughts – that he hasn't been near to temptation.

So she wouldn't be considering that he might have those ideas about her?

No, I don't think it's anything to do with her. That's why it's such a shock when he does make a move. She can't believe it. There was a fabulous seduction scene, which was minimally done. There was no ripping of corsets and tearing, or trying to kiss and grope. We sat side by side, facing the audience. As Angelo you very neatly pleated my skirt on my knee. With very neat fingers of just one hand, you made very neat pleats out of my grey serge skirt just above my knee, while you were insinuating really frightful things, like 'Will you let me have sex with you?' But it was never said in those words. There were two cases when she can't believe it. They're very different. There's that one with Angelo, and there's another with her brother. When Claudio says 'Sweet sister, let me live,' and begs her to sleep with Angelo [3.1], it is very, very shocking to her. But her vilification of her brother is also shocking, and it's not attractive. I don't think it's supposed to be attractive. It doesn't show her in a very good light. It shows her as a prude. It shows her as an hysteric, as a neurotic, and it shows her as a religious maniac. She has to break the fact to him that she's not going to save his life by having sex with Angelo. But she attacks Claudio in a very unfair way. And that's what informs the last scene, and the way we did it, with them not throwing themselves into each other's arms. They have a lot to get over.

It's an agonising scene, for both of them.

But you can understand, if you stand outside it objectively. I can understand Claudio. I find Isabella quite difficult, although I played her. That's why I had to make her such a severe person, so uncompromising. That's how I had to play it, because otherwise I couldn't have said those things.

Going back again to that line: 'Then Isabel live chaste, and brother die: / More than our brother is our chastity' [2.4]. It's extraordinarily difficult. I'm just wondering about modern echoes. The American 'Silver Ring Thing' for example – teenagers wearing silver rings as tokens of not having sex until they're married.

I suppose you could say (although it would probably not go down frightfully well, given today's climate, with extremism in religions around the world) that she's a religious fanatic in a personal sense. I don't think she's a religious fanatic in the broader sense, of expecting everyone else to follow what she does. This is a very personal thing that she has decided to do. There is extremism that says 'If you don't follow this path you're damned.' There was an item on the news only today about a large group of people who believe in honour killings. It's if the family has been disgraced – usually by a girl refusing to marry the person she's supposed to, or having an affair. But that's dictated by the men in the family. With Isabella, no one seems to have forced her to do anything. She has decided on this action, to go into a convent, to take up religious orders. The general climate of the play does seem to be quite lax. That's why the Duke appoints Angelo as his deputy, to bring back a more moral climate. Seemingly, that is the reason for him leaving.

You wonder about the Duke anyhow, he seems to be an odd character. He's a sort of Machiavellian type, a player of games, which I've never quite understood. It's fascinating. This is what makes *Measure for Measure* a problem play, because you never know quite where you are morally. Of course Shakespeare is never black and white. But there are other areas where you do know where you are, the characters are so rounded. Whereas the Duke seems to shift, the ground seems to be unstable when he's talking. He seems to make it up as he goes along – or has he actually thought it all out beforehand? You weren't sure whether you'd missed something! He seemed to me to be a very interesting character, full of contradictions. And a doubter of himself, filled with self-doubt. Probably his attraction towards Isabella is for that reason. She seems to be somebody with such strong beliefs, with no wavering, that he found her very attractive. And perhaps similarly with Angelo. Except I think Angelo really wants, in a way, to destroy what he sees. But I can't speak to you, because you played him!

When you do your soliloquy 'To whom should I complain? Did I tell this, / Who would believe me?' [2.4], do you tend to play it to yourself, or to the audience?

Well, on the whole, I do soliloquies to myself. Unless it has been decided in a production that they are played to the audience. But I think that takes you out-side. When I watch Hamlet, with hundreds of soliloquies, I always feel that he is talking to himself, working things out for himself. And if he plays it to me, I suddenly become outside the play. So for Isabella, it's like a voice in her head. She's thinking her way through, and her thoughts are spoken aloud. That's how I felt.

In the final scene [5.1] there are three particularly difficult key moments for Isabella. The first is when Mariana asks her to kneel, to help plead for Angelo's life.

It shows an amazing generosity of spirit. She's really asked, beyond the call, to do that. And I find it extremely moving when she does so. Her language then is very personal, and heart-rending, on someone else's behalf, at a very difficult time in her life. It's her saving grace. Because she can come over hard. I think it's true, she's a difficult woman. She's never going to be easy, Isabella. She's not pliant, she won't bend. She will do what she does, and she's alone. But she also has this exceptional warmth. It comes out when she's pleading for her brother with Angelo. And in the final scene when she tries to help Mariana by pleading with the Duke for Angelo. It's extraordinarily warm and human.

Then there's the finding out that Claudio's still alive.

Well, as I've said, that has been kept from her, when everyone else knows. The audience knows, the Duke knows, and a number of other people know. Angelo doesn't know, but I think Escalus knows. I don't know whether Friar Peter knows but he might, I can't remember. But it has been kept from her until the moment is right to reveal him. It's astonishing, this finale. The Duke sets up and stage-manages this big public set-piece for Angelo's undoing, for the unmasking of this seemingly pious but really villainous hypocrite.

But he delays and delays letting Isabella know. You reckon it's in order to stoke up her anger and indignation to the maximum?

I can only think that's what it would be. But it seems to me to be fantastically cruel. He's playing with her. Her emotions are played with throughout the play. She gives what she can, but she's used. She's used, and used, and used.

Finally the Duke asks her to marry him. Again, you've got no words. Nonetheless, you can play that in various ways. Do you suggest yes? Do you suggest no? Or do you suggest maybe at some time in the future?

Well, I played it as if she couldn't believe what he was saying. She was appalled. But her silence speaks volumes. Shakespeare, as I said before, gives her nothing to say. There are no words. If he wanted her to say anything, he would have given her something to say. But he doesn't. She's silent for quite a long time at the end of the play. It's a fascinating journey.

Do you think you'd ever want to do it again, and if so would you change anything?

Apart from the fact that I'm far too old to play Isabella now, yes, I would be interested. You never want to repeat something you've done before. But with a different cast there would be a whole lot of new energy thrown at you, so it immediately changes. So I would be interested to look at it again… Mind you, I don't know how different it would be. It seemed to me when we played it, given that we had set it in Freud's Vienna, that we were as truthful to the text as possible. If we'd set it in another period, I don't think it would make a great difference. The drama of the play is two people in opposite corners, coming out to box. And if they're not there to do that, then you don't have a drama. He has written opposites so that they will collide. So actually I don't think I would change it that much.

Synopses of the Plays

Antony and Cleopatra (1606-07)

ACT 1   Rome's great general Mark Antony, now middle-aged, is in Alexandria. He and Queen Cleopatra of Egypt are lovers. Antony's fellow triumvirs (the three supreme heads of the Roman Empire), Octavius Caesar and Lepidus, blame him for abandoning himself to debauchery, and neglecting his duties towards Rome. They need him urgently to help subdue a threatened rebellion by the pirate Pompey. 'Leave thy lascivious wassails!' cries the puritanical Caesar. When Antony's wife Fulvia dies, he tears himself away from Cleopatra and returns to Rome. Cleopatra thinks about him obsessively: 'Is he on his horse? O happy horse, to bear the weight of Antony!' He sends her an orient pearl and she resolves to write to him several times a day.

ACT 2   Pompey is alarmed to learn that Antony is back in arms. However, the triumvirs start squabbling as soon as they meet. Antony marries Caesar's sister Octavia in an attempt to heal the rift between them. But Antony's lieutenant, the sceptical Enobarbus, sees no chance of him leaving Cleopatra. He describes her dazzling appearance at their first meeting: 'The barge she sat in, like a burnish'd throne, / Burn'd on the water...' News of Antony's marriage to Octavia reaches Cleopatra, who vents her fury on the unfortunate messenger. The triumvirs meet Pompey and a truce is agreed, averting the danger of civil war. They celebrate drunkenly on board Pompey's galley.

ACT 3   The messenger prudently gives Cleopatra a most unflattering description of Octavia. Caesar and Lepidus break the truce with Pompey and

239

have him killed, then Caesar imprisons Lepidus. This infuriates Antony who returns to Alexandria, where he and Cleopatra are crowned rulers of Egypt and the eastern third of the Roman Empire. This in turn infuriates Caesar, and they prepare for battle. Antony's world begins to disintegrate. He loses the naval Battle of Actium as Cleopatra flees with her sixty ships and Antony follows her, leaving his fleet to ruin. He is deeply ashamed and his men begin to desert. He proposes peace terms, which Caesar rejects. In a futile gesture he dares Caesar to single combat. When Antony finds Caesar's messenger kissing Cleopatra's hand he flies into a jealous rage. She calms him down and he prepares to fight again, this time on land.

ACT 4   Strange noises appear to portend Antony's doom, but he returns from battle in triumph. Enobarbus, having deserted and joined Caesar, dies of grief and shame. Antony loses the following day's sea battle. He irrationally blames Cleopatra, raging 'This foul Egyptian hath betrayed me,' and resolves to kill her. She takes refuge in her monument. Hoping to soothe his anger, she sends a piteous message that she has killed herself, with his name on her lips. Antony thinks his own life is now worthless and attempts suicide, but bungles it. In great pain, he learns that Cleopatra is still alive. He is carried to her monument, where he dies. She is poleaxed with grief and calmly decides, in earnest, to kill herself.

ACT 5   Caesar's soldiers take Cleopatra prisoner. One of them reveals Caesar's intention to parade her in triumph through the streets of Rome. Rather than face such humiliation, Cleopatra arranges for poisonous snakes to be smuggled into her monument. 'Give me my robe,' she says, 'put on my crown. I have / Immortal longings in me,' before applying the serpents to her breast and arm. She dies joyously, anticipating a reunion with Antony in the afterlife.

As You Like It (1599-1600)

ACT 1   Orlando is persecuted by his elder brother Oliver. Rosalind's father, Duke Senior, has been banished and had his dukedom usurped by his younger brother Duke Frederick. Rosalind has remained behind to be with her cousin Celia, Frederick's daughter. Rosalind meets Orlando after watching him defeat Frederick's prizefighter, and they fall instantly in love. She tells him 'Sir, you have wrestled well and overthrown / More than your enemies,' but Orlando is tongue-tied. When the psychotic Frederick peremptorily banishes Rosalind, Celia promises to go with her. They head for Duke Senior's refuge in the Forest of Arden, with Rosalind disguised as a boy calling himself Ganymede, accompanied by Touchstone the clown.

ACT 2   Orlando is also forced to flee, along with his ancient servant Adam, under threat of death from Oliver. We meet Duke Senior and his pastoral court, which includes the melancholy Jaques. As the exiles arrive independently in the forest, Rosalind, Celia and Touchstone meet the old shepherd Corin and buy his cottage, while Orlando and Adam are welcomed and fed by Duke Senior. Jaques extemporises on the seven ages of man: 'All the world's a stage, / And all the men and women merely players...'

ACT 3   Back at court, Duke Frederick rages against Orlando's disappearance, and orders Oliver to find him. Orlando is meanwhile busily pinning love poems to Rosalind on trees in the forest. Rosalind discovers the verses, and becomes ecstatic when Celia tells her who wrote them. But she is in male disguise as Ganymede, so when Orlando appears she makes a virtue of necessity. 'I will speak to him like a saucy lackey, and under that habit play the knave with him.' Rosalind/Ganymede proposes to cure Orlando of his lovesickness: he must woo Ganymede, who will act out the part of his mistress. Other rustic lovers appear on the scene. Touchstone takes up with the country wench Audrey ('I thank the gods I am foul') and Silvius pines unrequitedly for the pretty shepherdess Phoebe. When Ganymede chastises her for being proud and pitiless, Phoebe at once becomes besotted by 'him'.

ACT 4   Orlando woos Rosalind-pretending-to-be-Ganymede-pretending-to-be-Rosalind. The love charade culminates in Celia conducting a mock marriage ceremony. After Orlando leaves, Rosalind tells Celia, 'O coz... that thou didst know how many fathom deep I am in love!' Meanwhile, Phoebe has written a love letter to Ganymede, who castigates Silvius for delivering it and tells him not to be such a wimp. A transformed Oliver arrives carrying a bloody napkin. He tells how Orlando has just bravely saved him from a lioness, having some flesh torn from his arm in the process. Ganymede faints.

ACT 5   Touchstone has resolved to marry Audrey. Oliver and Celia have fallen in love at first sight, and will be married next day. When Orlando envies his brother's happiness, Ganymede offers to make Rosalind appear by magic and marry him too. Silvius and Phoebe appear, leading to a daisy-chain of love declarations: Orlando for Rosalind, Silvius for Phoebe, Phoebe for Ganymede, and Ganymede for... no woman. Phoebe is persuaded to promise to marry Silvius if she cannot marry Ganymede. Two pages sing 'It was a lover and his lass'. Observing preparations for the multiple wedding, Jaques comments 'There is sure another flood toward, and these couples are coming to the ark.' When Rosalind reappears as herself, Phoebe realises her mistake, and Hymen, the god of marriage, unites all four couples. The play concludes with the news of Duke Frederick's conversion after meeting an old religious man, followed by an epilogue spoken by Rosalind.

Coriolanus (1608)

ACT 1   Rome is starving and its citizens are in revolt. A mob is on its way to attack the hated patrician Caius Martius, whom they blame for grain being denied them. They are calmed by Menenius, a revered fellow patrician. Martius arrives and is scornful and abusive towards the plebeians. News comes that Aufidius's Volscian army is about to attack Rome. Martius leaves to join General Cominius's retaliatory force. The tribunes Brutus and Sicinius denounce Martius's arrogance; meanwhile his mother Volumnia boasts to his wife Virgilia of her son's military prowess. At the battlefront Martius performs heroically, earning the title 'Coriolanus' for conquering the Volscian city of Corioles. The vanquished Aufidius contemplates revenge.

ACT 2   In Rome, as the tribunes continue to criticise Coriolanus, word arrives of his glorious victory. Menenius and Volumnia speculate with relish on his wounds: 'every gash was an enemy's grave'. Coriolanus returns in triumph. The tribunes are horrified when the senate elect him consul. But before being confirmed he must by tradition appear in public wearing the 'gown of humility', show his wounds to the people, and beg for their votes. His pride makes this acutely distasteful. He wins the people's support but with bad grace, and the tribunes soon persuade them to reconsider.

ACT 3   With Coriolanus about to be invested, the tribunes tell him his popularity has evaporated. Enraged, he rails against the plebeians and the concept of popular rule. The tribunes attempt unsuccessfully to have him arrested as a traitor. Volumnia persuades him to swallow his pride and return calmly to the marketplace to answer the people's objections. However, he loses his temper once more, execrating the citizens and tribunes alike. Coriolanus is banished.

ACT 4   After a hasty farewell, he goes to Antium and joins Rome's enemy Aufidius. Popular joy at his departure is short-lived. Rumour spreads that Aufidius is again marching towards Rome, with Coriolanus leading his army. Amid rising panic, Cominius lambasts the tribunes for their catastrophic blunder. However, Aufidius's private agenda becomes apparent: once they have taken Rome, he will destroy Coriolanus.

ACT 5   In desperation, first Cominius then Menenius attempt to win back Coriolanus. Both fail, but a when family deputation led by Volumnia makes a final plea, Coriolanus at last relents. He concludes a peace treaty, bringing relief to Rome. But Aufidius accuses him of treachery, and leads conspirators in his assassination.

Hamlet (1600-01)

ACT 1   Elsinore Castle, Denmark. Prince Hamlet is in mourning for his father's recent death. He is also disgusted by his mother Gertrude's hasty remarriage to his uncle Claudius, who has become King. He expresses his deep depression in the soliloquy 'O that this too too solid flesh would melt, / Thaw and resolve itself into a dew...' The pompous busybody Polonius is Claudius's chief adviser. His son Laertes is about to leave for France, and his daughter Ophelia is being courted by Hamlet. Both men warn Ophelia to beware of Hamlet's advances. They suggest he's only interested in sex. Hamlet meets his father's Ghost and learns that he was murdered by his own brother, Claudius. Hamlet promises revenge. He swears his good friend Horatio to secrecy, and confides that he may feign madness: 'put an antic disposition on'.

ACT 2   Ophelia is alarmed by Hamlet's sudden eccentric behaviour towards her. Polonius feels sure he is 'mad for thy love', and informs Claudius and Gertrude. They ask Hamlet's fellow students Rosencrantz and Guildenstern to discover the cause of his transformation. When Hamlet meets Polonius he calls him a fishmonger, but quickly realises that Rosencrantz and Guildenstern have been sent for. He tells them 'I am but mad north-north-west.' With the arrival of a troupe of actors, Hamlet hits upon a plan. In order to confirm the Ghost's story and his uncle's guilt, he will have the actors stage a scene like his father's murder, and watch Claudius's reaction. Meanwhile he castigates himself for delaying his revenge. 'Oh what a rogue and peasant slave am I...'

ACT 3   Hamlet's soliloquy 'To be or not to be...' is swiftly followed by a vehemently misogynistic confrontation with Ophelia in which he tells her 'Get thee to a nunnery.' Claudius and Polonius have been eavesdropping. The King, perturbed by Hamlet's highly erratic behaviour, resolves to send him to England, escorted by Rosencrantz and Guildenstern. The court gathers to watch the play. At its murderous climax Claudius rises, saying 'Give me some light,' and exits. Hamlet and Horatio take this as proof of guilt. Gertrude angrily summons Hamlet to her room. On his way there he passes the repentant Claudius kneeling in prayer – a perfect chance to kill him. Hamlet rejects the opportunity, however, reasoning that death in prayer would send his soul to heaven. A row breaks out between mother and son, causing her to cry for help. A man shouts out from behind the curtain. Hamlet assumes it is the King and stabs him, mistakenly killing Polonius. He proceeds to inveigh passionately against Gertrude's remarriage: 'Nay, but to live / In the rank sweat of an enseamed bed, / Stew'd in corruption, honeying and making love

243

/ Over the nasty sty!' His vehemence causes the Ghost to reappear and calm him down. He and his mother end the scene reconciled.

ACT 4   Claudius is now convinced that Hamlet is dangerously mad, and must be sent to England immediately. Once alone, he reveals his intention to have Hamlet killed on arrival. Hamlet meets the army of Prince Fortinbras of Norway, and soliloquises again on his own procrastination in revenge: 'I do not know / Why yet I live to say this thing's to do...' Polonius's death causes Ophelia to become demented with grief, and Laertes to return in fury from France. Claudius convinces him that Hamlet, who has returned unexpectedly to Denmark, was to blame. They hatch a plot for Laertes to kill him in a duel, using a venom-tipped rapier; Claudius will have a cup of poisoned wine in reserve. The act ends with Gertrude's report that Ophelia has drowned.

ACT 5   Hamlet and Horatio meet a gravedigger preparing for Ophelia's funeral. He unearths the skull of a court jester whom Hamlet remembers: 'Alas, poor Yorick. I knew him, Horatio...' Ophelia's funeral procession arrives, leading to a brawl between Hamlet and Laertes. Hamlet tells Horatio the story of his sea voyage, how he turned back and sent Rosencrantz and Guildenstern to their deaths instead. Osric, a 'waterfly' courtier, invites Hamlet to the duel. When Hamlet wins the first two bouts, Gertrude toasts his success, unwittingly drinking the wine poisoned by Claudius. The play reaches its corpse-strewn climax as first Hamlet then Laertes is mortally wounded by the envenomed rapier, before Hamlet uses it to kill Claudius. As Hamlet expires he asks Horatio to tell the world his story. His last words are 'The rest is silence.'

Henry V (1599)

An opening Chorus laments the impossibility of representing, on a bare Elizabethan stage, the mighty battles and multiple locations evoked in the play. The audience are encouraged to use their imagination. 'Piece out our imperfections with your thoughts.'

ACT 1   The prelude to war. The Archbishop of Canterbury convinces Henry V of his right to the French throne. The Dauphin sends Henry a gift of a 'tun of treasure', which turns out to contain tennis balls, mocking his reputation as a young wastrel. This enrages Henry, who promises 'His jest will savour but of shallow wit / When thousands weep more than did laugh at it.'

ACT 2   The Chorus describes battle preparations: 'Now all the youth of England are on fire', but also mentions a conspiracy to assassinate Henry.

After a short scene involving Pistol, Bardolph and Nym (favourite low-life characters reprised from *Henry IV*), Henry deals ruthlessly with the conspirators. We hear that Henry's friend and surrogate father, Sir John Falstaff, that 'huge hill of flesh' so loved by Henry in his youth, has died. Henry's uncle Exeter delivers an ultimatum to the increasingly nervous French court.

ACT 3   Henry's army sails for France. At the siege of Harfleur he urges on his troops: 'Once more unto the breach, dear friends...' He is parodied by the cowardly Bardolph, shouting 'On, on, on, on, on, to the breach, to the breach!' Four captains, from England, Ireland, Scotland and Wales, argue about the disciplines of war. The Governor of Harfleur surrenders, rather than face the atrocities threatened by Henry. We meet the French Princess Katherine, having an English lesson. The French nobles are smarting after Harfleur, but their King rallies them and sends a defiant message with a ransom demand to Henry. Bardolph is executed for stealing from a church. Henry admits to the French herald: 'My people are with sickness much enfeebled', but rejects his demands: 'My ransom is this frail and worthless trunk.' In the French camp the nobles wait impatiently for battle to begin, and mock the braggart Dauphin.

ACT 4   Early dawn before the Battle of Agincourt. The odds now favour France. 'The confident and over-lusty French / Do the low-rated English play at dice,' says the Chorus. Henry visits his demoralised troops in disguise, argues with a soldier, Williams, about the moral responsibility for soldiers' deaths, and soliloquises on the burdens of kingship. With the fighting about to commence, he inspires his army: 'This day is called the Feast of Crispian... gentlemen in England now abed / Shall think themselves accurs'd they were not here, / And hold their manhoods cheap whiles any speaks / That fought with us upon Saint Crispin's Day.' Against all expectation the English win the battle, suffering a mere twenty-five fatalities compared with ten thousand French.

ACT 5   The fiery Welsh captain Fluellen settles a score with Pistol, forcing him to eat a raw leek. The French have surrendered. During a peace conference Henry woos Katherine, countering her reluctance to kiss him before marriage with 'Oh Kate, nice customs curtsy to great kings.' All of Henry's terms are accepted by the French and a treaty is concluded, uniting the two countries. However, as the action concludes, the Chorus looks forward to the chaotic reign of Henry VI, and gives notice that the peace will not last long.

Macbeth (1599)

ACT 1　Macbeth and Banquo, generals of King Duncan's army, return from battle as conquering heroes. Three witches greet them with prophecies, notably that Macbeth shall become King. He becomes obsessed by the idea and communicates it to his wife in a letter. When Duncan visits the Macbeths' castle, Lady Macbeth plans to murder him and secure the throne for her husband. Macbeth has pangs of conscience but Lady Macbeth persuades him.

ACT 2　Macbeth's nerves are frayed. He hallucinates: 'Is this a dagger which I see before me, / The handle toward my hand?', before murdering Duncan in his sleep. The deed leaves him so shaken that Lady Macbeth takes charge. Early next morning Macduff arrives, and discovers Duncan's corpse. He suspects Macbeth, but does not reveal his suspicions.

ACT 3　Macbeth is crowned King of Scotland. However, he remains uneasy about Banquo, who the witches had prophesied would father a line of kings. Macbeth's hired assassins kill Banquo, but his son Fleance escapes. A banquet follows, where Banquo's ghost appears. Macbeth becomes frantic: 'Avaunt! And quit my sight! Let the earth hide thee! / Thy bones are marrowless, thy blood is cold; / Thou hast no speculation in those eyes / Which thou dost glare with!' The banquet ends in disarray.

ACT 4　Macbeth returns to the witches. They tell him to 'beware Macduff', but also that 'none of woman born / Shall harm Macbeth'. Despite this reassurance, Macbeth determines to assassinate Macduff's entire family. Macduff, who has taken refuge in England with Duncan's son Malcolm, is informed: 'Your castle is surprised, your wife and babes / Savagely slaughtered.'

ACT 5　Lady Macbeth becomes racked with guilt from the crimes she and her husband have committed. She sleepwalks and tries to wash imaginary bloodstains from her hands, all the while speaking of the terrible things she knows. Macduff and Malcolm lead an army against the tyrant. Macbeth delivers the soliloquy 'Tomorrow, and tomorrow, and tomorrow' upon learning of Lady Macbeth's death. A battle culminates in Macbeth's confrontation with Macduff, who declares that he was 'from his mother's womb / Untimely ripp'd' (i.e. by Caesarean section) and was therefore not 'of woman born'. Macbeth realises the witches have misled him. Macduff beheads Macbeth, and Malcolm is crowned King.

Measure for Measure (1604)

ACT 1   Vienna. The Duke declares he must depart, leaving government to his deputy Angelo. The city has become lawless and licentious, but Angelo is known for his puritanical zeal. He immediately announces that the brothels are to be pulled down. Mistress Overdone and Pompey, a 'madame' and her pimp, are lamenting this news when Claudio arrives. His betrothed Juliet is pregnant. Although they were about to get married, Angelo has sentenced him to death for fornication. Lucio visits Claudio's sister Isabella, a postulant nun, and asks her to plead with Angelo on Claudio's behalf.

ACT 2   Elbow, a half-witted constable, accuses Pompey and Froth of corrupting his wife. Isabella visits Angelo, and begs him for mercy. At first he is unyielding, but then her virtue and passion touch him. He becomes lustfully attracted to her and eventually offers to spare Claudio's life on condition she will yield him her virginity. Isabella is appalled and threatens to expose his hypocrisy, but then realises that, in view of his spotless reputation, no one would believe her.

ACT 3   The Duke has in fact remained in Vienna, disguised as Friar Lodowick. He visits Claudio in prison and advises him: 'Be absolute for death: either death or life / Shall thereby be the sweeter.' Isabella arrives and tells Claudio of Angelo's proposition. When he begs her to consent to it she is horrified. She becomes hysterically enraged, exclaiming 'Die, perish! Might but my bending down / Reprieve thee from thy fate, it should proceed.' The disguised Duke, having eavesdropped, suggests a tricky solution. Angelo's ex-fiancée Mariana is still in love with him. If Isabella will say yes to Angelo, Mariana will take her place in his bed, under strict conditions of darkness and silence.

ACT 4   The 'bed trick' works, but Angelo breaks his promise. Claudio still faces immediate execution, and his head is to be sent to Angelo as proof of death. Friar Lodowick hastily improvises a 'head trick', substituting that of another recently dead prisoner. But he doesn't tell Isabella, whose anguish and resentment against Angelo become extreme.

ACT 5   A complex last act. The Duke returns in his own person. Isabella publicly denounces Angelo, but the Duke pretends to find her claims incredible. Mariana is called to give evidence, and says that Angelo slept with her. Friar Lodowick appears to be implicated in these confusing claims against Angelo. The Duke departs, leaving Angelo to be judge of his own case, immediately returning in disguise when Lodowick is summoned. In a scuffle, Lucio pulls off Lodowick's hood, revealing the Duke. Angelo is exposed, shamed, and begs for his own execution. The Duke agrees, while insisting he first marries Mariana. She, however, pleads for Angelo's life. She begs Isabella to kneel beside her. With astonishing charity Isabella consents, arguing 'I partly think / A due sincerity govern'd his deeds / Till he did look on me.' The Duke reprieves Angelo. Claudio enters, still alive. Not a word is spoken between brother and sister. Finally the Duke proposes marriage to Isabella, who again says nothing. Her silence has been variously interpreted.

Running parallel with these events is a colourful low-life subplot, much of it concerning Claudio's friend Lucio and the disguised Duke. Lucio amusingly slanders the Duke to Lodowick, and later Lodowick to the Duke, eventually landing in deep trouble when the Duke and Lodowick are revealed to be one and the same person.

Richard II (1595-6)

ACT 1   A duel between two nobleman, Bolingbroke and Mowbray, is aborted after a long, ceremonial build-up. King Richard arbitrarily banishes both men. News arrives of a rebellion in Ireland. Needing to put it down, and having squandered much wealth, Richard announces widespread tax levies. His waning popularity declines even further.

ACT 2   Bolingbroke's father John of Gaunt delivers a deathbed speech in praise of England – 'This royal throne of kings, this sceptred isle...' – and lambasts Richard for his neglect of it. Richard is unmoved. Gaunt expires, and Richard seizes his estates. Gaunt's brother York remonstrates, to no avail. Richard departs for Ireland. During his absence, Bolingbroke returns with rebel soldiers to claim his inheritance. Richard's faction is thrown into panic and York (who has been made regent in his absence) feels his allegiance divided. When Bolingbroke and his troops arrive at Berkeley Castle, York has no option but to allow them to enter.

ACT 3   Returning from Ireland, Richard finds his army has dispersed, two of his favourites have been executed by Bolingbroke, and York has defected. In despair, he meets his enemies at Flint Castle. He vacillates between imperiousness and submission, at one moment asking 'How dare thy joints forget / To pay their awful duty to our presence?', and at the next 'What must the King do now? Must he submit? / The King shall do it.' Bolingbroke protests that he has no wish to seize the throne, but Richard admits he is powerless. However, the Queen overhears her gardeners discussing Bolingbroke's plans, and a coup seems likely.

ACT 4 Richard's abdication is announced to Parliament. He upstages his successor with a histrionic and self-pitying performance. Gazing at his own refection, he asks 'Was this the face / That like the sun did make beholders wink?', before smashing the mirror. He refuses to acknowledge the legitimacy of his deposition. York's son Aumerle and others are persuaded that Richard's cause is valid, and vow to fight back. Nonetheless, Bolingbroke is crowned King Henry IV, and Richard is imprisoned at Pomfret Castle.

ACT 5 Richard, under armed guard, bids a sorrowful farewell to his Queen: 'Go, count thy way with sighs, I mine with groans.' York and his Duchess are discussing Bolingbroke's soaring popularity in contrast to Richard's plight, when they discover that Aumerle is guilty of plotting against Bolingbroke. York pleads with the new King that his son should be punished, but after the Duchess's impassioned plea for mercy, Aumerle is pardoned. Richard, now alone in prison, muses on his fate: 'I wasted time, and now doth time waste me.' Believing that Bolingbroke has ordered Richard to be murdered, Exton assassinates him. On hearing the news, King Henry vows to go on a penitential pilgrimage.

Romeo and Juliet (1595-6)

ACT 1 The play begins with a street brawl between servants of two noble Verona families, the Montagues and Capulets. The Prince restores order. Lord Montague's son Romeo tells his cousin Benvolio of his unrequited love for a girl called Rosaline. The eligible bachelor Count Paris wants to marry Lord Capulet's daughter Juliet. She is only thirteen so Capulet counsels patience; however, he invites Paris to attend a masked ball. Juliet's Nurse and mother tell her what a great catch Paris would be. We meet the madcap Mercutio; he and Benvolio persuade Romeo to gatecrash the Capulet ball. Romeo and Juliet fall in love at first sight. But he is recognised by Juliet's cousin, the fiery-tempered Tybalt.

ACT 2 Midnight after the ball. Romeo climbs over the wall into the Capulets' orchard, below Juliet's balcony. He overhears her proclaim her love for him, despite their families' mutual hatred: 'O Romeo, Romeo! Wherefore art thou Romeo?' They declare their passion for each other and agree to marry. At dawn Romeo visits Friar Lawrence, who, with the Nurse as go-between, marries them secretly the following afternoon.

ACT 3   Tybalt challenges Romeo for invading the Capulet ball. Romeo, now considering Tybalt his kinsman, refuses to fight. Mercutio draws his rapier on Romeo's behalf, and is fatally wounded: 'Ask for me tomorrow and you shall find me a grave man.' Romeo, enraged by his friend's death, kills Tybalt. As a result he is banished from Verona by the Prince. The lovers are distraught at the prospect of separation. The Nurse and Friar arrange for them secretly to spend the night together in Juliet's bedroom. The following dawn, Romeo flees to Mantua. Juliet's parents misinterpret her tears as grief over Tybalt, and agree to an immediate marriage with Paris. When she refuses they threaten to disown her.

ACT 4   Friar Lawrence suggests a plan to the desperate Juliet. On the eve of her wedding to Paris, she takes a potion that plunges her into a death-like sleep. Next morning, instead of going to church as a bride, Juliet is laid in the family crypt, apparently dead. Meanwhile the Friar has sent a message to Romeo, promising that he can be reunited with her when she wakes.

ACT 5   The crucial message fails to reach Romeo; instead he hears that Juliet has died. Grief-stricken, he buys poison and goes to the Capulet crypt. There he encounters Paris, who is also intent on mourning Juliet. They fight, and Paris is slain. Romeo marvels that death has not diminished Juliet's beauty, before proceeding to drink the poison. Juliet then awakens and, seeing Romeo's dead body, stabs herself with his dagger. On arriving at the corpse-strewn tomb, the Montagues and Capulets are reconciled and agree to end their feud. The Prince delivers a final elegy for the lovers: 'For never was a story of more woe / Than this of Juliet and her Romeo.'

The Tempest (1611)

ACT 1   The play opens with a violent storm and shipwreck near a remote island. Cut to the magician Prospero and his daughter Miranda further inland. In a long scene of exposition, he explains that they have been marooned on the island for twelve years. Prospero is the rightful Duke of Milan; but his jealous brother Antonio, helped by Alonso the King of Naples, usurped the dukedom and set father and infant daughter adrift in a small boat. His faithful counsellor Gonzalo secretly supplied them with basic essentials, including Prospero's prized books. Arriving on the island, and possessed of magic powers due to his great learning, Prospero is served by the 'airy spirit' Ariel, who is invisible to all but Prospero. The only other native is the deformed savage Caliban. He showed Prospero how to survive on the island, and in turn was taught religion and language. But Caliban attempted to rape Miranda, and consequently Prospero and Miranda view him with contempt and disgust. Prospero, having divined that Antonio and Alonso were on the ship, raised the storm that caused it to run aground. Also on board were Alonso's brother Sebastian and son Ferdinand, as well as Gonzalo. Alonso and Ferdinand are separated, each believing the other drowned. But Ariel has magically arranged the survival of all on board the ship. Prospero arranges a romance between Ferdinand and Miranda. They fall in love at once, but Prospero worries 'lest too light winning / Make the prize light'. He pretends to suspect Ferdinand of being a spy and a traitor, and threatens to imprison him.

ACT 2   A long scene between survivors of the wreck leads to Antonio and Sebastian plotting to kill the sleeping Alonso and Gonzalo, and make Sebastian King of Naples. Ariel wakes the sleepers in the nick of time. Stephano and Trinculo, two eccentric servants from the shipwreck, meet Caliban and get him drunk. He thinks they are gods and offers to serve them, promising to show them 'every fertile inch o'th'island'.

ACT 3   Ferdinand has become a willing log-carrier, to prove his devotion to Miranda. Stephano, Trinculo and Caliban plan to murder Prospero and install Stephano as King of the island. Ariel stages a fantastical banquet. In the guise of a harpy he paralyses Alonso, Antonio and Sebastian, then reprimands them for their betrayal of Prospero.

ACT 4   Prospero relents towards Ferdinand, and arranges a masque to bless his betrothal to Miranda. The plot to murder Prospero is foiled by Ariel, who beguiles Caliban, Stephano and Trinculo with Prospero's fine clothes, then has them chased by spirits in the shape of hunting dogs. Prospero promises Ariel that he will soon be free.

ACT 5   Whilst Alonso, Antonio and Sebastian are still 'distracted', Ariel persuades Prospero to forgive them. In a soliloquy ('Ye elves of hills, brooks, standing lakes, and groves...'), Prospero declares that he will renounce his magical powers. He breaks the spell on the lords and reveals his true identity to them, before showing Ferdinand and Miranda playing chess. Alonso is overjoyed to find his son alive, and to learn of his imminent marriage to Miranda. All are reunited and reconciled. Caliban is forgiven, and Ariel is finally liberated. Prospero announces that after the wedding in Naples, he will return to Milan and reclaim his dukedom. In an epilogue, having surrendered his power, he invites the audience to set him free from the island with their applause.

Titus Andronicus (1591-2)

ACT 1   The Emperor of Rome has died, and his sons Saturninus and Bassianus squabble over the succession. However, the veteran general Titus Andronicus is named as the people's choice. He has returned victorious from ten years of fighting the Goths, bringing as captives their Queen Tamora, her three sons, and her secret lover Aaron the Moor. Having lost twenty-one of his own sons in battle, Titus sacrifices Tamora's eldest boy as part of their burial rites. She vows revenge. Titus refuses the throne in favour of Saturninus, who agrees to marry his daughter Lavinia. She, however, is already betrothed to Bassianus, and the couple escape together. Saturninus marries Tamora instead, thus transforming her at a stroke from captive to Empress.

ACT 2   Tamora's sons Chiron and Demetrius lust after Lavinia. Aaron suggests they rape her. When a hunting party arrives in the forest, they kill Bassianus and drag off Lavinia. Aaron frames two of Titus's remaining sons for Bassianus's murder. Lavinia re-enters, raped, and with her tongue and hands cut off. She is discovered by her uncle Marcus.

ACT 3   Titus pleads for his sons' reprieve, describing Rome as 'a wilderness of tigers'. When Marcus enters with the mutilated Lavinia, Titus is overcome with grief. In response to a deal which, so Aaron claims, will save his sons' lives, Titus allows his hand to be cut off and taken to the Emperor. In return, a messenger brings Titus the heads of his sons. Titus sends his eldest son Lucius to raise an avenging army among the Goths.

ACT 4   Titus and Marcus learn about Lavinia's ordeal when she writes a message in the sand by holding a stick in her mouth and guiding it with her stumps. The Empress Tamora gives birth to a black baby, Aaron's bastard, which he abducts. The increasingly demented-seeming Titus shoots arrows carrying appeals to the gods for justice into the Emperor's palace, enraging Saturninus. When news comes that Lucius is marching towards Rome with an army of Goths, Tamora promises to avert the danger.

ACT 5   Aaron and his baby are captured by Lucius's soldiers. Tamora, believing Titus to be deranged, visits him impersonating 'Revenge', and offers to wreak vengeance on his foes. Titus pretends to be duped and agrees to summon Lucius to a banquet at his house. When Tamora leaves he cuts the throats of her sons and cooks them in a pie. Saturninus and Tamora arrive for the banquet. During the meal Titus kills Lavinia, to spare her the shame of her rape. When Saturninus summons the rapists, Titus exclaims 'Why, there they are both, baked in that pie, / Whereof their mother daintily hath fed.' In rapid succession Titus then stabs Tamora, Saturninus kills Titus, and Lucius kills Saturninus. Marcus and Lucius are left to tell the story. Lucius is elected Emperor.

Twelfth Night (1601)

ACT 1   Duke Orsino is in love with Countess Olivia, but she is in mourning for her dead brother and rejects all suitors. Viola has survived a shipwreck, but believes her twin brother Sebastian to be drowned. She disguises herself as a young page, assumes the name Cesario, and enters the service of Orsino. He sends Cesario to plead his case to Olivia who, fooled by the male disguise, is immediately attracted to the messenger. Viola, however, has become besotted by Orsino. So far, so good? The play has a rich comic subplot involving Olivia's puritanical steward Malvolio, her debauched uncle Sir Toby Belch and his rich but dim-witted friend Sir Andrew Aguecheek, her maid Maria, and Feste her jester. Both Malvolio and Sir Andrew are also in love with Olivia.

ACT 2   It turns out that Sebastian has survived the shipwreck, having been rescued by the sea captain Antonio. Like Viola, however, he assumes his twin to be drowned. He also heads for Orsino's court. Malvolio chastises Sir Toby, Sir Andrew, Maria and Feste for their rowdy late-night drinking. In revenge Maria forges a love letter apparently in Olivia's handwriting, addressed 'To the unknown beloved'. Orsino tells Viola/Cesario of the intensity of his passion for Olivia, while Viola's own love for him remains undeclared. The plot against Malvolio is a triumph. Already gripped by fantasies of marriage to Olivia, he is easily gulled by the coded letter. 'I may command where I adore,' it reads; 'Thou canst not choose but know who I am. If thou entertainest my love, let it appear in thy smiling.' Malvolio falls for it hook, line and sinker.

ACT 3   Olivia is desperate for the unresponsive Viola/Cesario. But Sir Andrew, jealous of their apparent intimacy, is persuaded by Sir Toby to challenge Cesario to a duel. Olivia is startled by the arrival of Malvolio, who, obeying Maria's letter, is not only smiling incessantly, but wearing yellow stockings and cross-garters. She assumes he must have gone mad. A reluctant duel between Sir Andrew and Cesario is interrupted by Antonio, who has mistaken Cesario for Sebastian.

ACT 4 Confusion mounts as the real Sebastian is in turn mistaken for Cesario. As such he is challenged by Sir Andrew and Sir Toby, before being willingly seduced by, and hastily marrying, Olivia. Meanwhile Malvolio has been locked in a dark cellar, and taunted by Feste on account of his supposed insanity.

ACT 5 After further mistaken identity mayhem, the twins finally appear simultaneously and rejoice to find each other alive. 'Most wonderful!' cries Olivia. When Viola reveals that she is in reality a young woman who has loved him since they first met, Orsino loses no time in proposing to her. It is learned that Toby has married Maria. Malvolio is released from his dungeon in high dudgeon. When told of the trick that was played on him, he storms off, threatening revenge. Feste's song, 'When that I was and a little tiny boy, / With hey-ho, the wind and the rain...', ends the play on a subdued note.

The Winter's Tale (1610-11)

ACT 1 For nine months King Polixenes of Bohemia has been visiting his childhood friend, King Leontes of Sicilia. Polixenes decides it's time to go home, but Leontes wants him to stay longer. When Polixenes reluctantly refuses, Leontes asks his Queen Hermione (who is heavily pregnant) to persuade him. Hermione succeeds. Leontes is suddenly consumed with paranoia that they are lovers and that her baby is his friend's bastard. He orders Lord Camillo to poison Polixenes. Instead, Camillo warns Polixenes, and they hurriedly leave for Bohemia.

ACT 2 Hermione is playing with her young son Mamillius. Leontes learns of Polixenes's flight and takes it as proof of his guilt. He accuses Hermione of being a 'bed-swerver' and of conspiring against his life, and has her arrested. She gives birth to a daughter in prison. Paulina (one of Hermione's ladies-in-waiting) shows the baby to Leontes but he becomes frantic and orders Paulina's husband Antigonus to burn it. He later relents on condition that Antigonus take the baby 'to some remote and desert place... Where chance may nurse or end it'. Messengers sent by Leontes to the Delphic Oracle are about to return.

ACT 3 At Hermione's trial the Oracle's verdict is announced: she is innocent. Leontes declares that the Oracle is false. News arrives at once that Mamillius is dead. Hermione collapses and is carried out. Leontes immediately repents his appalling misjudgements. Paulina returns in a paroxysm of grief to berate Leontes and to report that the Queen has also died. Leontes is distraught.

Meanwhile, Antigonus deposits the baby with a box of gold on the seacoast of Bohemia, christening her Perdita – 'the Lost One'. He meets his end with Shakespeare's most famous stage direction: '*Exit, pursued by a bear.*' Perdita is adopted by an old shepherd. He says to his son (who has just witnessed Antigonus's death): 'Now bless thyself: thou met'st with things dying, I with things new-born.' Simple prose, at the crux of the play. Death and rebirth.

ACT 4   Bohemia, sixteen years later. Polixenes hears that his son Florizel is wooing a shepherd's beautiful daughter (Perdita, unaware of her royal parentage). He and Camillo attend a sheep-shearing festival in disguise, to investigate. The con man Autolycus, 'a snapper-up of unconsidered trifles', is fleecing the locals. During a long and joyous pastoral scene, Prince Florizel proposes to the shepherdess. Polixenes, now revealing his identity, is furious, violently threatening both them and the shepherd. Camillo helps the couple escape to Sicilia.

ACT 5   In Sicilia, Leontes continues to mourn. He promises Paulina never to marry again without her consent. Florizel and Perdita arrive, hotly pursued by Polixenes, whom Leontes – beseeched by Florizel to be his advocate – goes to meet. Three excited gentlemen report the Kings' reconciliation, and the old shepherd's revelation, 'like an old tale', that Perdita is Leontes' long-lost daughter. Her marriage to Florizel is approved. They all visit Paulina to see a statue of Hermione, and marvel at its lifelike quality. 'Would you not deem it breath'd?' says Leontes. Then 'Oh, she's warm!' as the 'statue' (in fact the living Hermione) very slowly begins to move. Paulina tells Hermione what she has waited sixteen years to hear: 'Our Perdita is found.'